I0807955

Photograph by Man Ray, Paris, 1927.

A Sacred QUEST

The Life and Writings of Mary Butts

Edited by
Christopher Wagstaff

McPherson & Company
Kingston, New York

A SACRED QUEST

Copyright 1995 by McPherson & Company.
All rights reserved.

Published by McPherson & Company, Post Office Box 1126, Kingston, New York 12401. No part of this book may be reproduced in any form without written permission from the publisher. Typeset in Baskerville at Delmas Type, Ann Arbor. Printed on pH neutral paper by Braun-Brumfield, Inc. Manufactured in the United States of America.
First edition.

Library of Congress Cataloging-in-Publication Data

A sacred quest : the life and writings of Mary Butts / edited by Christopher Wagstaff.
p. cm.
Includes bibliographical references (p.).
ISBN 0-929701-45-3: $25.00
1. Butts, Mary, 1890–1937. 2. Women authors, English—20th century—Biography. 3. Women and literature—England—History—20th century. I. Wagstaff, Christopher.
PR6003.U7Z87 1995
823′.912—dc20
[B] 95-15818

ACKNOWLEDGMENTS
The Publisher extends thanks to the following for their kind permissions to reproduce copyrighted materials. The frontispiece photograph by Man Ray is from the collection of Timothy Baum. Works by Mary Butts and most of the photographs appear courtesy of Camilla Bagg and The Estate of Mary Butts. Additional photographs have been lent by Robert H. Byington. The Jean Cocteau drawing on page 107 is from the Monroe Wheeler collection. "Re Mary Butts" by Robert Duncan is reprinted with the permission of The Literary Estate of Robert Duncan. "Recognition Not Farewell" by Bryher is reprinted by permission of Mrs. Perdita Schaffner.

Published with the assistance of grants from the literature programs of the New York State Council on the Arts and the National Endowment for the Arts, a federal agency.

To Patricia and Everett with deep gratitude.

CONTENTS

IV: DATA

PREFACE

WHEN IN 1937 Mary Butts died suddenly at the age of forty-six in a Penzance hospital, the loss to English letters was mourned by the small band of her devoted readers. A review of her autobiography in the *Times Literary Supplement* began: "Nearly three months ago there passed almost unnoticed from the world a woman who possessed an intent awareness of its natural beauties." And the novelist Charles Williams remarked in the daily *Times:* "Her books supplied the reader with provocation hidden in quietness; she concealed power in peace, and made herself a style that was like burning glass." Despite the praise of Williams, Ezra Pound, Ford Madox Ford, Jean Cocteau and others, Butts's reputation underwent an eclipse following her death, and almost the only information available about her has been the tantalizing glimpses of her in memoirs by Stella Bowen, Douglas Goldring, Jimmy Charters, Nina Hamnet, Elsa Lanchester and Virgil Thomson. This volume is the first one to present a more comprehensive look at Mary Butts's life as well as to consider the significance of her rich, allusive and often unsettling work.

Although she was early hailed as "the English Chekhov," many critics in the 1920s found Butts's novels and stories "bewildering," "uncomfortable," "lacking in lucidity" and "too difficult." Like T. S. Eliot, James Joyce and Gertrude Stein, she was decidedly modern in dissolving logical, rigid causality in her writing and in seeking a matrix of meanings not fully apparent to, or comprehensible by, the mind or the senses. About her early masterwork *Ashe of Rings,* one commentator observed: "If you don't like to be confused, avoid this book. If you are ready to pierce through confusions, you will enjoy it." Another reviewer said: "If you can imagine the stylistic influence of James Joyce, combined with Miss Richardson's soliloquizing method in a writer whose theme has the incoherence of an nightmare, you may realise how bad and mad is 'Ashe of Rings' by Mary Butts." By the early 1930s, critics who had absorbed the undermining of rational certitude and of the substantiality of space and time in *The Waste Land, Jacob's Room* and *Ulysses* came to appreciate the piercing directness of Mary Butts's incantatory, ever-shifting prose. In 1933 *The Bookman* noted: "She is able to probe, with a quite remarkable dexterity, the subtler phases of the human consciousness. She stands somewhat alone among the writers of to-day."

In a span of about eighteen years Butts wrote five novels, three collections of short stories, an account of her childhood, a large number of essays and reviews, and about thirty poems. Late in her life she said, "Our world is dying for want of a *restatement* of final realities, serviceable both to the heart and head of every man of good-will." Each of her novels includes an encounter with such lasting entities. Her characters' anguish and conflicts push them to relinquish their self-identities, and with this surrender comes the discovery of a transcendent power underlying and unifying the plurality of psyches, attitudes and egos encountered in everyday life. In *The Crystal Cabinet* Butts speaks of a "perception of a hierarchized universe, quickening the visible order." And in her sparest novel, *The Macedonian,* Alexander has a vision of the holy Spirit at a shrine of Zeus Ammon in the oasis of Siwa, after which he begins to imagine the fusion of the races of the world: "He wants to make the earth and its various peoples plastic, interpenetrated, one with the other, capable of exchange of resources and excellences." Like Simone Weil, with whom she shared a passion for Greek literature and the truth, Mary Butts preferred to leave this integral awareness largely unstated, to suggest rather than to define a noumenal realm beyond formulated thought and words.

* * * * *

It was Robert Duncan who first introduced me to Mary Butts one afternoon in 1983, when I inquired about the woman whose strange-sounding name appeared on a row of books high up on one of the shelves of his third-floor library. Duncan told my wife Barbara and me about this fun-loving and genuinely bohemian writer whose searing style and artistic integrity had meant so much to him as an impoverished young poet in New York in the early 1940s. He said that, unlike his beloved Virginia Woolf, Butts did not observe the world through the screen of her own sensibility, and he mentioned regretfully the neglect of her writings. We left Duncan's home in San Francisco that day with four or five of

Butts's books; as we began to read them that night and in the days following, we were struck by the rare wonder infusing the landscapes and scenes as well as her characters' inner lives, and also by the subtle shades of thought and sensation mirrored in her sentences. About a year later, in hopes of stimulating interest in our new-found discovery, Barbara and I organized a conference on the Davis campus of the University of California, at which Barbara, Robert Duncan, Robin Blaser, Robert H. Byington and Kenneth Irby presented papers and talks on Butts's work before a small, attentive audience. Following the two-day meeting, I gathered the papers together for what was intended to be a slim volume; however, over the next five years, as further valuable materials on Butts came to light, this compilation expanded to include many more views of her life and work.

The opening section of the book gives perspectives of Mary Butts by some of her fellow writers, as well as by young friends, protégés and scholars. The memoir by Harcourt Wesson Bull, probably the most complete single portrait of Butts we have, was written in the early 1960s at the request of Robert Byington. Also in this section are interviews with four notable figures in the arts who knew her in the 1920s and observed her personal and artistic struggles. A reminiscence by her daughter tells of Butts's efforts to rebuild her life in Sennen, a village on the coast of Cornwall, at the close of the decade-long celebration and dissipation of the 1920s.

The second part offers a sampling of Mary Butts's writings, beginning with the short story "Angèle au Couvent," which describes adolescent anguish transmuted and illuminated. Gerrit Lansing has written in a letter: "It is arguable that in the form of the short story Mary Butts's genius found its most felicitous and satisfactory expression." This story is followed by answers to a questionnaire in *The Little Review* in 1929; by selections from her journals; by two probing book reviews from the early 1930s which point out the need in the 20th century to rediscover sacred truths and values; and by a sampling of letters to Glenway Wescott and Hugh Ross Williamson, evoking her native Dorset and clarifying the mystical experience. The section closes with a complex, powerful poem, "Pythian Ode," which pictures Delphi before the 5th century B.C. and extols the intelligence as a "delicious enquiry" rather than a calculating process.

The third section, "Reappraisals," includes extended discussions of two of the author's major novels. Robin Blaser's searching meditation on *Armed with Madness* explores the relation of modernism to the sacred or unseen, and Barbara O'Brien Wagstaff examines the sublime metaphysical romance *Death of Felicity Taverner,* in which what Coleridge called "the power of the informing Word" subdues the forces of cruelty and oppression at work in a small English community. These two essays are preceded by a short comment by Robert Duncan, who had intended to contribute a study of the short stories, to be titled "Daimon and Demon in Mary Butts," but was unable to do so because of his last illness.

The final segment of the book is comprised of a chronology of Mary Butts's life and a preliminary checklist of her published writings, as well as of selected articles about her and notable reviews of her works.

* * * * *

A number of people deserve recognition and warmest thanks for helping to make "A Sacred Quest" a concrete reality. Special appreciation is due Bruce McPherson for his continuing effort to bring all of Mary Butts's work back into print and for including this volume in his publishing program. Professor Robert H. Byington has been most generous in sharing his wealth of knowledge and materials on this writer, and this book would not exist in its present form without his thoughtful and timely assistance. I am much indebted to Camilla Bagg for having clarified many details about Mary Butts's life, for her interest in this tribute to her mother, and for the great hospitality she has shown in many ways, most memorably in visits to places in Dorset and Cornwall important to her mother. Elena Storer-Nitzberg showed early enthusiasm for this volume for which I am very grateful. Robin Blaser, Kenneth Irby, Robert Kelly and Gerrit Lansing offered helpful advice and encouragement, and Marilyn Kinch meticulously typed final copies of the text. Lastly, behind the scenes, my parents Everett and Patricia Noonan gave abiding inspiration, guidance and love; William and Aileen Hillman patiently shared their deep understanding of spiritual things; Lois O'Brien has been always generous and supportive; Harry Jacobus has been an example of integrity and dedication; Margaret Mirk and Jess have been the best of friends; and, above all, Barbara O'Brien Wagstaff has tirelessly assisted at every stage of the preparation of this volume: without her sensitive counsel, care and enduring affection, this book could not have been undertaken or come into being.

—CHRISTOPHER WAGSTAFF

Portrait at age 18 by her aunt, Agnes Briggs.

FOREWORD

The Dream of Badbury Rings

WHEN IN the early 1950s I first read Mary Butts—my introduction to her work was like Robert Duncan's, the reading of the two novels *Ashe of Rings* and *Armed with Madness*—plus the little essay *Traps for Unbelievers,* which I presented to John Ashbery—I was at once captivated. It was her sense of significances other than social or psychological (again my experience echoed Duncan's) moving behind the surface of mere happening in intercourse of daily life. Behind the human encounters and attractions, sexual and initiatory, shadowy presences hovered and hinted at awareness beyond the physical or psychological. I had already read D. H. Lawrence, and I recognized her affinities, though I felt her insights more subtle. The same excitement hissed in my ears when later I read her short stories (often more finished than her novels) and the brilliant autobiographical memoir *The Crystal Cabinet.*

Rereading her now (1985), I can distinguish two seemingly opposed themes and attitudes in her work, one which could be labelled "rebellious," and the other "conservative." At first I recognized and identified with chiefly the pole of rebellion. An entry in her Journal, dated London, Sept. 18, 1917, reads, "Notes for *Ashe.* Take for the central theme the hatred of age for youth, of the old for the new, of yesterday's 'rose' for today's, expressed in a cruelty, part intuitive, part consciousness." But the other pole, expressed in her extraordinary sense of place as embodiment of time and secret spiritual tradition, is active in her work from its beginning, implicit where not overt.

In her brief memorial of Mary Butts, "Recognition Not Farewell," Bryher remarked that she felt Mary Butts's work was essentially complete at her death: "Nor do I think that she had much more to do. Her last work already repeated itself." The truth in this is that her work is "of a piece throughout," one web from beginning to end, and that though the *Last Stories* do resound themes heard before, the stories are in no way inferior. In fact the collection contains some of her most refulgent writing.

Refulgence is a special quality of her writing. She is not, like the novelist Henri Bosco, a poet of night and solitary lamps. Her daylight dazzles; "like the white cliffs, miles off, you watched in summer from the sea; burning white and blue waves dancing at them and up the floor of the cave called the Parson's Barn." Like Bosco in this, her countryside is a warm "South," Heart-land, opposing the cold Northern Scottish scape of her short story "Angèle au Couvent."

In the web of her stories and novels the same themes recur, without the monotony Bryher hints, although the early work may emphasize the pole of youthful rebellion against the sexual and social tyranny of the old British order, and the later work a social conservatism (hatred of the ill-bred city-bred masses, the notorious polarity of City-Country) and exaltation of an imagined pastoral. In *Warning to Hikers* some of her diatribe can be appreciated as early awareness of ecology. Her method is always autobiographical. Friends and family are barely disguised in all her work, and the speed of her impressions is translated at once to her paper. Alien to her would be the elaborate mathematical coding underlying a masterpiece such as Michel Butor's *Portrait of the Artist as a Young Ape.* Her metaphors for creative process evoke organic process rather than procedures of construction and technics, even if, like Butor's, related Pythagorean magical operations.

But pattern is always present, of words, refrains of songs, quotations, recurrences that speak of magical intrusions into everyday reality. And Chance and Luck (of whose magical aspect she writes in *Traps for Unbelievers*). The Omen. It was not idly she studied and practiced magic. Aleister Crowley credits her with giving him essential assistance in the final form of his major treatise *Magick in Theory and Practice.*

Her later conservatism was not like T. S. Eliot's, up tight and puritanical—she never repudiated her joie de vivre or the liberation she found in French culture. (A journal entry records her eventual "seeing through" T. S. Eliot, though she continued to love his poetry, which haunts her fiction.)

Her mediumistic sensibility was formed in childhood, like John Ruskin's, whose *Praeterita* can be compared to *The Crystal Cabinet.* In both, the sense of alienated isolation was extreme, and at times Mary Butts may have felt herself brushed by the wings of that madness that overwhelmed Ruskin. Her reliance on Earth and the numinous powers of *things,* which she consciously absorbed, was for her a saving grace. She was a passionate collector of all sorts of divine *baubles,* jewelry, gay ribbons, crystals, the lovely found junk of the tides of living. And in the solidities and embodiments of the past she found reconciling symbols which enabled her to persevere, to endure, to go forward.

When with her brother she visited the remains of the old Roman fort situated at the Badbury Rings in Dorset, near Salterns, the house she had grown up in, she found there her temenos, a primordial sacred place where she experienced an epiphany of supernatural patterning, "the makings of a correspondence, a translation which should be for ever valid, between the seen and the unseen."

That midsummer night, after reading about Helen looking out from the walls of Troy she fell asleep, she writes at the close of *The Crystal Cabinet,* and

> I was again approaching the Rings, driving very fast, from a dance, in a small white car. It was in winter: "pendant l'horreur d'une profonde nuit," but just before dawn.
>
> Driving the car was the boy who had sat beside me at lunch. He drove it into the ditch beside the road under the hill to the Rings. "I get off here," he said, and vanished.
>
> Instantly I was on the Rings again, the same and not the same as the Rings awake and by day. Another version, taller and stranger, their loveliness and power, as it were, extended into other terms, not to be described. Above them, above the grove that crowns them, there were people. People I knew, one person at least I was to come to know; and persons who were not people at all. There was a great voice like a bell, and I woke up. For some reason more inspired than by anything that had ever happened to me.

That inspiration would continue to sustain her all her life, "Experience that would provide in the end, not the answer, but the way to the answer . . . ," and this dynamic likewise would empower the dance of fiery and airy particles that is the shimmering body of her writing.

—Gerrit Lansing

I

PERSPECTIVES

Mary Butts, ca. 1920.

BRYHER

Recognition Not Farewell

I READ "Angèle au Couvent" and, because of identical experience, wrote. It must have been March, blowing and rough for Florence, when a cab came beside the Arno, stopped, and my first, my lasting impression was of Mary's hair, flaming and red, no Tuscan scarlet but the torque-gold of windy islands.

There were weeks when we met every day. It was light when I walked along the river to her room, but eastern dark, the perched chimneys seeming minarets, when I returned. I heard the outline of *The Crystal Cabinet* then, told, not written, history handed down as in the tenth century the skalds taught it. (Who has noticed that there is a spoken, as well as a visual, quality in Mary's work? We call them stories because of the way they are printed, actually they are poems.) Of course, the book is more static than the tale, for writing it, Mary had desperately the need to record her experience while time lasted, whereas in 1924, in Florence, we both smelt laurel, felt we had the right, even the obligation, to be reckless.

I didn't know Dorset. I had passed through it but my country was west, west even of Cornwall, the Scillies; these, perhaps, were simply stepping stones to the States. I could see the Persian bridges against the majolica hills yet with all the power of Italy about us, those evenings all that mattered was the region of Mary's childhood. Here was someone who so loved England that her chance words could push away one of the world's most famous landscapes, yet nobody has commented on this quality, she is not recommended in the

Originally published in *Life & Letters To-Day,* Vol. XVII, No. 9, Autumn 1937, pp. 159–64.

lists of English authors distributed to foreign universities, she is unheard of in any school (for immortality this is just as well), and one reviewer even found her Dorset dull. The city amused her and she loved Paris, she was no false nationalist believing that praise of another land could harm her own, but she loved her woods and sand so utterly that I can still see them (rather than hear her speaking); turning the chapters over I feel cheated, for the hours, the pictures, she has chosen to leave out.

I do not know if we can speak, with poets, of tragedy or doom. They have their own reward. Yet when the notices of her death refer to a distinguished young writer, is silence possible? Mary was young, but she was not distinguished, no, never in that grudging sense; she was from the start one of the few who matter, a builder of English, and I have never doubted since I read her first story that she belonged to the immortals.

Nor do I think that she had much more to do. Her last work already repeated itself. If people are as blind to the quality of her mind as most of the reviewers have appeared to be, what else could she have done to make her readers believe in her? Her mixture of clarity and metaphysics, of charity and intolerance, made easy fame impossible. They speak of her use of English; it was superb, but the day of the *mot juste* is past. I should not feel so easy if we had to rely for her living upon the way she made her sentences. What she had, more than most other writers, was pity and understanding and a new to literature sense of the psychological nuance of emotions exaggerated or created by the war.

The Crystal Cabinet is the least difficult book that she has written, a dictionary for us to look up references, for to understand Mary we must examine history and perhaps she will forgive me this once (later we were on opposite political sides and so as not to quarrel, did not write) if I speak of her relationship to her time.

When Mary was born, England was at the full flower of the industrial age. It had developed a culture, false today but not necessarily false then. There was a tradition usually honoured, of responsibility towards the less fortunate, of truth and respect for principles. It is true that it shut its eyes to industrial abuses and was frankly imperialistic but at least it would have prevented the Abyssinian fiasco and the attempted blocking of aid to shell-pursued refugee children; it was less corrupt than the political generation (not party) succeeding it in power and its programme was coherent if narrow. On the other hand, the close of the nineteenth century was a black moment for women. They had not the responsibilities of the time when everything from bread and jam to cloth was made at home, nor the modern opportunities for education and movement. Repression's usual end is selfishness and the result was a generation of frustrated lives whose aim was to keep opportunity and progress from their children.

We shall find in Mary's work a revolt against the attempt made by school, family, or world to keep her from knowledge, to ban as "dirty" or "morbid" all learning not of strictly conventional pattern, while she had absorbed from her surroundings a fanatical belief in truth that no contrary experience was to shake; disastrous equipment for a society where survival depended largely upon the ability to disguise or to fake the answer temporarily demanded.

To go back to the beginning. In the early nineteen hundreds, so many harmless things were forbidden us. We might not feel water nor sand nor earth, when "two kinds of drawers and two kinds of petticoats, a pinafore and serge frock imposed, as I can still remember, a very real strain on one's vitality." Prohibitions were imposed for whose reason we might not ask. We were pruned of every form of self-expression, like the single flower on an exhibition stem, until everything in us went into a single desire, freedom, which we saw only in wind or in the breaking waves and as we could not hold these, into what was nearest to them, poetry. I do not think that the present generation feels literature as we did. They love it, of course, but they have no need of our intense and concentrated passion. They sunbathe at two, have some of their questions answered. It was, however, the sign of our age, the identification students will tag to us, when we are dug out, as the Elizabethans were in the nineteenth century, after the night of forgetting almost sure to come.

When outside conditions become unbearable, people take refuge in what is to be or what was. It is a quite normal state, nothing to be ashamed of, it is, in fact, a sign of our will to live. Naturally, cases occur where it is carried to excess, but we might just as well refuse to go to bed because there is sleepy sickness in Africa, as to deny it in reason. Most of us make up some wished-for future, a few, like Mary, return to an ideal past. Apart from inevitable fears, she had been completely happy in childhood, so throughout her stories there is always the sense of the perfect world before history happened and, as a child can see no deliverance from harsh uncomprehended laws other than a miracle, so it is always some missing word with her that will unlock the gate, explain, make a new realm possible.

There was free, inquiring babyhood, a reasonably kind first school and a father interested in her development; then he died, her mother married again, and though she got on well with her stepfather, there must have been psychological difficulties. At this moment the blow fell that, together with an experience in war, she was never to get over; she was sent from her home, her own landscape, all that was familiar, into veritable exile in a cold and wind-swept part of Scotland, into a school so alien and uncomprehending that a part of her died. Those who understand will read the end of *The Crystal Cabinet,* wondering at her understatement. She forgave (and that was like her) where she should not have forgiven. Whatever strange and reckless actions happened in her later life, were the direct result of these unhappy, neglected years.

People accept without question the fact that physical illness may leave lasting traces in the body; why is it so hard for them to realise that the wrong treatment of a child's mind may have far more serious effects? It is not a single act of recognisable brutality that is harmful but the forcing of immature thought into a mould it obviously does not fit. Neither a country nor a school can be run for the benefit of a minority but in its own interest, civilisation should provide help for the specially gifted child, often a little information or special study prevents all maladjustment. It was an additional tragedy for Mary that she was not a rebel, she would not then have been so isolated, she wanted to cooperate with authority; her revolt was only against the system that crushed her overwhelming desire for scholarship and insistence that she conform to a pattern they never even troubled to explain to her.

No wonder that she turned to her home and the companionship of her brother, during the holidays, with too intense a concentration. They were an affirmation that she was not alone, not the last of something that she wanted to preserve, a culture, perhaps, that had only ever existed in the dreams of someone like herself.

"It was at Salterns that the important things happened, and the proper end of this book, a short time after the end of my university life."

The rest was repetition. There was another story, too terrifying to be told. Hints there were, incidents and hours, but it was something that she wanted to forget, that will never now be written. It was one of the nightmares that creep sometimes into her pages, where we feel Mary pause, herself frightened of a dark catacomb way, wondering if the ordinary, companionable world will ever be restored to her?

It was not easy to be of the minority in 1914, and Mary was a pacifist. With her upbringing, it brought her into conflict with her own loyalties. It would have been so easy for her to have driven a lorry, nursed, broken in mules, done anything other than follow the difficult course she set herself, that flung her into personal loss, extreme poverty, the opposition of people in all the small incidents of life, with air raids overhead and uncertainty for companionship. Her only weapon was the memory of a childhood world where she had once been happy. In the middle of these years something happened worse than school and that must have revived the shock of it. I do not think that she ever recovered.

A little of it was told but even at the time I had the feeling that she wanted me to forget it. She never wrote of it, only, as I have said, sometimes the feel of it is in the frightening undertone of a dream.

Much is left on the sand. Hooks, pebbles, shells, fish, often in the wrong places. So the war, when it ceased, scattered exiles and misfits about the capitals of Europe. It might have been kinder to have shot them, row after row, so that there was neither cold to face, nor hunger, nor the intermittent alms they took with a bad grace, being mostly young and not repentant, only bewildered by their fate. It is easy to say that in an ideal world such people could not happen. They were facts, not theories, forming a new kind of underworld, debris of a civilization. Mary understood, pitied, and did not judge them. She wrote of them without sentiment, knowing that they would take from her as mercilessly as from a stranger, but seeing them as dropped playthings of the gods, always as worth saving. "The House Party" and "Scylla and Charybdis" seem deeper and more important to me than some of her longer novels.

I saw her again in Paris in that "grey and green map, of stone and trams and trees, whose noises were American voice noises and street cars and wind"; under her gayer voice and clothes, I was startled by her detachment. I have an impression of amused eyes watching me being frightened of someone who was a pre-study for Boris (her glorious sense of humour was too seldom in her stories), yet if she were apparent audience for the suddenly born books, the painted intrigues and the foolish hopes of that moment's group, they remained external. She was exploring the new type of emotion for which we have not yet words, we shall grow them in time, and to understand is first a judgment on the self.

We can summarise her work: a happy childhood, this was the background for it all, then loss, loneliness, and shock, a brief moment of uneventful development, war, and again upheaval. She clutched at Dorset and at her brother as a last barricade, attempted readjustment abroad, then found a home in the county nearest in spirit to her own, and what was not surprising, in view of her experiences, renewed her early interest in religion. For her there was always the magic land, the visible one that was sometimes an echo of it, the fairy tale people, evil and good, hating and loving, that threatened and protected it.

It is true that she was not "left," nor in any way political, yet her life was communal enough; in spite of her own poverty she was always looking after people. She broke down barriers of whose existence the present generation are unaware (though, with Brecht, she seems to have influenced their work the most), and was left without the strength to push forward into another phase of civilization. If they will remember this, take her as historian of twenty years and poet of them, from 1910 to 1930, the occasional sentences in her last books that seem surface reactionary, will not disturb them. She was free herself, and in the bulk of her work, from any belief in a society of greed and war.

We met in London for the last time, hurriedly, for we were both going away. I never worried sometime we should stroll again into the same room, the saga would go on as if no interval had happened. The final message was prophetic. "The work I was trying to do in Florence never quite came off. I finished it and put it away. Of course, I thought no end of it at the time, but later I saw that it was only 'exercises on a theme.' Since then I've written far more than I've published, than any one will publish, or ever will publish until, maybe, I'm dead."

She wrote her own epitaph in her autobiography: "The kind of poet whose books people will not read until after he is dead, and then they are very, very sorry." (The first half has come so true that one only hopes that the other will follow.)

The girl she nursed, the boy she kept out of prison, will they remember her, do they even know that she has died? Perhaps I am of the last generation to understand fully what she was trying to do, the last to remember the flannel petticoats, the "don't be so morbid, darling," how difficult it was not to be muffled by these and silent; it may be that for a time her conception of beauty will simply seem subversive or incomprehensible. She was too close to the truth of art that is at once Gorgon's head and Perseus, not to come at last to her rightful place. I should have written to her had she lived; as it is, I can only prophesy, wonder what we could give her for memorial, record what I know of her courage, her understanding, and her loyalty, in recognition not farewell.

GLENWAY WESCOTT

The First Book of Mary Butts

MISS BUTTS'S COLLECTION of stories can be likened only to master-work: *Dubliners* or Mr. Lawrence's *England, My England*. It is the announcement of a new intellect, acute and passionate, to scrutinize experience with an unfamiliar penetration and to substitute for it, as it ceases, new form and light.

The light is tragic. Funereal mother, she hurries her exact heart-breaking figures into rigid graves or silence; without explanation or complaint; in a bare parti-coloured light, "all the epiphany you've got for the fine clothes, and the fine movements, and the sensual elegance, and the silly imagination, and the pain." What is done, is still; the memory can make these events a part of itself, but cannot turn them into theory or proposal. The result in sorrow and sweetness is great; halted by an aesthetic intuition at the exact point where it would become sensational.

English to the core, her good is serenity. Something over and above the décor of passion and inquisition of pain, like a David and Jonathan pact, is its nearest equivalent in conduct. The elaborate genius of her race enchants or bewilders a foreign mind: of two common labourers, "They were pleased that they recognized without philanthropy, or commiseration their contrasted pride and grace." Beyond that, there is no "impulse of malice, indignation, despair," and little comparative appraisal.

Therefore, the tales are sinister when not idyllic. No emphases are made for the benefit of society; hungriest youth could not regard these parables as aid. The fierce

---

A review of *Speed the Plough and Other Stories,* reprinted from *The Dial,* Vol. 75, September, 1923, pp. 282–84.

passions belong to the author's mind; it has not pretended, or spied on civilization. Particularly in "In Bayswater," the absence of praise and blame gives a terrific tragic tonality to the whole; one choir of instruments stilled, for a purpose. The purpose is an artificial savagery, deliberate and strong; furthered by Miss Butts's refusal to employ any modern convenience of interpretation or terminology. The parent devouring its young; the cold girl warming herself by male catastrophe; the erotic friendship, drawn out and frustrated; "Festus like a thin rod incapable of evasion or compromise or the least adaptation," intolerably a suicide; the final reckoning of the friends—Homeric waste and slaughter, needless, pitiful: it draws from her no remark. The theme is a "hard, bright and sweet" male reality wasted and wounded by old female instincts, not swiftly enough altered to a new order—unrequired and perverted. The story is not as perfect as later ones will be; but they also may present no solution and no surcease.

For her work is an irresponsible evocation; the first and strangest resource of the human intellect, and, in our literature, longest in abeyance. Of all forms of utterance, narrative, the description of a mobile cluster of experiences, is the least easily comprehensible; the contrary appears to be true only because debased romancers have too long imitated a redundant theatre. The latter's devotees are bound to find "that which is done" in these stories much overlaid by that which merely is, the plot by something as displeasing as poetry. Their demands are in fashion; but fine writers have always differed from petty by understanding that the relation between experiencing itself and mere events is exactly that between the music and text of an opera.

As to mechanics and her system of speech, she combines a minimum of linear fluency with a maximum of swift continuity in emotion. Each movement or image stands out crisply, in full relief; intermediate phrases have been cut away. Very rarely her meaning depends on grammatical relations which take place in the ellipsis, and a part is lost. The eye does not predominate, and analogies are not made to prolong its portion of experience; but to illustrate or to probe into meaning: "A huge motor gauntlet like a dead animal." This prose is not something stretched between one mind and another, a mere telephone wire; it has weight and substance, "definitely an object of whatever shape lying upon the paper" (Dr. Williams). In the dialogue, work of genius, the obliqueness of talk, its wide palette of meanings, are used with brevity and elegance; the violent atmospheres, the muscular haste, the sensual tints, the symbols and diagrams are handled with the balance of Congreve. The rhythm is subtle, short fluent jets retarded by spondaic forms. Never unnoticeable, it keeps the intellect nervous and watchful, before which the illustrative violence, the extremes of tenderness and sweetness, bud and increase and burst, incredibly primitive and bright.

Once more, beauty is not featureless. By these means of style it has boundaries, differentiating figure and surface and scent: "By the centurion's hard fire there was another arrangement of life like a base scale played firmly." To see and exist, and to see exist: the appetite of a race of navigators, with large stone eyes:

> "There were little pieces of meat classified and no carcasses. The poor like thick gold watch-chains, and little earrings stuck on cards." "Into a city of charwomen. They climbed out of deep areas. Soon he saw they were everywhere, descending, rising, in their rhythm; young in glazed cotton furs, mature and very pregnant, old with scum in their eyes. . . ." "Rain began. Wetted at dusk, the streets' patina of filth gleamed like stale fish, and out of the crests of the houses came noises of weeping that never was, never could be comforted."

Beyond these collected slums, England "hammered by the sea," its "naked sun" and "grey, savage grass" and "cows, that sharpen their teeth on their sides"; the Holy Land's "pool of hot wood," its "grey tent and its gilt bird"; France full of trenches, and Greece—a world heavy with characteristics.

Now that religion has been broken which lay embedded in faith, the shivered emotion attaches again in crystals to objects: a kind of awe and apprehension of meaning. This moody haughty mind, essentially religious, collects no drawing-room symbols; but gathers exactly the sense of ploughs, blades, and blood. It is rich in the scholarship of a golden bough, of a stamen of wood twelve feet long hung with a fox-pelt and feathers, of a dark grail. Strictly contemporary experience is lit by an antique fiery light; life an "infernal saga ... coming up-to-date." The racial memory, the animal memory, has been strangely extended; and memory is the identifiable soul.

HUGH ROSS WILLIAMSON

Who Is Mary Butts?

"Who is Mary Butts?" That was the question which I asked unavailingly of dozens of literary acquaintances in the summer of 1925. I had just read her contribution to *The Calendar* entitled "The Later Life of Theseus, King of Athens," and I wanted to read more. What else had she written? No one seemed to know. Very few seemed to know even her name.

That autumn, by a happy coincidence, a green paper-backed novel, printed in English but published in France, arrived in a pile of books for review. It was entitled *Ashe of Rings* and was written by Mary Butts. Never before and never since have I read a book for review—or for anything else, for that matter—with such eagerness. And it did not disappoint me. It was "difficult"—with that difficulty which may perhaps always limit Mary Butts's appeal to a limited audience; it created an atmosphere which added to the difficulty, because it defied rational analysis; its staccato style, combining the direct narration of prose with the elliptical suggestiveness of modern poetry, produced something of the effect of a rhythmic incantation: the story itself, though contemporary in its setting, dealt with forces and fears reminiscent of *The Golden Bough.* To read *Ashe of Rings* is to surrender to an experience, at the end of which one feels moved to quote: "How wonderful, how glorious—but what an escape!"

Ashe of Rings remained one of my treasured hooks. As for a year or two I could find nothing more of Mary Butts's work, I re-read it, and it survived that test. Then one day I came across an old second-hand copy of *Speed the Plough,* a book

---

This essay first appeared under the title "Mary Butts" in *The Bookman,* Vol. 81, December, 1931, pp. 188–89.

of short stories which, though written later, was published earlier than *Ashe of Rings*. The tales vary considerably in quality, but "In Bayswater" is an absolute masterpiece of the macabre. By comparison any other uncanny tale I have read seems merely an exercise in conventional sentiment. Again there is created that elusive atmosphere heavy with dark and evil forces which the reader cannot altogether understand and which (I feel) the writer cannot altogether express. But here the scene has become completely modern. The Greeks, whose lives and beliefs form the theme of "Theseus" and the undercurrent of *Ashe,* are far away. And with them has gone security. The elemental forces are now oppressive and frightening: they are unreasonable and undirected, and modernity becomes menacing.

"Theseus" was one of many contributions in the fourth issue of a magazine which had not a very long life or a very large circulation. *Ashe of Rings,* though it had an American edition, was never published in this country. *Speed the Plough* met with the predictable fate of any book of intelligent stories by an unknown author. And when, in 1928, Mary Butts made her bow to the English public with a novel, it was unfortunately a work so difficult to understand that it was almost a despair to her admirers. For *Armed with Madness* marks no advance on her previous work either in thought or in technical achievement, and it is representative only in the sense that it is an epitome of it. What a reader unacquainted with *Ashe* would make of it I cannot imagine. As an introduction to the public it was foredoomed to failure. And her critical essay on Aldous Huxley in the second volume of *Scrutinies* is too slight to give a just sense of her capabilities.

It is her as yet unpublished work, "Episodes in the Life of Alexander of Macedon," which I have had the privilege of reading in manuscript, that seems to me to sum up her real genius, for here everything that is essential to it is utilised to the full. Her scholarship, her knowledge of Greek life, her intense feeling for family, her archaeological interests, her power of suggesting elemental forces, her irony, her vivid sense of colour, all contribute to make "Alexander" a little masterpiece of its kind. It has the wit of "Theseus," the style of *Ashe,* and the atmosphere of "In Bayswater," but it is written so simply that those who were frightened away by *Armed with Madness* will be charmed back into allegiance.

Behind all Mary Butts's work one is conscious of a very definite and challenging personality. In searching contemporary literary memoirs for some portrait of her, I found only one reference—and that one not very enlightening. It was in Sisley Huddleston's *Back to Montparnasse* and there, among the artists and writers of the Left Bank, which is still the cultural dictator of the world, flitted the figure of "dear, delightful Mary Butts." The adjectives, though doubtless justified of the person, were obviously misleading as applied to the writer. No "dear, delightful" author could ever have written with such power, such insight, such ruthlessness. The "dear, delightful" are predestined to recommendation at the circulating library counter.

In spite of my knowledge of her work, I was still asking "Who is Mary Butts?" six years after my discovery of "Theseus." Her life, I felt, must explain her writings. And when she told me the story of it, I found that her experience of life and her creation of art made a perfect unity.

Mary Butts was born in Dorsetshire, in surroundings which were an epitome of the English countryside. The house was surrounded by fields and woods, heath and marsh: facing it was an inlet of the sea and beyond the sea, hills. Here, among country folk, living close to the earth and sharing its magic, she lived till she was eighteen, oblivious of towns. Here at a very early age she learnt Greek from a scholarly father and found a universe in Homer and the great myths. The gods and heroes became real people to her. That was the second magic, which explained and was explained by the first, the primal magic of earth. The two were one, inextricable.

There was another influence, strangely combining with

and acting upon these two—the magic of mystical art which had been preserved for her by the continuity of a family tradition. Mary Butts's great-grandfather was Thomas Butts, the friend and patron of William Blake. It will be remembered that Captain Butts was for thirty years Blake's admirer and customer, whose interest made it possible for the poet-painter to spend so much of his energy on those works which made him famous but were never financially remunerative. The twenty original water-colour illustrations for *The Book of Job* for instance were bought by Thomas Butts, who had recognised their genius long before Linnell ordered the duplicate set which resulted in their publication in book form. And thus many Blake treasures, MSS., engravings, and the whole collection of the tempera water-colours which was later acquired by the Tate Gallery, surrounded the growing girl. Mary Butts, to use her own words, "spent a childhood saturated in Blake." Here she found the very antithesis of the Greek vision, with its simple directness and its masculine dislike of unnecessary complications. Here, too, was something which had little in common with Nature. But there was a spell in it nevertheless—the spell of the compelling imagination of an artist-prophet.

From a knowledge of these things in her early life one could almost deduce her work. Country-writers we have had in plenty. There are those who turn to Nature as a highly idealised form of escape from urbanity; and there are those, inspired by reaction from this school, who delight in exhibiting the sordidness and narrowness of rusticity by reminding us that a picturesque village may contain more squalor than a hideous slum. With neither class has Mary Butts anything whatever to do. In the first place she accepted the country without comparisons. To live there was not a mode of existence to be contrasted with the lot of the city-dweller; it gave her the only background for experience which she knew. If she judged it by any standards, they were the historical ones of family tradition. She was the heir of Hellas. It was on a hill that Endymion slept; Aphrodite had risen from the sea, and in the woods Adonis died; Persephone haunted the meadows and Pan the pursuer still lingered by the reeds in the marshes. She had inherited their land. Gradually she came to understand them. If they began as real people, they ended as equally real forces, which refused to be moralised over but demanded acceptance. The earth had magic, but it was not necessarily good magic—and, good or bad, it could not be explained away. More, in certain cases it could not even be explained. All she knew was that she was the child of it. She must express it as well as she could, but Blake had taught her that the perception of a mystery does not carry with it the power or the necessity of rational and logical interpretation.

At eighteen she went to London to study for her degree at the University there. The urgent life of the city, the new contacts, the strange rhythm of modernity, imposed themselves on the old quiet certainties. But the older was the stronger, and by the light of it the newer was interpreted. In "Theseus" the narrator says:

> Before the Argo's voyage and the hunt of the calydonian boar, life moved quietly in this land, arranged on certain antique forms. These I have upheld against the innovating heroes. There are dark spots in nature; let them stay dark. Man need not try to illuminate them. His business is to keep harmony by due propitiatory sacrifices to the infernal powers. I would offend no Sacred Snake. Omit no libation of honey, milk, or blood. Especially not blood. It is, when you think of it, the cheapest of the three.

Those "dark places," it seems, are unaltered by centuries of civilisation. But we do not perceive them because our normal approach leads from the end to the beginning; we accept the twentieth century and research into antiquity. Mary Butts reversed the journey; she grew up in antiquity and applied its lessons to the twentieth century. So she came to "Bayswater."

This mental process was however largely subconscious.

At the time, life was to be lived not written about. A spell of feverish activity at the London School of Economics (where the study of Economics turned her into a Socialist) was followed by her first job, undertaken at the beginning of the War. Always she had been devoted to children, and she worked for the L.C.C. as secretary of the Children's Care Committee in Hackney, writing experimentally in her spare time. Soon afterwards she married, had a child of her own—a daughter—and settled down to write in earnest. The greater part of *Ashe of Rings* was written at her house in Hampstead during the latter part of the War.

When war was over, she went abroad, leaving her small daughter in the care of a devoted aunt to be brought up as she had been brought up, in the heart of the country. And for five years Mary Butts wandered over Europe, making Paris the headquarters to which she returned regularly from her journeys in Italy, Germany, and Southern France. It was during this time that she wrote the stories of *Speed the Plough.*

When she returned to England, the focus of the life of the artistic world was the Russian Ballet, whose great seasons under Diaghileff were influencing all the arts. She took a flat in Regent's Park, which soon became a salon both for those performing in the ballet and for many of the spectators. But London palled, and once more she returned to Paris and the intense vitality of Montparnasse. There she continued her work.

Only in the spring of this year did she come back to England again and after a short stay in London, went north, and on the Border moors wrote *Alexander.* Now she and her husband (who is Gabriel Aitken, the artist) are living in Chelsea.

At thirty-seven she has come, I think, to the end of her wanderings. She has observed life in its most varied forms; her experience of it has left her without bitterness; and, for the recording and interpretation of it, she has perfected an intensely individual style as befits a unique vision. Her admirers await a masterpiece.

DAVID HOPE

Mary Butts, Fire-Bearer

HERE IN THIS peaceful backwater, where a few thatched roofs still cover strongly built pre-jerry walls; where the winds of heaven blow free from the dust and soot of cities; here where life is simple, and beauty catches the throat, lived Mary Butts, rightly called a Fire-Bearer.

Her posthumous autobiography *The Crystal Cabinet* (Methuen) represents her last known work, but it is hoped that the notes of her promised book on the Holy Grail will be edited at a later date and given to the world. Who can tell what painful travail was hers in the search for the elusive Grail?

The little house in which she lived stands on a cliff overlooking Sennen Cove, until recently a dreaming unspoilt bit of Cornish coastline, and from her windows she could watch every mood of the restless tides which ebbed and flowed beneath her garden fence.

There is an old saying that every man is immortal till his work is finished, and if that be true then it is certain that sooner or later the value of Mary Butts's finished work will be realised, for her pen was certainly the instrument of a message which, though ended, is not yet fully known.

This is a strange age. Artists with beauty in brain and fingertip find themselves shouldered aside in competition with modern indifference; writers with an inspired message fail to find publishers or, if found, see their books buried beneath the latest thriller—and yet if one of these Fire-Bearers passes on to that place whence inspiration comes, the indifferent world, moved by sympathy, fashion or curiosity, awakes to the fact that some divine spark has vanished

---

First published as Sennen Pamphlet Series, no. 1, 1937.

from our midst, and whips up a jaded and momentary interest.

Mary Butts was original in thought and outlook, blessed with a knowledge and sensitive emotion which informed all her output. Although somewhat of a dreamer (at times she would not recognise friends who greeted her in passing) her writings are not ephemeral words to be hurriedly scanned as one scans a mechanical novel, but require deep study if one is to enjoy a glimpse of the spiritual gleam which infused her labours.

Her love for the country and sea was emphasized by her choice of this lovely spot in which to make her home, and the environment undoubtedly coloured her opinions on the question of rearing children in country surroundings.

She believed that from earliest infancy the budding child imbibes and retains impressions which influence the whole after-life, and it was one of her great arguments that children bred in a city environment, no matter under what luxurious conditions, were deprived of some vital principle best illustrated by suddenly leaving a darkened room for the bright light and clean air of the open.

That was Mary Butts's passing last March: she suddenly left this darkened room we call (with such irony) "life" for the light and freedom of a wider sphere, and at the early age of forty-six dropped the Torch for other hands to bear.

Although her principal joy was found in the beauty and peace of Sennen, she still retained delight in what we term civilisation and its amenities, but one fancies that those amenities were discounted by comparison with the simple things she loved.

Her tiny garden typifies the fate of most Fire-Bearers. A few weeks ago it was tended with care, and held all the promise of summer glory; now, in June, it is overrun with weeds, the empty house looming sadly in the background seeming to express desolation at the owner's absence.

Hidden beneath much of her writing is that pagan enjoyment of the ancient gods which obtrudes from some of her works, and gives proof of her wide reading and wider application. She believed in the creed of blind old Homer:

> "I bid thee know
> Gods in the garb of strangers to and fro
> Wander the cities, and men's ways discern;
> Yea, through the wide earth in all shapes they go,
> Changed, yet the same, and with their own eyes learn
> How live the sacred laws—who hold them, and who spurn!"

She knew a great deal about the spurning of the sacred laws, and learned "what happens to Fire-Bearers in this wicked world, and what they must expect and what they must endure." But a heart communing with the gods must acquire some of their secrets, and the translation of those secrets gliding smoothly from her pen would be much clearer to her open vision than to those of us overshadowed by material things, to whom any form of contemplation is a waste of time.

Mary Butts inherited much of her great literary talent from her father's love of books, as well as from her avid reading in early youth, and she had a peculiar gift of being able to "de-bunk" things. We are told that "It's the Bunk" was a phrase often on her lips, and the uncanny power to penetrate to the root of a matter did not always make for friendship in this superficial world.

In common with so many other Fire-Bearers, Mary Butts suffered neglect and met indifference during the many years when her works should have commanded respect, and it may be that had she been less passionately a lover of the country, and more tolerant of city life, her publicity value might have been discovered, and popularity would have given prominence to her books.

A noted writer, whose criticism is beyond appeal, places Mary Butts with D.H. Lawrence and T.S. Eliot, but some of her admirers go further and claim that she saw visions denied to both those writers. The woman who had been with

Apollo to the back of the North Wind brought back a message which she passed on simply, and without any veneer, which is the tragedy of her lack of recognition.

* * * * *

In this one-time smugglers' haunt, where Athelstan, Stephen and John made history, and where the ghost of Perkin Warbeck can still be sensed, many famous artists, scholars and writers have sojourned, but none more inspired or worthy of the world's approbation.

The winding road from her little house is wind-swept and stony, something like her passage through life, but some of us miss the small figure whose inner communion with a greater world allowed little time for conformity to the conventions and trimmings of modern life.

There are some who discern a Law of Contrariness in fate, and it is interesting to learn that, now she has passed, the Press contains full and excellent notices of her book. Knowing the value of her message she rather exulted in the neglect which did not daunt her, and perhaps in some other place she is now moved to laughter by the veering winds of popularity.

In any case the time will come when her books will command respect for their spiritual value alone, and none may dabble with sacred things without being scorched. Least of all a Fire-Bearer.

> "The sacred fire the soul of him shall scorch
> Who seeks in life to bear the flaming Torch:
> If rough the track and sharp the flints we tread,
> Soon Zeus calls—Olympus lies ahead!"

Sennen Cove, Cornwall
June, 1937

ROBERT H. BYINGTON

Interviews with Virgil Thomson, Eugene MacCown, Quentin Bell and Hugh Ross Williamson

I

VIRGIL THOMSON lived in the Hotel Chelsea on 23rd Street. It had sheltered writers Thomas Wolfe, Dylan Thomas, and Brendan Behan, among others, at different times, and its literary associations lent it for me a certain romance that made a virtue of its complacent seediness. There was a plaque by the front entrance attesting to Thomas Wolfe's satisfaction with the place, should a visitor entertain any doubts. We announced ourselves at the desk, and in a few moments took the appropriately dowdy but obviously functioning elevator up to Thomson's apartment. A black man, who I assumed was Thomson's houseman and who did not stay very long, led us through a narrow hall into a larger room crammed with furniture, where Thomson awaited us.

Short, dapper, pink-faced and bald with a round head that tapered slightly at the top, Thomson greeted us pleas-

---

The following interviews are excerpted from "The Quest for Mary Butts," a valuable biographical study which Robert H. Byington began in the fall of 1963 and completed in early 1974. Partly an effort to fathom why Mary Butts's work disappeared from view and who she was, this unpublished volume contains a wealth of material, including discussions with Camilla Bagg, Djuna Barnes, Kitty Cannell, Angus Davidson, Robert Gathorne-Hardy, Sheelah Hynes, Man Ray, Mary Stanford, Glenway Wescott and many others. In his conversations with Virgil Thomson and Eugene MacCown, Mr. Byington was assisted by the musicologist, Glen E. Morgan.

antly and then left us alone for a moment while he talked briefly with his houseman in an adjoining room. [Glen] Morgan and I looked around. The room was richly if idiosyncratically furnished, with large, upholstered chairs, a sofa, a love seat, Persian rugs, and every available foot of wall space covered with paintings and photographs. There were also filled bookshelves and a grand piano. It was cozy and personal, suggesting the intimacy of its inhabitant with various eras and media of artistic achievement. I knew Thomson principally as the author of lucid and witty articles of musical criticism I had read in the *Herald Tribune* back in the early '50s, when I had spent a lot of time in New York, and thought it would be better if Morgan carried the ball in the interview, which he did.

Thomson had met Mary Butts in March of 1927, and had stopped seeing her in November or December of that year. As he remarked, "It was all in a single year ... very intense, and very nice, but it was all in a single year." His opinions coincided with Glenway Wescott's on certain matters, and differed on others. He, like Wescott, not only accepted the grandeur of Mary Butts's family, but vehemently insisted upon it. At one point, when Morgan had casually referred to Mary's background as "middle class," Thomson literally pounced on Morgan's presumed error, and reminded him intensely that Mary had been "very, very, very upper class." Indeed, he opined that part of the Russian refugee, Boris's, appeal for Mary had been his aristocratic heritage, so similar to Mary's, the English country families having their counterpart in the Russian country families. "All those people that Turgenev wrote about are the Russian equivalent of the English landed families," Thomson said. In fact, Thomson himself had a more favorable view of Boris [Sergei Maslenikof] than he had earlier expressed to Morgan back in Pennsylvania. While admitting that Boris was a sponge, Thomson added that he "had so much grace and sweetness about him that he could get away with that.... He unquestionably had considerable charm, he was gracious, and upper class, and nicely elegant." All this preoccupation with social class, I thought, on everybody's part, Mary's, Wescott's, Thomson's, but I said nothing. Neither did I mention [Douglas] Goldring's description of Mary's unfortunate "passion for befriending odd persons of apparently aristocratic origin."

If there had been any question of Mary's gentility in our minds, Thomson wanted it laid to rest. It was as if something very important to him depended upon his establishing that fact, even when what one would have thought unrelated matters were under consideration. At one point Morgan asked him whether, when he knew her, Mary had been a heavy opium smoker; and, again, the vehemence of Thomson's reply surprised us.

"No!" Thomson retorted with what seemed almost resentment. "Mary was *not* a heavy opium smoker. She smoked in a genteel fashion, like a lady. No more than you would say she was a heavy drinker. She was brought up in an English country house, where she'd been taught to drink, and she could hold a good deal of liquor and never show it.... Mary was a lady and acted like one." Thomson's insistence upon Mary's presumably class-related propriety was a recurrent theme throughout the interview. At another point, after Thomson had identified for us a number of people Mary had known in the literary world, Morgan somewhat superfluously remarked that Mary had known a lot of people and a lot of people had known Mary. Rather than ignore the banality, Thomson used it as an opportunity to drive home his lesson:

"Mary knew all the people of her class and age.... [He paused for a moment.] Don't ever get the idea that there was anything wrong about Mary, in her appearance, or her style, or anything. She was immaculately turned out, and if she wore the British national costume which was a sweater and a skirt, it was a good sweater and a good skirt, and she was likely to wear a man's hat, from a Bond Street establishment.... the body was very beautiful. You'll see the face is not exactly beautiful, but it's not ugly! If Mary had a little tuckup here and there, or a lover here and there, she did it as a lady would do it."

A lady who, for whatever reasons, had a steadfast champion in Virgil Thomson. I decided to try and get those reasons into better focus. Earlier, while discussing Boris, Thomson had said that Mary "would have liked him to be her lover, but he was queer and wasn't doing it." Then he paused for a long time and remarked, "I was her lover for about six months, I suppose. [Pause.] Were there others who lasted that long? I don't know."

After that it would not have been tactful to mention either his own ambiguity about his and Mary's relationship in the Hoover/Cage biography, or Glenway Wescott's doubts. So I settled for an "approach oblique" as perhaps the heaviest the circumstances would tolerate. I asked Thomson what about Mary had chiefly appealed to him initially. I might just as well have used the "approach direct," because for the first time in the interview he expressed some irritation.

"Look," he snapped, "this book's about her, not about me."

"That's true," I said, somewhat startled, "but we wanted to get your opinion."

His response was hurried, as if he wanted to get it over with.

"It's very difficult, it's very difficult to psychoanalyze yourself. Mary and I got on like a house afire from the beginning. We understood each other, we laughed together, we told each other stories.... I was an old back country American just as she was an old back country English girl, and we understood each other but *perfectly!*"

I let it rest there, and Thomson quickly regained his amiability. He asked us if we wanted to see Man Ray's* photograph of Mary (of which, it later developed, he may have

*The photograph described appears not to be by Man Ray.—*ed.*

the only copy extant), and we jumped at the chance. Taken from the left, its subject carefully posed, it revealed a Mary Butts suggested by the Cocteau drawing, but far more glamorous. In a large cartwheel hat, and a huge jade earring pendant from her left ear, she seemed strikingly handsome. No laundry bag here. We were still looking at it when Thomson asked us if we were ready for dinner. He remarked that he had nothing suitable on hand, but that there was an acceptable Greek restaurant across and down the street a bit, and we might try that.

Over dinner Thomson told us the story of Mary's black tooth. It seems that Mary had a front tooth which had been broken, and she didn't have the money to get it fixed. So, when Thomson came into a little money in the fall of '27, he gave her a number of presents as well as the money to have the tooth repaired. Mary had taken the money and spent it on something else; as a consequence (for a couple of years), she had to go around with a broken tooth that first turned black and finally fell out. Thomson said that people were always making jokes about Mary and her tooth, and I remembered that Wescott had referred to it, but declined to tell the story because he considered it "Virgil's."

Morgan and I both laughed because it seemed to be the response Thomson expected, but I thought it more pathetic than funny. So, when Thomson invited us back to his apartment for an after-dinner drink, and we were settled with our brandy in his comfortable chairs, I brought up the subject of Mary's finances.

"Mary had a little bit of income," Thomson said, "but it was never enough for her to live on, and certainly not enough to buy opium on. I do know that she was always overdrawing on that account, as you do in England."

"Whether or not her income was adequate, would you say that Mary's financial problems resulted chiefly from the fact that she spent money foolishly, if not on opium, on other things?" I asked.

He agreed, and added, "She was *terrifying* the way she

could spend money. Any money she could lay her hands on, she'd spend."

That seemed to settle the matter for the moment, so we passed on to other things. Thomson didn't know anything about Mary's desire to get to America, which cast considerable doubt upon Wescott's explanation of Virgil Thomson's principal appeal to Mary. Whatever it had been it seemed not to have been that. Like Wescott, however, Thomson was disinclined to attribute any Lesbian leanings to Mary, and said firmly when the question was raised, "I don't know of Lesbian adventures on Mary's part." On the other hand, he also mentioned that on one occasion he had been with Mary on a visit to Camilla attending a school in nearby Nice, and they had taken her for a day's outing. This suggested at least some concern on Mary's part for her daughter, whereas Wescott had told us that "Mary would have cheerfully *drowned* Camilla!"

Thomson obviously knew little of Mary's life after her return to England, and had heard of her death second-hand from Kirk Askew, the picture dealer, who had presumably been informed by Angus Davidson. Since we had already uncovered a number of agreements and disagreements between Thomson and Wescott, who had known Mary at the same time, if not equally long, I thought it would be helpful to cross-check their opinions on one or two other matters. Remembering that Wescott's opinion of Mary's work was that it had showed early promise and then petered out, I asked Thomson what he thought of her work (without mentioning Wescott's opinion). As I had suspected, he held a very different view. He tended to discount the novels for reasons he did not present, but maintained that in her short stories, poetry, and *The Crystal Cabinet* Mary Butts was "the best of the lot." He characterized them as "bigger than any Sitwell, and less phoney than Elizabeth Bowen" and "really extraordinarily good."

He also maintained that the English publishing houses, controlled by the "Bloomsbury crowd," had discouraged any serious consideration of Mary's work, and reported a conversation he had had with Raymond Mortimer, whom he had asked what people in London thought of Mary Butts. Mortimer had replied, "Well, we don't really think of her at all." Thomson added, "It was by a kind of tacit agreement that they didn't mention her."

When I tried to get at the cause of what sounded to me like a conspiratorial boycott, I asked the foolish question "Why?" which drew from Thomson a testy response.

"Oh, you ask such foolish questions beginning with 'Why?'! I don't know these things."

He went on to say somewhat vaguely, however, that it was probably a combination of factors, of "events," as he called them, rather than any one thing, such as Mary's desertion of [John] Rodker, which I had suggested as a possible cause of Bloomsbury's enmity.

Braced by brandy (I think we were all getting a little tiddly by this time), I made one more assay. I mentioned to Thomson Glenway Wescott's statement that there had been two camps of expatriate writers and artists in the 'twenties, British and American, and that they did not overlap much. Thomson considered this a moment and then disagreed.

"Well," he said, "there were several groups. Several English groups and several American groups. But no special chasms between the English and the Americans."

He then made a very telling point, I thought. He recalled that while of course Mary Butts had English friends from her London days, Nina Hamnett and Duff Twysden, for example, she consistently spent most of her time with Americans—Philip Lasell, McAlmon, Glenway Wescott and Monroe Wheeler, Mary Reynolds, et al.—and not very much with the English, not even with Duff. I thought this was important, and did not remind Thomson that it seemed at some variance with his earlier statement that Mary had known "all the people of her class and age." It also appeared that Wescott had been projecting from his own tendency to stay away from Americans, at least the Hemingway and

Fitzgerald breed. So Mary had traveled mostly with Americans in France. And avoided the English? Did this tie in with her rejection by Bloomsbury?

As if Thomson had been aware of my train of thought, he qualified his comment about Mary's preference for Americans:

"Of course, Mary had known in London a man named Allington, Napier Allington, who later became Lord Napier (and if he's still living, he is Lord Napier). All that very posh, gay English set, not the stuffy ones, but the gay young ones that Mary used to refer to as 'the tall tight boys.' She wrote a lot of poetry about them. She called them 'the Achilles set.'"

These were the English with whom Mary did get along, and mingle, however she may have been rejected by the Bloomsbury set. In other words, the non-Bloomsbury homosexuals.

Our remaining time with Thomson that evening was chiefly spent in taking down names and frequently addresses of people in Thomson's incredibly large circle of friends and acquaintances who had known or might have known Mary: Tommy Earp, a good friend of Mary's in London (until Thomson suddenly recalled that he had died not long ago); Eugene MacCown, "a man here in New York who knew her quite well"; Marcel Duchamp; Harold Vursell (Managing Editor of Farrar & Straus, Publishers); Janet Flanner ("Genêt," the Paris correspondent for *The New Yorker,* who knew Mary and would also know the address of Jean Guérin and Walter Shaw, both of whom had known Mary well and were particularly qualified to fill us in on the "dope business" and Mary's involvement with it); Natalie Barney; Raymond Mortimer, English man of letters; Alexander Calder; Hilaire Hiler (painter and pianist in Paris when Mary was there); Margaret Anderson; Anthony Powell; Morrill Cody (American newspaperman in Paris); Osbert Sitwell; Sir Cedric Morris and Lett Haines; Laurence Vail; Man Ray; Djuna Barnes; Kay Boyle—in fact, almost the entire cast of characters, still living, who had acted in that phenomenal cultural drama the 'twenties had produced in London, Paris and elsewhere.

Some, of course, were already lost to us. Mary Reynolds, for one, who had been Marcel Duchamp's girl friend and Mary Butts's fellow tenant at 14 rue de Montessuy in Paris. But her papers had been collected and deposited in the Ryerson Library at the Art Institute of Chicago, and we could check to see if there was anything pertaining to Mary Butts among them.

We asked Thomson about Boris, but he had no knowledge of what had happened to "the little Russian," or whether he were still alive. Our question reminded him of *Imaginary Letters,* however, which we had not read, and he said it was a collection of imaginary letters to Boris's mother which Mary had composed discussing the problems of her relationship with Boris. Thomson described it as "concerned with the whole problem of homosexuality in our time, which"—he said with a chuckle—"the women have got to deal with."

I was about to turn off the tape recorder when it occurred to me to inquire of Thomson whether he thought Mary had been a very disciplined writer. He confirmed that she was, and attributed it to her upbringing and education. The properly schooled English, he said, "A. Get up in the morning, B. Keep a notebook." Our ears pricked up. Had Mary kept notebooks? "Oh my dear, yes. Black notebooks, bound black notebooks. Fountain pen handwriting." He described them further as containing diary items, opinions of people, accounts of things she was doing, quotations from her reading, "the same notebook," he said, "that all the English literary ones keep, full of ideas, references, the picture of their intellectual life." It was with that picture very much in our minds that we said a grateful goodnight to Virgil Thomson, and made our way out to 23rd Street.

II

Eugene MacCown's response to my most recent letter had been cordial enough, but brief, and merely suggested that we call him when we reached New York. A year earlier (replying to my first communication, which had failed to produce a meeting), he'd been a bit more responsive and I remembered now what he'd written: "That you and your colleague are experiencing an interest in the world of Mary Butts gives me great pleasure. Lord knows the poor dear enjoyed precious little of it during her lifetime." It expressed the same note of kindliness and concern that Mary's descriptions of him, written forty years ago that very fall, had somehow conveyed; and I was anxious to meet him. In his note I'd received the week before he'd said that he was in the throes of moving from his present apartment, hence the need to arrange a meeting elsewhere. I reflected about what little I knew of him, and it didn't take long. He had been a painter in the 'twenties, and for a while was fairly prominent in the artistic-social swim of Paris and that of Villefranche, where he'd known Cocteau, Glenway Wescott, Monroe Wheeler, and met Mary. He had also painted her portrait, according to a letter she had written Tony. That about summed it up. Morgan had reviewed the references to him in the journal and had found nothing more. Well, at the very least, he had known and liked her, and we didn't need much of an excuse to spend a night in New York.

When we reached our room in the motor hotel where we always stayed, I called the number he'd given me; and while the phone rang at the other end I glanced at his address on the letter I'd written him: 1107 Second Avenue. Not a very attractive neighborhood, I was thinking, when there was a click in the receiver and a tense, tired voice said hello. I identified myself and reminded him of our appointment. He remembered it, but not with any apparent enthusiasm, and when I suggested we have dinner—Morgan and I, as usual, were hungry—he said he'd rather not, but would be happy to meet us for a drink at a bar he knew on 59th Street, the "Queensborough." So we agreed to meet there in forty-five minutes. He said he would be sitting at the bar and wearing a black shirt.

Our tape recorder was not battery-powered, so we grabbed a pad of notepaper apiece, and headed uptown. The "Queensborough," on 59th Street between First and Second Avenues, was a typical workingman's bar in a business section of small retail stores and mercantile companies. It had a worn black and white tiled floor, with a bar extending down one wall and a row of booths the other. There were stools along the bar, and behind it the usual tiers of liquor bottles, mostly inexpensive brands. But it was clean and well-lighted.

There were only two or three customers in the place when we arrived, all of them sitting at the bar. The man closest to the door was wearing a shabby brown overcoat with its collar up and sat hunched over a drink. He turned as we entered, and we could see his black shirt. We were obviously who we were, so he left the bar and walked over to us with a slight, forced smile on his face. He was a thin man of less-than-medium height, which may have been what made his overcoat seem too large for him. He had a narrow face with a yellowish complexion and eyes slightly pinched at the sides, which gave him a somewhat oriental look. His thin grey-brown hair was combed straight back. We shook hands, and he suggested we sit in one of the empty booths, gesturing toward those in the rear. We followed him back and sat down, he on one side, Morgan and I on the other.

MacCown asked us if we'd like a drink, and when we said sure, he turned and called out the name of one of the bartenders in an imperious tone. There were no waiters or waitresses. To my surprise the summoned bartender came around the bar at the front and walked the entire length of the quite large room back to our booth (had it been me in such circumstances I would have gone to the bar, ordered the drinks and brought them back to the table myself). He was a big man in his mid-forties, and looked about as servile as the bare knuckles champion of the block, which, given his job and the location, he might well have been. But he took our orders, whiskey for MacCown, beer for us, and returned shortly to place them in front of us. MacCown thanked and then dismissed him so superciliously I expected blood to flow. But the bartender only looked at him with what seemed to me a kind of rough compassion, glanced indifferently at us and walked away. This interaction would have been somewhat clearer to me if I had known then what I learned later about MacCown.

He had been a painter, but not just any painter in a time and place when the woods were full of them. He'd known everyone in almost every expatriate group during the 'twenties and early 'thirties; he had been friends with Nancy Cunard, Norman Douglas, Osbert and Sacheverell Sitwell, Clive Bell, Raymond Mortimer and others among the English; Bernard Faÿ, André Gide, Jean Cocteau and others among the French; Hart Crane, Harry Crosby, Bob McAlmon, Janet Flanner, Kitty Cannell, Virgil Thomson and many others among the Americans. He had done portraits of Nancy Cunard and Norman Douglas, had been the piano player at Cocteau's Le Boeuf sur le Toit, designed the cover for Nancy Cunard's *Parallax,* published by the Hogarth Press, designed the catalog published by Nancy Cunard's Hours Press for the first exhibition of his own paintings in Paris. Hart Crane had lived at his house in Paris, and he had been present at Le Sélect the night of Crane's famous donnybrook with the gendarmes and instrumental in setting up Crane's defense fund. Furthermore, he had been a close friend of Virgil Thomson's, and they had once danced folk dances in Austria together.

One would have guessed little of that from the appearance of the sallow-faced man who sat quietly in the booth across from Morgan and me that Thursday evening in the fall of 1964. Only his way with the bartender, perhaps (natural to him and obviously accepted as such), suggested a lifestyle different from the one symbolized by the thick, false-bottomed shot glass of cheap whiskey he now held in his hand. He was alert, however, somewhat suspicious, and very noncommittal when we first began to ask him the questions we had prepared from Morgan's review of [M.B.'s] journal. Then he slowly began to open up, and for a while we were able to elicit from him rather extended answers, even to questions that had evoked "No comment" from him when they were first raised.

He had gone to Europe in the early 'twenties and stayed until 1933. He had seen Mary most frequently in Villefranche when they were both there from the early fall of 1925 to the spring of 1926, but he had seen her occasionally after that until her final departure from Paris in 1930. Much of what he told us, that she was interested in magic, that she "adored" her brother Tony, e.g., we already knew. He himself had thought Tony, whom he'd met in Paris, "beauty personified," but noted that he "faded, very, very fast." MacCown claimed not to remember certain episodes that Mary had mentioned but not elaborated upon, such as a "perfect day" that she, Cocteau, Georges Auric and MacCown had spent together on March 3, 1926. On other points he seemed quite clear. He maintained that Mary's final quarrel with Glenway Wescott and Monroe Wheeler had not been over Murray Goodwin and money, but, rather, had its genesis in an occasion when Mary went to their room looking for them, found a bottle of Monroe's hair-dye, and kidded him about it, which made Monroe very angry. We had no way of verifying either story because other than the enmity toward Glenway and Monroe she expresses in her journal after 1928, Mary makes no reference at all to the quarrel.

Other subjects that MacCown seemed to know a good deal about were Mireille Havet and drugs. We knew from the journal that Mary's relationship with Mireille Havet, the Lesbian actress who, among other roles, had played "Death" in Cocteau's *Orphée,* had been far from casual. They appear to have met in the spring of 1928 in Villefranche, and later, in the last half of 1929, were together in Paris. Mary even lived at Mireille's house in Paris for a while. Whether or not their relationship was sexual is not clear from the journal, but Glenway Wescott's comment that Mary had used Mireille as an entree into certain sectors of French society was true only if one recognized the sectors in question comprised the drug culture. MacCown described Mireille as a man in travesty, who always wore tight-fitting, very tailored, masculine clothes and men's slouch hats. She was, nevertheless, "pretty as she could be," and "bright as a cricket," with a husky voice. He was also of the opinion that Mireille had played a pivotal function in Mary's later drug addiction by introducing her to French sources of supply that would not otherwise have been available to her. The journal entries for the latter part of 1929 indicate that Mary's and Mireille's relationship at the time was drug-related if not dependent, and reveal one of the most painful periods in Mary's life. When we asked MacCown about Mary's use of drugs at this time, he said flatly that she was "definitely addicted to an injection procedure"—which suggested heroin to us—and that Mireille had so bungled it that she had sores on her thighs.

When we told him that in Cornwall Mary had boiled poppy heads in water to make an opium *tizane* and had used both Camilla on her wanderings through the fields and the local Boots as sources of supply, MacCown scoffed and said "Nonsense," as if it were impossible. We knew from the journal alone that it was not only possible, but true. On the other hand, we were inclined to respect, if not entirely believe, his other comments on drugs. We had noticed almost from the time we sat down that the pupils of his light brown eyes were as small as the head of a pin.

Mary's journal had made it clear that when she was living with Mireille Havet in Paris, Mireille had been quite ill, but the nature of the illness had not been specified. MacCown's story suggested it was connected with her use of drugs, and when he mentioned that Dan Mahoney had told him about the sores on Mireille's thighs, we remembered Arthur

Mizener's letter and asked MacCown who Mahoney was. MacCown replied that Mahoney had been the "unofficial doctor for the Quarter," and that while he had not been licensed to practice medicine in Paris, he could still write prescriptions, which were much in demand. MacCown went on to say, somewhat critically, that Mahoney was a "monologuist" who "held forth" interminably, and made it impossible to carry on a conversation with him. That sounded vaguely familiar. Then, when MacCown said he had been the model for Djuna Barnes' incredible character, the renegade doctor, Matthew O'Connor, in *Nightwood,* a light went on, and I had a clearer idea of what he must have been like. Not knowing who he was at the time, I had taken very few notes on Mary's journal references to "Dan," and recalled now only her irritation with him when he'd failed to return a book of Cecil Maitland's that he'd borrowed ("that animal Mahoney," she'd called him), and a remark he'd made about fucking that had amused Mary (and us): "All I really care about is kissing someone I love," he'd said. "Fucking is so intimate. It's sort of lewd." I mentioned this to MacCown, and he smiled painfully, as if the thought of Mahoney was just a little much for him that evening.

When we asked him about himself, we could almost see his mind retreating from us, like a snail into its shell; and all we managed to get out of him was that he had gone to Villefranche in order to get away from Paris to paint, that he no longer painted (what he did do he didn't say), and that he'd come originally from Missouri. Morgan quickly mentioned that he, too, had been born and raised in Missouri, hoping to establish some common ground with our informant, but MacCown only smiled, briefly and bleakly. The mention of Missouri did serve to bring up the subject of Virgil Thomson (also from there), however, and about him MacCown suddenly had a good bit to say.

He didn't move from his slouched position in the seat of the booth, but he was concentrating now on something in his mind, and I had a flash impression of a snake coiling to strike. He said—matter of factly, at first, then more cattily as he went on—that Thomson was a homosexual, who liked to play up his relationship with Mary. Of the latter contention there seemed to be ample evidence. He said that Mary and Thomson had not lived together, and that their relationship had been sporadic even before it ended. MacCown then said that all during the nine months or so that Thomson had known Mary, he had maintained a constant association with a man he had known and would continue to know for years, and who had been a "complacent husband" to him. There had been no reference to this in the journal and, if true, Mary seems not to have been aware of it. That she was aware of such possibilities, however, is at least suggested by certain journal entries in the spring of 1927:

> I first arrived at a special and enduring love for Virgil when he told me . . . that a miracle was always possible.
>
> For Virgil: If you are going to trouble about women at all, and have a very sensitive one, it becomes the question of how to get the best out of her. For example, the first night at Juan les Pins [where they had gone together from Villefranche] . . . it took me a night and a day to get over the spiritual bruising. I didn't mind about that boy, but suppose just for that night you had wanted nothing but me, or had even denied yourself for me.

MacCown's tone as he talked about Thomson was bitter, and I wondered if they saw each other now. It was Thomson who had first suggested we contact MacCown, but there did seem to be a gulf separating their present stations in life and I doubted that either made much of an attempt to cross it. Not for the first time I felt the poignancy of the fate that had overtaken so many of those who had ridden that merry-go-round in the 'twenties. Only the very good or the very lucky had caught a brass ring to take home, it seemed. Gene MacCown had not been among them.

He stopped talking about Virgil Thomson, and simply sat there looking at us. We asked him some more questions.

About Murray Goodwin, whom we knew Mary had thought of putting under MacCown's tutelage when he'd been rejected by Cocteau, Wescott and Wheeler, MacCown would say only that he had been a "rich little boy [that was not the impression we'd received], an unguided young man" in whom Mary had taken an interest. Had he known Gabriel Aitken? No. Sergei? No. Had he painted a portrait of Mary? He couldn't remember. Then he lapsed into silence again, staring at us. We asked him if he had any letters of Mary's, any papers that might be of interest to us. He shook his head, which was beginning to nod, fixing his eyes more frequently on the table top than on our faces. For some reason—and it wasn't the whiskey, since we'd ordered only the one round of drinks—we were beginning to lose him.

Morgan and I looked at each other. There seemed to be little point in continuing. I reached across the table, shook MacCown's arm slightly, and said that we would have to leave. I also told him how grateful we were for the time and information he'd given us; and at this he roused himself sufficiently to say he was glad to be of help, for Mary's sake. We got up from the booth, and he walked to the entrance with us, where we shook hands and said goodbye. He turned then and sat down with his back to us on the same bar stool he'd been sitting on when we came in. I can bring the picture of that slight, hunched figure in the worn overcoat readily to mind, but it has always been difficult to associate it with another picture that was placed in my mind later: one of him and Virgil Thomson, dressed in leather britches, dancing the *Schuhplatteln* together in the Austrian Tyrol.

III

Quentin Bell had invited me to be his luncheon guest at the Reform Club, and our appointment was for 12:45 p.m. I was interested in this interview, and not simply because Quentin Bell had known Mary "fairly well from about 1929 until the time of her death and did once write a little memoir about her," as he had written Morgan years before, or because he was the author of the recent and widely acclaimed biography of his aunt, Virginia Woolf. Nor was it because Mary had been quite fond of him, once referring to him in the journal as "the delightful, enchanting Quentin Bell." Rather, it was because he was by birth, personal experience, and acquired knowledge the veriest living embodiment, the last true representative of Bloomsbury. The son of Clive and Vanessa Bell, the nephew of Virginia Woolf, he had personally known everyone in the indisputable core of the famous group, from Roger Fry to Lytton Strachey to Maynard Keynes to Duncan Grant, and I thought if anyone could settle the still somewhat vexing question of what Mary's relationship with any or all of them had been, he could. Gabriel Aitken, who had known Quentin Bell at the same time as Mary, had once remarked to her that Quentin's manner of speech was "vintage Bloomsbury," and I looked forward to hearing his voice. He had written in his last letter to me that an hour's conversation would probably exhaust his recollections of Mary, but in fact they required almost three.

I arrived at the Reform Club some minutes before he did, and waited a bit nervously for him to make his appearance. I had not at that time seen any photographs of the young or middle-aged Quentin Bell, and when he came in through the front door and started up the steps to me, smiling, with hand extended, I thought for a moment I was looking at a reincarnation of Lytton Strachey—the same length and shape of beard, the same kind of spectacles, and so forth, that I'd seen in numerous photographs. The opportunity for closer and prolonged inspection of my affable host made clear what physical differences there were, but I have never quite shaken the impression that I lunched that day with more than the detritus of Bloomsbury, "delightful, enchanting" though he unquestionably was.

We went into the dining room immediately, and Quentin Bell said at the outset that he had been introduced to

Mary by Robert Medley and Rupert Doone in the fall of 1928, when he was eighteen years old and had gone to Paris to study art. Their friendship had extended through 1931, and he had once visited her in Cornwall after that. He said that Mary "was a delightful person to drop in on when one happened to be in Paris," although his impression of the quality of her life at the time was that it had been "rather ramshackle." He remembered with amusement one occasion when he had gone to see her, taking a girl with him. The girl was the daughter of the headmaster of a public school, with the values and opinions one would expect such a girl to have. They arrived at "14" around 4:00 p.m. to find the flat decorated with lighted candles, the electricity having been cut off, and Mary in bed, not alone. The conversation that ensued did not amuse Quentin Bell's friend, and came to an abrupt end when Mary put her hand under the covers on the bed, drew out something, and exclaimed, "Oh, my God. This is the end. Bugs!" Bell received an awful scolding afterward from his friend, and since he later told me his unpublished memoir about Mary was entitled "Bugs at the Rue de Montessuy," I gathered this incident was central to it.

Bell went on to say that, Mary's living conditions notwithstanding, dropping in on her was just normally one of the things he would have done at the time. He would occasionally bring people with him to meet Mary, and remembered that Gene MacCown was there one time, apparently on bad terms with Mary and probably, he opined, over money. That reminded me of something, and I asked Bell what he knew about Mary's drug-taking. He replied—and this was contrary to Wesson Bull's experience—that Mary was "a proselytizer for drugs," and would promote the benefits of taking them, "the only sensible way to write poetry," he remembered her as saying. He said, laughingly, that she rewrote English literary history in such a way that "mandragora plays a quite disproportionately large part." He said that Mary had smoked opium in his presence and had tried to persuade him to have a pipe. He also said, however, that when she was in London after leaving Paris, she must have been off drugs at least for a time, "and not having much to drink, either." The transformation in her physical appearance at the time had impressed him as almost miraculous. "She looked so young and pretty," he said; "it was incredible. She really looked quite charming," whereas she had been "a bit blowsy" when he'd seen her in Paris earlier. All of that coincided pretty much with what I had learned from others.

When I asked him about Mary's relations with Bloomsbury, to the extent any existed at all, Bell said that Virginia Woolf, for one, considered Mary to be a "member of the underground," so to speak, and that when Mary died and John Raynor's memorial poem referring to her as a firebearer appeared in *Time and Tide,* Virginia Woolf had remarked, "I think the fire was fed by alcohol." On the other hand, he felt that the influence of Bloomsbury was greatly exaggerated, and that they could not have kept Mary from being published. He concluded that while Bloomsbury had little interest in Mary, there was no enmity or hostility; Mary's world and his father's were simply very different and did not impinge upon each other. At the same time, he recalled that Mary had always been very polite to him, one example of which, he believed, was that she never mentioned Bloomsbury, as such. It seemed to me, therefore, that while Bloomsbury had ignored Mary as much as possible—as Raymond Mortimer's remark to Virgil Thomson indicated—when awareness occurred, it was coupled with dislike. What had been responsible for this was probably no longer possible to isolate, but I was satisfied it had been a combination of Mary's outré nature and behavior, her treatment of Rodker—with whom Bloomsbury had had some sympathy, Lytton Strachey having been a CO during the War—and, quite possibly, her association with Roger Fry and, later, with Gabriel Aitken.

Quentin Bell told me that Gabriel, whom he had met at Mary's, had been Maynard Keynes' "boyfriend" years before; and he noted that although in 1929 Gabriel "had lost his youthful bloom ... you could still see that he'd been a great charmer—rather decidedly pretty." Bell also said that when Gabriel left Mary in 1930, she had asked him to ask Maynard Keynes to help get Gabriel back. He said that he had mentioned the subject to Maynard Keynes, but not with much enthusiasm. Gabriel had been a Catholic, Bell said, and had left the Church because he felt the priests to whom he had confessed his homosexuality were "rather narrowminded." Aitken's former Catholicism surprised me, and it immediately suggested that there had been more than their mutual alcoholism and decrepitude linking Aitken and Cecil Maitland in Mary's view. If I would never be able to *fit* all the pieces together, I was certainly seeing some relationships I hadn't discerned before.

As our long and very enjoyable luncheon extended into its second hour, I mentioned Mary's practice of alchemizing or modifying reality to suit her needs, and Quentin Bell strongly testified to it. "She was a myth-maker in an extraordinary way," he said, and recalled that Mary had once urged him to go see Gertrude Stein. He had asked her, "Well, what will happen?" Mary had replied, "What will happen will be that you'll come back to me with a cup of cold poison in one hand and a dagger in the other. . . ." "And," Bell said wonderingly, "she was only *half* laughing."

I explained what I now considered to be Mary's motives for her assertive/defensive myth-making about herself, at which Quentin Bell nodded as if to indicate he did not at least *dis*agree, and I mentioned how "tiresome" it had all seemed to Angus Davidson (a handsome photograph of whom as a young man appears in Bell's *Virginia Woolf*). At that Bell smiled, shaking his head slightly, and said, "Dear Angus is so squeamish. He's very easily distressed by irregularities of any kind." I had never looked at it quite that way. Bell then went on, musingly, to give me his own reasons for remembering Mary quite fondly.

"There was something generous about her ... something big about her," he said, "although lots of people did dislike her very much. I was always slightly shocked at hearing that. And yet," he continued softly, "I should have found it difficult to build up a reason to defend her."

As if that troubled him, he immediately proceeded to her defense.

"If she was self-centered, it wasn't in a boring way," he said, and I couldn't help comparing him with Wesson Bull expressing much the same sentiments.

"She was congenial, in some way," Bell continued, and then, very thoughtfully, said, "I suppose she flattered me. Which, of course, is never disagreeable.... She was very kind. She made one feel important. She made one feel one's good company."

It occurred to me that I had just heard as succinct an explanation of Mary's appeal to younger men, uncertain of themselves, just beginning their careers, etc., as I was likely to. By this time Bell was looking back to the last time he had seen her in Cornwall, and in apparent reference to her sickness, her game knee, her dauntlessness in decrepitude there, he summed up his obviously approving view of her.

"She was rather splendid, Mary," he said. Mary had made at least one friend in Bloomsbury, I thought, even if one discounted Roger Fry, which I was not about to do. The journal indications and reinforcing anecdotes, such as Oswell Blakeston's story, while providing only circumstantial evidence that Mary and Roger Fry had been lovers, certainly made it clear that they had known and liked each other for a time. It was hard to believe their relationship hadn't reached the bed, at least once or twice. It had certainly been on Mary's mind, and Roger Fry wasn't likely to have put up much resistance. Quentin Bell didn't know anything about it one way or the other, but he told me an amusing anecdote about Roger Fry and T. S. Eliot that I had never heard before. Quentin Bell had been told it by his mother.

It seems that Vanessa Bell and "Tom" Eliot had been having dinner at Roger Fry's one night, and the credulous Roger (who, among other similar interests, kept track of the tides with a tide clock of some kind) gloomily announced that, according to his instruments, the tides were not on time. Ergo, something was wrong with the moon, hence the solar system, meaning very probably that some dark star had entered and might shortly destroy the earth. No one else thought too much about it, but Eliot's anxiety had been aroused immediately, he was silent for the rest of the evening, and his continued perturbation at the thought of such a dark star destroying the earth had caused him to leave the MS. of *The Waste Land* (which he'd taken with him) on the tram to Tottenham Court Road, when he and Vanessa Bell went home. It had taken him two days to recover it.

Both Bell and I laughed at the story, which showed a side of T.S. Eliot I, at least, had never heard of before. Lunch over, we were now sitting in a second floor lounge lazily sipping cognac and smoking large cigars. Bell began recalling, enjoyably I think, some more Mary stories. He said that she had told him one evening how, shortly before the Easter Uprising in 1916, she had been friends—Quentin Bell opined lover—with a young man named White, who took part in the Uprising, was captured, tried, and sentenced to death, but later reprieved because his father had been an important general. Mary recounted dramatically a meeting between White, DeValera and the others (just before the Uprising) at which White had said, "Do it at the end of the War. If you do it now, you'll be crushed." Which was, of course, what happened. Mary, apparently, went on sheltering IRA gunmen on the run, and told Quentin Bell of one who came to her London flat one time, absolutely exhausted, and collapsed on the sofa. When she went to wake him in the morning, "he woke in a flash and was gone." Bell credited these stories, and accounted for the absence of any reference to them in the journal on the basis of prudence.

I wasn't sure, but there was some evidence that Mary had aided the Irish revolutionaries. For one thing, the journal does not begin until some months after the Easter Uprising, so the lack of evidence in it is hardly material. For another, the journal does record with no further comment that on January 4, 1917, a "Jack White" had dropped in. When this entry is coupled with a letter Mary received from a "J. R. White" written in Swansea Prison on May 22, 1916, only a month or so after the "Risin'," it seems there may have been *some* basis for at least one of the IRA stories she'd told Quentin Bell. The letter makes clear, however, only that Mary sympathized with the prisoner and whatever cause he represented, which appears to be revolutionary, although White contends he has done nothing for which they can legally imprison him. It does not sound as if he had been one of those who seized the Dublin Post Office, as Mary had maintained to Bell. I suspected her stories were dramatic alchemizations of some peripheral and not particularly dangerous expression of sympathy for the IRA that would have been quite consistent with her volatile rebelliousness, generally, in 1916.

When I asked Bell whether he had ever encountered Mary Reynolds or Kitty Cannell at 14 rue de Montessuy, he answered "No." He then said, "I have a dim memory there were 'wounded princes' lying stricken around, but I don't remember other people with Mary very much. Except for Gabriel. And, of course, Robert and Rupert."

Bringing up the names of Medwell and Doone reminded him of the time—also referred to in the journal—when Rupert Doone had come excitedly to Mary to report his recent discovery of a perfectly marvelous thing called *The Symposium,* and what Bell considered Mary's kind silence on this occasion. Although he did report that later Mary had said, "You have to realize that when the rest of us were getting some education, Rupert was delivering the milk." It didn't sound all that kind to me, rather an indirect way of airing her own knowledge and asserting superiority; but Bell had a fixed impression of Mary's essential kindness and humanity—evidence of which he saw in her consistent record in the journal of stories other people had told her, indicating to him she had been a good listener—and I had no reason to try and change that impression.

It was getting well into mid-afternoon when we both decided we'd better attend to what other business the remainder of the day held for us, and rose to leave. As we retrieved our coats, Bell said that, whatever difficulties I had encountered in trying to define and fix the biographical truths of Mary's life, I was still lucky in a way because she had been "a marked character." I thanked him for the lunch, we shook hands, and just before he turned to go, Bell looked at me and said, "That'll be a fascinating book, you know."

IV

The evening at the Ross-Williamsons at 193 Sussex Gardens was one of the most enchanting and delightful I have ever spent anywhere, and extended through teatime and supper up to the very moment I *had* to leave in order to catch my train to Cornwall. Hugh, a large, handsome man, then in his very early seventies, was confined to his bed in a large room on the fourth floor of his narrow house; and, when I arrived, he conveyed the distinct impression of holding a congenial court, at which then, at least, Dawn Stilgoe, a young friend of Hugh's named Philip, his devoted wife and daughter, Margaret and Sheila, and very shortly myself, were in willing attendance. We talked and drank, and ate and drank, and talked through the swiftly passing hours; and although Hugh was not ever to arise from that bed without assistance and for the most unavoidable of purposes (such as a subsequent operation), he gave no impression of invalidism and his dauntless, happy spirit filled the room.

It was of Mary that we mostly spoke, at least at first, and his assertions about her actual and deserved positions in literary history were the most authoritative I had yet encountered, and I paid close attention. When I asked him where she'd *been* in the English literary scene of the 'thirties, when he had known her, he said: "She wasn't anywhere. Let us be frank, she wasn't anywhere. One saw it then [i.e., the literary scene] *almost* in terms of D.H. Lawrence and T.S. Eliot. And *I* saw Mary as a combination of both. I think it [i.e., her work] is a very impressive corpus, if you take the tracts [*Traps for Unbelievers* and *Warning to Hikers*] as well."

Although he characterized the conflict between the "ins" and the "outs" of the literary world at any given time as "a very nasty dogfight" in which the "ins" are "very nearly always wrong," he said that in Mary's case there was no hostility or antagonism on the part of the literary establishment towards her.

"Absolutely not," he said. "It was purely ignorance. They weren't aware of her existence. As a matter of fact, Edward Hoke [a friend of HRW] used to say that 'Mary Butts' was an alias of *mine.* [She was] totally outside."

He thought that the principal reason was that, in addition to her not having been "in" much, to begin with, she had simply been gone too long in the late 'twenties; and when she finally came back, she was totally lost because she no longer understood what was going on. When Hugh took over *The Bookman* in the last quarter of 1930, he said, he tried to do what he could for her as long as he was in a position to help, but it obviously hadn't been enough.

He had always been most impressed, he said, by her keen, intuitive understanding of the Dorset scene, with all its natural beauty, mystical power, and potential deadliness. That's the way Dorset is, Hugh clearly believed, and said of Mary: "I'm quite sure in those early days at the Salterns and all that, I mean she *would* chat with the gods and goddesses. And in *that* sense she knew more than anybody. There was nothing that Crowley could teach *her,* really. I mean not from that point of view."

Hugh then told an anecdote about a friend of his who, tired of the rat race and wanting to get away from it all, had gone to bucolic South Dorset for a vacation. Among other evidences of the underlying wickedness of Dorset which had upset the friend and sent him quickly back to sane, orderly London had been an old lady in the village where he was lodging. As Hugh told the story: "There was this dear old lady, everyone's idea of the good fairy grandmother, and she lived in a little cottage, at the head of a lovely slope which children loved, a green, grassy slope they could roll down. And at night she went out and sprinkled broken glass on it. It's so typical of Dorset."

And Mary understood that, Hugh maintained—whether it was Dorset or Cornwall made little difference—in a way that both Lawrence and Eliot sensed from their different perspectives, but never fully grasped. Hence, Mary's admiration/jealousy/resentment of Eliot, particularly. Hugh then mimicked, with a very punctilious articulation which he said was just like Mary's, remarks she used to make about Eliot:

"Poor Tom Eliot. I always thought he never had much fun."

"You are quite right to say he is one of the guardians of the Grail, but, *my,* how surprised he'll be when he finds out who the *other* guardians are."

Hugh, who had known Eliot well and liked him very much, considered those remarks two of Mary's most brilliant pieces of insight; but he was fonder of the latter because it suggested the synthesis of other and older forms of religion upon which her Anglo-Catholicism was grounded.

As the evening wore on, and the time when I would have to go sped toward us, Hugh asked what form my book on Mary would take; and I answered hesitantly that I hadn't yet made up my mind between a "personal" approach (which I did not define, although he seemed to understand what I meant) and a conventional critical biography.

"Can't you combine them in one?" Hugh immediately asked. "Can't you find another near *Quest for Corvo*? I mean that would be an ideal form. I think a Corvo-esque book plus the critical thing could be an absolute best seller."

I didn't know about the last point, but identical suggestions that [A.J.A.] Symons' *The Quest for Corvo* might be an appropriate model to follow coming from two such eminent men of letters as William Plomer and Hugh Ross Williamson, and at almost the same time, closed a circle that Mary's review of that very book years ago seemed to have started; and I saw no reason to try to break out of it. I think the matter was settled that night; and ever since I have considered the decision a collective one. As Hugh wrote me two or three weeks later: "For me it was a wonderful meeting. Mary, in her kindness, must have arranged it and then tactfully—as she could in her grande dame moods—retired into the background." But perhaps not very far.

In any case, by the time I left only Hugh and I remained in the room. He gave me as parting gifts inscribed copies of two of his books, and his blessing (he was still, I guessed, an Anglo-Catholic priest). Then, with the glow of the evening still on me, I walked to the station, reclaimed my luggage, and, as Mary had hoped Hugh would do in 1934, boarded the night train to Cornwall.

HARCOURT WESSON BULL

"Truth Is the Heart's Desire"

I

Villefranche-sur-Mer, Spring, 1928

IT WAS AT THE Hôtel de la Colline during luncheon on the day of my arrival in late April or early May that I first laid eyes on Mary Butts. She was not unbeautiful with her sandy-red bobbed hair and fair skin, and certainly "interesting" in her pale green boucle dress and one extremely large, light jade pendant earring, mill wheel shaped. (Later I saw just a touch of green make-up on her eyelids.) She was sitting alone and reading, but I knew she was taking one in—we had heard of each other. I had read *Ashe of Rings* in college and was pleased and impressed to be meeting her. I was twenty-three and she a decade, more or less, older.

We became fast friends at once. We both had friends in common living in the hotel or town, but they were engrossed in their affairs, and we, unattached, were thrown together more often than not which I found most pleasant. Almost always we drank a coffee and a Benedictine in the garden after lunch, alone or with others, and used to go off alone on walks or excursions in the afternoons or evenings. The first place she showed me was a house said to be haunted by a white horse.

Mary was fascinating, charming, gay, gracious, generous. "Dear delightful Mary Butts," someone writing of Paris in the '20s has called her. Her graciousness appeared to be carried almost to a fault at first, for she flattered one tremendously,

---

Another discerning portrait of Mary Butts in her last years can be found in Frank Baker's *I Follow But Myself* (Peter Davies, 1968).

calling me (and others) "Sweet Prince," and "My Bird." ("All the gods and goddesses," she murmured when a group of us had assembled for photographs.) But one soon discovered that this was her manner—even a part of her good manners. And she liked to see good manners in others. Once she said mine were 18th century and praised my mother. Furthermore, this graciousness was part of her generosity. Giving friendship, she was particularly outgiving of herself. She always seemed to be there for one, a lovely trait. Naturally I realized that her life was full of people, some celebrated (though Mary was never a "name-dropper" to impress): her reminiscences were rich—and I knew even better on reading her journals after her death how much else had been, and was then, going on!

This giving of herself was apparent in any company where she always held up her end with witty and humorous stories; a special tale of hers, told very well, was of the man in a train with a "m'guffin" in a basket. Much curiosity was aroused among the other passengers by his lifting the lid to peer at or feed it—but in the end frustration because the man left the basket behind and it was empty. (One sees how this appealed to Mary: its air of mystery and a puzzle.) Other stories were anecdotal, regaled in fun, clever and often profound observations of the foibles in the human comedy, sometimes critical, not malicious, sometimes rueful. The behavior of "all the gods and goddesses" was not always exemplary. I remember one description, with Mary-embellishments, of someone pursuing someone else through the night, standing agonized in the front seat of an open taxi. The mock tragedy made her laugh that quick laugh of hers on one middle note. She could gently tease. "X. has lost his, or her, knitting," she would chide if someone did or said a silly or stupid thing and showed confusion.

Mary herself was quite ready for lively adventure, joining in the fun of this group, if greatly above it, observing. I liked best adventures alone with her in Nice. I remember a particular evening when we made an occasion of it, Mary in white beaded evening dress, a white fox fur and her bee earrings (twisted gold-colored wire in the shape of bees, made for her, if I am not mistaken, by Man Ray). We dined at a quai-side restaurant where we liked the wine and she talked of Mary Queen of Scots, of such delicate beauty that "when she drank red wine one could see it passing down her throat." Mary seemed to really believe it, looking at me with serious face, eyes almost closed, her head tilted. That evening included a place of quite unusual entertainment. If extreme, and Mary had her extremes, as did I, we watched this together with perfect equanimity—again observing the human comedy. It went with the intimacy we now shared and was for the green youth of those days a glad weaning away from New England, a relief, in short, happy under Mary's auspices. I do not mean to let it seem inferred here that we were lovers, for we were not. I doubt if she greatly wished a lover at this time—nor did I. (I was deeply in love, and things were going wrong.) Yet that night, in the dark taxi returning, there were curious tears on the white fox fur and Mary's comfort in her sheltering arms. That we loved one another, and in a truer sense than most of those around us, is certain.

Perhaps the very special fascination Mary had for those who loved her and were her kind of person was her gift of "making magic," magic in which one saw many things: her fancy and imagination, her learning, indeed erudition, her old wisdom. How magically she made alive, made real and gay for one who responded, the persons of mythology and history, her intimates. "East of the sun, west of the moon," she crooned. She spoke of the *Emerald Tablet,* of "signatures," of many other matters of this sort I had never heard of and which were food and drink to me, so generously given.

I believe prime influences on Mary's whole thought and writing were Gilbert Murray, early, and *The Golden Bough,* then the Neo-Platonists (Plotinus?), and later, mystical Christian writings (as through Charles Williams).

Mary read her poems to me—in a high lilting voice lifted

to a tenderness—and all her gaiety, lightness and grace was in the reading; and all her magic in the poems for me. Though minor works, the quintessence of Mary is in them, not only her magic, her tender, generous attitude, her "knowingness," her comfort, yes, and her "swank," too, to use one of her own words.

In one of them she speaks of a loving sister-brother relationship which led her to tell me of Tony Butts, her adored brother in younger days, from whom she was now almost completely estranged. Was this adoration somewhat romanticized? I believe not. I believe that she felt the change in that relationship most keenly—and substituted others for him all the rest of her life.

Another poem or two would certainly appear to be opium-influenced: "Seas of glass," if I remember correctly, "jade cliffs." I have been told that Mary "smoked," and soon knew the sweet stench of opium in the corridor outside her room. She did not speak of it herself. There were times when friends of a different set descended on her, and she simply disappeared for two or three days. One of these friends was Mireille Havet, an actress who had played "Death" in Cocteau's *Orphée,* agitated, vivid young woman who died not long after. (Was it by suicide as I seem to remember?) With her, Mary made an eventful expedition to low places in Marseilles to get the raw stuff, followed by an hilarious night, not without its alarms and mishaps, cooking it at someone's flat in Nice, as she described to me later.

But it could not have been much later that Mary let me share the open secret with her. I used to lie with her on cushions on the floor in her room while she smoked a few pipes, I watching the process, fascinated—and perhaps slightly repelled. I knew it was not for me, not then at any rate, if ever, I told myself: I wanted other knowledge and experiences first. Be it to Mary's great credit that she never directly suggested I begin smoking; the temptation may have been strong since it could have meant another to share the expenses, or even to provide them.

She became quite free in talking of her smoking at this time, although she never reported its pleasures. She spoke of other people who smoked: T. G. and his Chinese robes and screens, or of things incidental to smoking, such as how she and women friends brought their pipes in and out of France hidden in their hair under cloche hats. (Incidentally—speaking of hats—Mary was good at making turbans out of men's silk neckties, two of them opened, ironed, intertwined and sewn together. She said she and Duff Twysden used to collect ties for this purpose to the despair of all their men friends.)

Mary's addiction to opium—or should I not say "addiction" because I have no idea how much she smoked nor when and how she ended it—Mary's opium smoking in this period leads me, just here, to remark on her journals. I began to read and discuss them with Angus Davidson in 1937, but I never cared to read them through since they became more and more painful to me. When I was first allowed to see them, however, turning to the date Mary left Villefranche—in late June or early July—I saw that she had written: "I breathed a prayer at the station," or words to that effect, nothing more. It is not surprising that she prayed. I had taken her to the Paris train, noticing among the pieces in her baggage a battered steamer trunk, unlocked, with most insecure hasps, and no strap. As the cab driver and a porter were removing it to the platform the lid came partly open—to disclose its entire contents of raw opium. Tut-tutting, the porter went off to find a rope. The danger was averted, yet what a risk she had taken—and why? since it was needless. Were the journals written for herself alone, and not for posterity, or much less for posterity? For example, I happen to be the only one in the world who can interpret Mary's entry re a prayer that day. Would it not follow, considering this very small instance, that there must be innumerable other passages as obscure?

Mary wrote me from the train that evening a very beautiful and long letter, something of ourselves, something of a lovely sunset and twilight in Provence. I regret so much I haven't this letter and a largish packet of others, all written before 1930, which were in a box stolen from an apartment house cellar storage bin at a later time. (There are a few other letters, pasted in her books, unfortunately also unavailable now—though intact in crates—which Yale will get one day.)

II

Paris, Summer, 1928

I was in Paris on and off during the summer and saw a great deal of Mary. Her inexpensive front flat, three or four flights up, at 14 rue de Montessuy, almost under the Eiffel Tower, had a certain charm for me. It was small: a sitting-room, bedroom and kitchen only, and I don't remember noteworthy furnishings, but it was Mary's, and there were a few interesting objects about. I especially remember a "snowstorm," a glass-domed paperweight ornament made, again, by Man Ray, its "scene" a large painted eye in a triangle.

There is a striking photograph Man Ray took of Mary in the early 20s when she was at the height of her beauty—and she was both beautiful and distinguished looking. In it she is fashionably dressed, great cartwheel hat and other fineries—a long cigarette holder, I think—in fact as she herself might have said, she is "dressed to the nines"—pure "swank."

It was interesting to see Mary in a domestic role, one had never thought of her like that. She could prepare a meal easily and simply, deft with salads. Sometimes we sat quietly talking while she sewed.

Of course we went out together often, Mary in her bee earrings and a Chanel dress, the skirt all ribbon streamers, given her by Tony a season or so before in a moment of reconciliation. At a time when sheer pleasure-seeking was neither shaming nor dull, many bars saw us, and the night-clubs and cafés one frequented in those days: the "Boeuf," the "Grand-Écart," the "Sélect," where Mary sat with a paper bag of the now famous raw opium at her feet. (It was to be picked up by someone.) We danced "Chez Bricktop." Bricktop called her "Miss Mary," and Robert McAlmon came over and said to Mary: "You'd better stick to him, he's the best of the lot," which pleased me. I would have thought that Mary might have had enough of all that, but she still liked observing the circus, so to speak, to be amused—and be amusing; sometimes we laughed over very simple things, the names she gave people. A friend of mine to whom she was not drawn, the German painter, Helmut Kolle, she called "Monsieur Faux-Col"; another, Peter Teigen, whom she found attractive, became, of course, "Nice Mr. Peter Tiger." But we had many, many serious discussions, and I think she was observing me as well, "one of the new young batch America was sending over." In a way I can see there was something of the mentor and pupil in us. She knowingly taught; her mind was always at work.

I told her of my impressions of Paris and how I sensed the change from what it must have been like in the years just following the '14-'18 War: the now well-known artists and writers of that wonderfully creative period yet unknown, it must have been vital, and certainly "magic." Mary agreed, "and we were all 'copains' then, and poor."

(Mary was never rich. From the way she lived I assume she had an income probably adequate—or just adequate?—to meet her needs. Nevertheless there were indications she was over-spending on her smoking, for frequently she seemed financially embarrassed. I tried to help, discreetly, by inviting her to many meals—not that it wasn't my pleasure and a privilege—and Mary, bless her, never refused. She did not ask to borrow money from me then—and a good thing since I also was never affluent.)

There were other quiet moments together; I remember sharing one of Mary's "signatures" with her. We were sitting talking in her flat one night when suddenly we heard an unusually frightful human cry in the street below. We looked up, startled and sobered. "Terrible days are coming, my Harcourt," Mary said like a sibyl. "Can you shoot? Strengthen your hands. Strengthen your long brown hands." My hands are neither long nor brown (if presumably then tanned), and the admonition sounded too dramatic, but her prophecy, made in all seriousness, could not have come more true as history turned out. (Mary showed a perspicacity in international and political affairs I hadn't looked for. She spoke discerningly on the problem of the Polish Corridor.) Here I have been reminded of another remark of Mary's, a sentence in one of her books: "'Goddess,' said I, 'keep an eye on your servants,'" also spoken after a noting of something untoward. And again:—how in lighter moments she often crooned the song (not *quite* in tune, I think she had no ear for music): "Lady be good—oh, lady, be good to me." She knew all the words. In her mind the Lady was, surely—Artemis? (Yes! how greatly Mary was of the moon!)

I met a few friends of Mary's in Paris—there was Kay Boyle, briefly, and poor Sergei Maslenikoff—not many: I think she was not seeing numbers of people at this time. But with Mary, possibly more than with any other friend, it was a case of not usually knowing whom she saw or what she did when one was not with her. She was the antithesis of one who "tells everything." This was even more apparent in her not speaking of her past. I was getting, however, glimpses and hints of that from the tales of others and a few of her own chance remarks. For me it was like a plot thickening. So many mysterious chapters in her background! Of her marriage to John Rodker, her leaving him directly their daughter, Camilla, was born for Sandy Maitland, *their* life in Paris, their observations of "black" magic, their trip to Sicily and Aleister Crowley, Maitland's death and what Mary did then, the history of her smoking—of these things I learned almost nothing—and to this day know almost nothing but the bare facts, even after the months of intimate companionship at the end of her life.

I did have a thorough insight into one present relationship, that with Sergei, the protagonist of her *Imaginary Letters.* It is an idealized portrait of him: the real Sergei was less attractive and far more of an incorrigible ne'er-do-well than one would have dreamed possible. I spent an evening or two with him simply because Mary asked me to look after him. Yet I cannot judge her here. If she wished to mother, worry, actually suffer over, give money to him who seemed unworthy—that was her affair. Was it not, in short, a positive good she did out of compassion? I have read somewhere lately that Mary was always seen with, and preferred, boys of this type, not much good, all perverted—a most unkind and false judging. To be sure there were some other Sergeis—varying degrees of Sergeis? I think their ways amused her: I have heard her giggling about them. (And, I repeat: it was because of Tony?)

And then: did Mary sometimes choose to suffer? There is the shortest of her poems in *Imaginary Letters* of an evening when an engagement was unkept:

Il ne vient pas ce soir,
Absent le bienvenu,
Le menu plaisir de ce soir disparu.

(I can clearly hear her uttering it now with rue in her lifted voice.) It comes to me, again not as a judgment, that she did sometimes make this choice; I believe I can discern it in other departments of her life; sometimes, I say, not habitually, because there was always the other side of the coin with Mary. I have seen her thoroughly philosophical over misadventure. Yes, in spite of everything, I think it was basically against the grain for her to be sad and self-pitying. (She had too much else up her sleeve!) Perhaps she even wrote off this certain sadness in the *Letters*?

Among the things I was glimpsing of Mary then was the

fact that she had become estranged from numerous old friends, or, at the very least, that there were some strained relationships. My feeling was then—still is—that the others involved were lesser persons. (One cannot go so far as to say she was never at fault.) At any event I have seen her feelings genuinely hurt by misunderstandings. Once Mary said to me: "Beware of those you don't invite to your party, of those to whom you have lent money, of those with whom you have refused to go to bed." Many variations on this theme are possible, and I supposed most of them had been experienced by Mary in her Paris life. At twenty-three I was learning much from her; some of the intelligence was heady—and some of it was oppressive and dark.

Mary's estrangement from her brother certainly had to do with money. This summer she bitterly complained to me about his treatment of her and firmly believed that he and her mother, Mrs. Colville-Hyde, were preventing her receiving her rightful financial income. Loving Mary, I sympathized but wondered how justified she was. She must have exasperated both her family and the family solicitor to whom I remember her writing "inquiries" and getting disappointing answers. Mary had many of those in her life! But if her family had their justified grievances, I know there were unkindnesses from them, and others too.

And less unkindnesses from Mary who had forgivenness in her nature. You see, I must stress, for I know it to be true, and beg you to bear it ever in mind in forming your portrait of her, Mary's outgivingness, evidenced to me in so many ways, her compassion, her comforting, were in sum greater by far than the total number of her mistakes.

In this manner of misjudging, the following story is somewhat pertinent. In Paris Mary showed me an American fan letter from a girl in Greenwich Village, or the like, which described in detail for her benefit and relish an odd scene of disenchanted lovers throwing eggs at one another—eggs which smeared the walls in streaks that had some deep significance for the writer afterwards. It was a silly, rather vulgar and pretentious letter from someone who obviously thought she "understood" Mary's writing and was very wide of the mark. But Mary (never silly, or in any way vulgar or pretentious) was completely puzzled. "What kind of people *are* these, Harcourt?"

Often, and in many ways, Mary was misjudged.

III

London, Winter and Early Spring, 1928–1929

Mary came to London some time, as I recall, in the late autumn or early winter of 1928, staying for a while with her mother. Possibly she returned to Paris for a few weeks, but was certainly in London again shortly and remained there until April at the earliest. I was living in Half Moon Street and recommended to her a bed-sitting-room in Clarges Street, the next street over, where she continued out her stay.

She invited me to tea at her mother's—a rather sticky occasion since Mrs. Colville-Hyde, obviously not in rapport with her daughter, plainly mistrusted me as one of her new friends. Mary, in spite of being ill at ease, did most of the honors with her usual graciousness. She showed me an Empire chair copied after the seat of Roman judges. The rounded knobs at the ends of its arms where their hands rested, she explained, were made of some metal or stone that remained cool and kept their judgements impartial. (Rather an appropriate conversational topic under the circumstances!) Mrs. Colville-Hyde listened in silence. The child, Camilla Rodker, bone of contention, was also present. She seemed not to belong to Mary in any way.

On the whole Mary appeared quite a different person in London, out of place at least in circles she had once turned her back upon. There was an air of hesitancy about her. A former friend of hers in France had said to me: "She is declassé," a remark I resented for her at the time; but now I had to accept some meaning in it, largely, I think, because Mary herself seemed to feel it and made one aware of it in certain instances. Society's viewpoint doubtless meant little or nothing to her when she had run away to an unconventional life. I think her mother and Tony must have, directly or not, often reminded her that she had too flagrantly flaunted the rules of their world and was different now. And the fact that she was poor aggravated the situation, made it harder for her to hold her chin up proudly (which she did). One can ask, especially in the present day, what did it all matter, and to a creative artist with all her knowledge? But the point is it did matter to Mary, born in the Victorian era, who never forgot that she was not ill-born, who was sensitive, not made of brass (a toughness with her sensitivity was something else again), and she made me too feel that it mattered. We never openly discussed this thing; but in its light there were many small indications that seemed to signify. She didn't like someone for the way he put his coat on, it showed he wasn't a gentleman. "*You* don't put on your coat that way! X. doesn't."

Of course Mary was seeing other friends who couldn't have cared less about all that—Nina Hamnett and the scholar, Dr. Tancred Borenius, were two, and I dare say there were more of whom I didn't know. I brought new friends to her, but they were young, and I felt they sometimes tired her. All in all I recall this as a time of triste for Mary. I remember that she was not always well and do not think she was writing with any regularity. Why did she stay in London so long? To rearrange her affairs? It was a marking time, a waiting process for personal reasons? I can imagine it to have been a kind of interim in her life, a turning point, when, no longer young, thoughts of the future were presenting problems. One couldn't make light of it and suggest she had merely wanted to come over and see what everyone was doing in London: she didn't give that kind of impression at all. No, my best answer, after some consideration, is the suggestion that perhaps she was bravely disintoxicating herself at this time and preferred to be apart from drug-taking companions. (There wasn't the slightest indication of Mary's smoking in London.) It would account for her general malaise and also her being better in the spring. If I am right, a "brava" to her—and out with all my other conjecturing!

I didn't conjecture then. I accepted what I saw—Mary, one day when she didn't see me, walking down a wintry street in her utilitarian brown tweed coat and plain brown felt, mannish hat, a seemingly lonely, "unlucky" figure. I felt, curiously, both compassion and an impatience I couldn't possibly have explained. Today I know that we choose tristesse and suffering as we choose anything else. But was I right about her then?

Not that we didn't enjoy unmelancholy moments alone, yet—how one comes back to this!—I seem to remember few evenings of unmitigated pleasure as in Villefranche and Paris. There was one bad evening with the brother of Edgell Rickword, a contemporary of Mary's, in his cups, accusing me, an American, of being responsible for so many of their generation being killed in the War. "It's your fault for not coming in sooner!" he savagely reiterated over and over. Mary, for once, didn't come to my aid. "I'm afraid he's right, Harcourt," was all she said. She was momentarily carried away by her own memories, although she did retain some of the anti-American sentiments fashionable in her youth and after. "Keep the American from our shore," is a line in one of her poems. She had interjected, however, when she read it to me: "No offense meant," and I cannot believe that this feeling was deepseated.

Something happier? This was the period of the great parties with names. I remember before going to the Wild West Party I went by Clarges Street to show myself to Mary who was bright, gay, laughing and mocking, dying to make me up. "Harcourt, you're *en beauté* tonight—just a little blue around your eyes, *please!*" (I refused.) "Tu es beau, et bien fait, et bien né," she sang, quoting herself.

Mary was completely in her element at the time of the Greek Party in the early spring. I had introduced her to some of the so-called Bright Young People I had met, in this instance Elizabeth Ponsonby, "Babe" Plunkett-Greene, Eddie Gathorne-Hardy, Brian Howard, who asked her to plan their costumes: there were feathered caps and almost indecently high tunics. Mary tried, without success, to persuade Jean Cocteau to come over from Paris, an incident not without its contretemps. She had left exposed her unfinished letter to Cocteau, and gone out. In the meantime Brian Howard came to consult with her, and, waiting in her room, read the letter. In it she had described him as "moitié genie, moitié idiot," perhaps a not unfair appraisal, unappreciated, of course, by Brian. "Even *she!*" he expostulated to me. (This is one of the ways estrangements occurred with Mary—not always quite her fault, yet through some carelessness.) I regret that 'flu kept me away from the Greek Party; I would have liked to have remembered Mary in her long chiton and high headdress and blue wig a caryatid or goddess. I have a photograph of her taken at the party by Olivia Wyndham (too faded now for your use, I fear), and she is lovely. I heard that she had a wonderful time and was seen under a table with the octogenarian, Harry Melville.

IV

Paris, Late Spring, 1930

I had gone home for some months but returned to Europe at the end of May and landed in France, for one reason, I expect, to see Mary at once. In Paris I hurried eagerly to 14 rue de Montessuy. The following excerpt from a periodic journal I kept at the time sets the mood for our far from expected, sad meeting. I give it unchanged: "After I had knocked and knocked and gone down into the street again, I looked up at her window and saw a frowsy head furtively appear. At the sight of it, and remembering this was the behavior pattern when creditors were calling, I knew on the spot that our relationship was not going to continue as before." (That "frowsy head!")

Mary's flat was unkempt, she had been ill in bed, and there were medicine bottles and unwashed plates and glasses about. Immediately she asked to borrow money. Because the sum she wanted was large for me, and because I felt sure it was either for opium or for paying pressing debts that had accumulated while she spent the rent money on opium, abysmal, repeated process that meant I'd be embarrassed unless repayment were prompt, I said I could not make the loan. Indignantly, I thought it unfair of her to put me in that position. I have no recollection of what else we said that day. There is a reproachful letter from her to me in the Beinecke Rare Book and Manuscript Library at Yale which refers to our conversation. Her indignation matched mine. I think I went out and bought her some medicine (so small a gesture!) but of this I am not certain: I had done that before.

On one level my attitude could be said to have been perfectly justified. Why, I reasoned, should I shoulder her ill-met responsibilities at a cost to my budget where I had to be careful? I had seen Mary in somewhat this situation before; there wasn't the slightest indication it wouldn't happen again. Naturally it was her drug taking that influenced me most. Others had had the same reaction and bowed themselves out, though I didn't want to be like them. But on another level I was almost entirely wrong, and I am ashamed of this picture of the youth I was then, something selfish and hard in him, thinking of himself only, giving another no benefit of doubt, uncharitable. I get a very bad mark here.

"Uncharitable," that is the key, not enough love. Mary, at the lowest ebb I have ever seen her, needed love and comfort, which I did not give and which I truly know she would have given me had our positions been reversed. On that day something was spoiled, a friendship that had been good was impaired. Whatever else, it was unworthy of me, and in a sense, not worthy of Mary, either, as a matter of fact, for both of us were capable and worthy of loving one another as time was to prove, and this unhappy episode, fortunately, more than redeemed.

But in the meantime our relationship did not continue as before; I had been quite right there. While in Paris I saw her a few more times—there was no open break—but we were not to meet again for nearly five years, and if at Yale there are no letters during this interval, then we did not correspond. I went on to England, to Germany and Italy, and later back to the States, seeking, and getting, the experiences I thought I wanted. Many absorbing things happened to me, but I always regretted what had happened between Mary and me, and I was sorry that she was not more fully in my life.

V

Sennen, Cornwall, February—August, 1935

In a very different environment I met Mary again. She was living simply in the tiny Cornish village of Sennen. Here too had come our friend Angus Davidson with whom I was to stay for many months.

Mary, for reasons of her own, had told Angus she wished our re-meeting to take place at the upper pub, and so, on my first evening there, we set eyes on each other once more at "The First and Last." I was surprised by her changed appearance. She was far less thin, almost stocky, and had really lost the beauty of the Villefranche days only seven years before. She wore no make-up to speak of, and the extreme paleness of eyebrow and eyelash in her somewhat freckled face gave me rather a shock. Her clothes also were decidedly countrified: beret, short, blue serge skirt and blouse, man's worn tweed jacket, "sensible" low shoes—costume that was rarely varied—and she carried a sturdy cane. She seemed nervous and keyed-up; her mind was working furiously, I suppose; she may have had qualms about my being there at all. I realized the importance of rebeginning on the right foot and took the cue to be perfectly natural. There was no doubt that we both preferred to be good friends again—and so we were.

The next day Mary and I went for a walk, first to a rock where local tradition had it five kings (or was it more?) had gathered. She indicated barrows and pointed out the headland up the coast where Phoenicians and Romans had worked in tin mines—and Carn Brae, rounded hill in the distance where, she said, on a certain night all drowned sailors crawled out of the sea to its summit. "It isn't a night to be out, Harcourt!" Her magic-making was with her still—and presently I saw the old lightness and gaiety too.

Then began again between us a dear and valued friendship that lasted until her death—days unmarred by shadows of any consequence. And I rejoice that Angus Davidson and I—for she saw hardly anyone else and had no other intimate friends in Sennen—together contributed toward making happier that last short chapter of her life, she less alone in it.

Mary's last husband, Gabriel Aitken, was still alive, but he never came to Sennen while I was there, nor I believe after that while Mary lived, though their separation was amicable, and Mary referred to him easily. "Gabby" (she pronounced it to rhyme with "Ah, me") said or did this or that. "He wouldn't wash his face. He said shaving cream on it in the morning was enough." Yet this unexplained late marriage and separation was another enigma for me. Why had she married him, "The Archangel Gabriel"? For companionship? He had failed her, I thought—though it did not appear to be of any importance. He was off somewhere living with an aunt and going to pieces, it was said, with drink. They corresponded.

I think that living in Sennen was the best and happiest kind of solution that Mary, given her past experiences and reduced circumstances, could have found.

The entire first weeks after my arrival were taken up in sandpapering and painting the interior of the thatched cottage which Angus had restored, "No Place," set back in the fields from the Land's End cliffs. Mary came up often to advise and help in various ways. When the furniture was installed she polished some of it and oiled all of Angus's leather-bound books with some favorite preparation. One should use this, never that, she said, and talked of beeswax. Indeed, she had her stock of household lore.

When Angus and I had moved into "No Place" to live, a wonderfully satisfying order in our days became established. We were both writing, as was Mary, and spent the mornings at our desks. In the afternoons we always walked, sometimes took very long walks in that marvelous countryside, inland or along the coast, came back for tea and more work, with reading, writing letters, and so on, in the evening. But there was scarcely a day when we didn't see Mary: she came for lunch or tea or dinner, and we went to her together or separately. Well I recall her brief little notes brought up by Lucy, her devoted Cornish "daily," when it was my turn: "Harcourt, pink soup, wreck wine, seven o'clock!" Pink soup, wreck wine! The soup was a tomato bisque I had praised. "It's not just out of a tin," Mary said. "There's all sorts of things in it, herbs, and it takes a long time to prepare." The delicious and strong red wine came from bottles that had floated in on a certain ocean current from Portugal and been collected by fishermen, in this case Lucy's "wrecker" brothers who had a fascinating illegal cache of things from the sea, planks of mahogany, for instance. With the soup and wine Mary often made a pilaf of rice and fish, and we ended with fruit and cheese.

As well as in her meals, Mary took pride in her housekeeping in that commonplace little villa, for her who loved big, old gracious houses! But it stood on the edge of a steep, gorse-grown bank above Sennen Cove with a superb view of sea and sky and overlooked Whitesand Beach and Bay, ever-changing. What blues and jades and purple-reds over sand and rock in sunlight! I remember these better than what was inside the house except that it was well cared for.

At first Mary went on shorter walks with us. Later she became less inclined to go very far afield: I see now that she may have been less well. And there was her game knee which gave her trouble at stiles. She would lean on her stick and agitate her right leg in two or three little circles to fix her knee in proper place before mounting any steps. After her first explaining that her knee could be thrown out easily, she didn't like to have it noticed or referred to.

For days when Mary remained indoors I taught her how to hook rugs which I had learned by watching an invalid make one. I said it was a nerve-soothing but creative pastime she might enjoy, and she agreed and learned readily. It was the type of hooking with knots, on a wide-meshed backing, a three inch or so length of heavy yarn. Soon piles of these colored snippets covered Mary's sitting room floor—she called them "little worms." I had recommended she attempt some striped design initially, but she would have none of that and immediately worked quite a creditable Butts coat of arms, and secondly, a primitive of Sennen Cove complete with boats and figures, a splendid sun. The latter rug was for the No Place thatcher's family of innumerable children and a wife with one arm. Mary used to visit them bearing small gifts for the children.

Shortly came gardening days—spring arrives early in Cornwall. Both Mary and Angus were good gardeners. Angus was starting his garden from scratch, and there was much planning and talk between them. I expect Mary had a green thumb. I can see her sowing seeds at No Place—a quick scattering motion, a swift and light smoothing over of the earth as she moved along. I thought of Ceres. In Mary's garden I remember scarlet poppies and clumps of cultivated goldenrod, mullein too, surprising to an American. I helped Mary in that special task of destroying slugs. We used to go about in the evening finding them with flashlights and dropping them in a jar of vinegar (after which, well pickled, they were thrown to the seagulls). One night I shone my light into a miniature rock garden grotto, all green with a tiny-leaved plant, and there sat, perfectly ensconced, a gleaming jewelled toad. "Mary, come and see the toad in its bower." "The toad in its bower, the toad in its bower," she sang. How much she liked a turn of phrase.

Collecting slugs reminds me of the story I told her of another kind of slug which positively delighted her. Gertrude Stein on her American lecture tour had happened to be housed overnight with a cousin of mine in Springfield, Massachusetts, and there had been taken to see the printing process of a local newspaper and been given a printer's slug with her name on it. "Ho-ho!" Mary exclaimed with tremendous glee, "a slug named after Gertrude Stein!" She was to improve on this theme more than once afterwards until it became: "A new species of slug has been discovered and officially called 'The Gertrude Stein.'" She almost seemed to believe it—and perhaps in time she did? Mary made fun of Gertrude Stein's writing and intensely disliked the woman whom she considered evil. She told me she was surrounded in Paris by a shocking group of people who practised the refinement of causing others to fall in love with them that they might be treated with sadistic cruelty.

I remember other moments in Mary's garden. Once coming upon her there in the early twilight, I told her of my afternoon's walk, when, wandering into a stand of pines, absorbed by its beauty, I had encountered, in a pit, the rotting body of a cow and its terrible odour. It led Mary to speak of pairs of opposites—"Great abominations—and great beauty," she murmured, nodding toward the evening star limpid and liquid over the quiet sea.

But in May we had an abominable storm that devastated both gardens, a high gale like a hurricane. Angus had gone down to tea at Mary's and I followed him later, surprised by the strength of the wind and the driven rain stinging my cheeks like hard pellets. My hat swirled off and out of sight. Staggering alone, there seemed danger from the howling, tautened telephone wires and stones being blown off hedges—they littered the road up which I could see a metal windmill bent double. Mary, whose house was exposed to the very worst of the gale, met me with horror on her face. Why had I come out? How had I even managed to get there? As we struggled with the door a long rug in the hallway lifted its full length, and I was hardly aware of the comparative quiet inside before there was a rip and clattering above our heads: loose slates were being torn from the roof. "Christ!" cried Mary. "The roof is going!" The roof held, we tried to reason with her, but she was wrapped in the drama of the situation. The gale's whistling reminded her of the story of a man who had found a Roman whistle and called up a malevolent wind. "Someone has found that whistle again!" And it was not hard to think of that wind as a curse. The sea was a troughed mass of white, torrents of rain hurled against the shaking windows as if to break them, and just outside a row of young ash trees we had helped to plant, stake and water, had been stripped of their few leaves, the wind's fury holding them down unnaturally: they would not recover. Mary kept crying over her garden, the new plants laid flat or carried away. We had an uneasy tea, continually interrupted to wring out the soaking towels we had placed along the bubbling window sills. Next morning showed the No Place garden a ruin of blackened leaves, they looked frost-killed (and indeed there had been a frost in parts of England and Scotland that unusual spring). Mary sent up word not to uproot and discard our plants, that she believed they would recover. And it was true: they did.

It took one, as well, a little while to recover. Although I could not read as much as Mary did in portents and auguries and changes, by queer coincidence we learned within a day or two that T.E. Lawrence had lost his life in a road accident, and I heard that my brother had been killed on the same day in much the same way. It was an unsettling time.

And Mary seemed more tired. I can recall evenings now when she admitted it. I cannot say that she was ill then, but in the light of future events I think she may have been in pain at times. I know she took medicines, a quantity of cascara—and also her infusions. Angus and I had been carrying down to her from the Post Office many mysterious cartons, some of them quite large, sent by garden supply houses. One day a partly damaged box revealed the fact that it was full of dried poppy heads. "What is in all these boxes?" one of us, too innocently, asked. "Oh, just little bits of wood," Mary answered. From then on in the evenings there was always a brew of those "bits of wood" simmering away in a small saucepan at the back of Mary's stove, and I couldn't refrain from asking, one night while we washed the dishes, what *it* was. To be sure my question from one point of view was impertinent, but it was not meant impertinently. Knowing her as well as I did, sharing daily all we shared, being possessive about her, I wanted a truthful reply so that our intimacy and trust would be even greater. If she had said: "It's an infusion of poppy heads—a mild opium substitute," which I knew it to be, and had not treated so near a friend—childishly in this case, for she only said casually: "Something for my knee,"—I would have been content. Never once had she referred in any way to the old days when I lay beside her as she smoked, though I gave her opportunities, and I felt it unnatural of her not to do so. To this day I have no idea why she was so reticent, actually secretive, on this subject at any rate, and at least with me who knew, and shared her laughing jokes about it. Whether she now felt shame, or a shyness, or wished to avoid criticism and discussions, I could not tell. (I think these infusions may have been a contributing factor to her being slightly unwell these months, and to her terminal illness.)

But even when she was tired (and confounded me by her secretiveness), always, always her generosity. When Angus and I had friends to see us from America, from London, she put herself out to be entertaining and gay with them—and once seemed to outdo even herself. A group of four or five American college girls touring England had stopped to see me, and Angus and I gave them an elaborate Cornish tea, inviting Mary to meet them. She did not appear early, but then a knock at the door and Mary stood framed there wearing a wide-brimmed hat turned up on one side and a dark silk dress I had never seen, in her arms and a gloved hand an enormous sheaf of long-stemmed flowers. "Mary!" I'm afraid I gasped. And to what perfection she played the part of lady bountiful, very gracious lady, yet a little distant and untouchable—terribly interesting to me, for there were the other roles she might have chosen and this one, for the young females from overseas, was so different from the everyday Mary we were accustomed to.

Speaking of visitors and manners, during her Easter school holiday, Mary's daughter, Camilla, was with her that year. I noticed that Mary was strict with her and frequently admonished her to be "a little lady." However, Mary felt rather put upon by her presence at times. One day Camilla came up to No Place and hung about. "What can we do for you?" "Oh—nothing." Mary had merely sent her up to get rid of her. "They'd love to see you," she confessed she had said and that it was rather naughty of her. I took Camilla for a few long walks to "help." Mary could rely on my good nature, and did.

Later Mary herself had a kind of holiday, and I was glad for her. She saw Dr. Tancred Borenius, among others, in London—was he not made Camilla's guardian?—met her greatly admired Charles Williams, and stayed with Mrs. Betty Montgomery at Windsor. It was a huge success, and she told us all about it on her return. She had motored up with a departing guest of ours. "He drove like a bird," Mary said. "His hands scarcely touched the wheel." Small wonder an accident was narrowly averted? "I saw the lorry and had just time to commend our souls to God." Mrs. Montgomery lived within the Castle close, and one day they had glimpsed Queen Mary alighting from her car. "The Queen saw Betty and waved. Betty swept into a most beautiful courtesy—but I had trouble with my knee." (Poor dear, she felt she had disgraced herself.)

Mary's meeting Charles Williams undoubtedly meant the most to her. She used to mention him at times and spoke, too, of an intention to write one day on Christianity in connection with Julian the Apostate. Lacking her erudition on the subject, and her interest then, I was not always able to follow her allusions. But I do not think that even the local Church of England rector was helpful to her here. When he came to call on her the length of his stay made her a little restive, and I never knew her to attend his church. On the other hand she conversed at length with the excessively high church rector of a parish beyond Penzance. I went with her to one or two of his services and was not impressed by the general atmosphere, the silver witch balls that hung in every window. It is too easy to say they were just Mary's "cup of tea," though I think she was not disapproving.

What a perfect subject Julian would have been for Mary if she had lived to write that book! I wonder how she would have treated the old gods and goddesses, her onetime intimates? I do not see her unsympathetic, however, to true mystical worship in any religion. Once when we were looking through a book on Egyptian art she breathed, "Holy. Holy," as we turned a page to a picture of the goddess Hathor giving suck to a believer. At this time Mary was writing *The Crystal Cabinet.* She used to read chapters to Angus and me as they were completed, and very good we found them. I firmly believed (and believe) that after some fallow years—indecisive years? but who can know the inner story of that sequence?—Mary's best work lay ahead, that with *The Crystal Cabinet* a renaissance was beginning for her. I had no tangible proof of this, I simply felt it in my bones. Once she said to me: "Harcourt, you have great strengths—and great weaknesses." I acknowledged it as I think she would have acknowledged it about herself; she too had strengths and weaknesses to a degree, and here to me was a sign of great strength: a not giving up, a determined giving herself to work again. There had been a time earlier when I was afraid Mary might have grown too discouraged. A manuscript refused, she had said to me: "It's not good at my age." But I saw I need not have been concerned, for I felt it in my bones also that she had found a way to resolve her past—perhaps in several volumes?—and that it was "right." The writer's true and curious joy was wonderfully evident. When she read the description of her old home and what it had become, "its back broken," her voice broke.

We used to talk of writing, of words and their usage, the permissibility of repetition, such as the "broken" and "broke" above. Angus and I told Mary we thought some of her phrases cliché: "her cap of curls," for example, "her travelling kit." And what was wrong with them? she questioned. (Ah, but of course, that was Mary herself, that was part of her gay "burden," and we were wrong.) More often we read our finished work. I brought her something I had done in which there was a portrait of her. I called her Diotima (she of whom Socrates had said: "perfectly skilled in this and many other doctrines"); Mary was pleased—how much more pleased I, surely, when I found in a packet of letters Angus showed me in 1937 some letters from me under the label: "From writers who are famous or may become famous."

Returning to phrases and redundancy, Angus and I teased Mary when she spoke of an acquaintance as "a gentlewoman of good family." She didn't like to be teased; it made her knit her brows in protest, albeit she knew we meant no unkindness. (I had seen her when she had been cruelly hurt by some lesser person's malice. "I didn't do that, I *didn't,* Harcourt," she wanted me to understand. "Ouf. *Ouf!*" and she shook her head vigorously.) In playful teasing she could get her own back at us. One day Angus and I, walking to her house, had entangled ourselves, not very brightly, in the question: "If an airplane can travel faster than light and you leave a place at dawn, fly around the world, and arrive at the starting point a minute before dawn, what happens to you in that minute? What indeed?" We presented the puzzle to Mary. "You idiots, you arrive the next day," she said quickly, and blinked her eyes at us rapidly and mockingly. No fourth dimensional problem for her there!

Mary read a great deal. I remember carrying to her parcels of books from Boots' lending library: biographies, histories, detective stories, five or six at a time. And she wrote other things apart from her more serious work: reviews for *The Sunday Times,* an excellent description of a local mullet catch that season for *The Manchester Guardian.*

They were really wonderful, those days in Sennen. But a day came, at the end of July, for me to leave, to be with my mother for a while after my brother's death. I had a last meal with Mary, little dreaming I would never see her again, for I planned to return as soon as possible. It was a dinner with pink soup, wreck wine, candles on the table, an evening of easy and peaceful talk. Nevertheless when we embraced good-bye and I was about to turn to go, I blurted out compulsively: "But, O Mary, why have we never talked about the days when you were smoking, and all that? It seems so strange we haven't." Still that unresolved, unfinished, most personal question for me: in spite of our intimacy, her strange reticence. Mary said, not easily: "You are asking something that only lovers can talk about." At this I said no more, and she answered nothing, sat brooding. Even when I reached the door and looked back at her she did not look at me, I could not tell what she was thinking, brooding there in the flickering candlelight and shadow.

But the next day she answered, writing to me in London, en route, a sweet note beginning abruptly: "Because we love each other and everything is right and shall be right. . . ."

We exchanged letters until her death only months later.

Once she gave me a difficult commission: to determine the exact price an American museum had paid for the Butts's Holbein. (So it still went on: her fixed idea that her fair share of family moneys was being withheld from her?) I tried to find out what I could from museum directors I knew and hoped that their cautious replies satisfied her. And once she wrote that she would like to dedicate to me her *Julian the Apostate.* It made me profoundly happy. I knew that such a gift is from the heart and that Mary had forgiven me my lack of charity in Paris. Now, finally, I could forgive myself.

VI

Sennen, Autumn, 1937—Summer, 1938.
After Mary's death. Conclusions.

I returned to Sennen where Mary would not be returning. I wished so much I had been with her in her last days to give what comfort I could. She comforted. I was afraid she may have suffered considerably. After the emergency operation—for appendicitis!—and her death in Penzance, the hospital matron told Angus she had never seen so appalling a case of stomach perforations. (I have a theory here that the years of cascara—cum drugs, and the infusions later, that necessitated it?—had done its damaging work, though this is my private conjecture only.) Surely the sudden end was merciful.

Mary's presence, naturally, was everywhere in the many memories of her. Furthermore Angus had received all her papers and allowed me to look them over with him so that we were discussing her constantly. In fact a day could not have passed during the nine or ten month period I remained that we did not speak of her. And presently, in my room, always seen, was the flat silver bowl dug up in Greece, a treasured possession of mine I had once laid at Mary's feet, now kindly given back to me. In it she had kept her beads and the crystal pendant on a chain she often wore. Her one-time possession of the bowl gave it an added meaning and aura.

At least once, was she herself, something of her, at No Place as more than a memory? I hesitate to give an account of this very personal experience, wondering if it has a proper place in these notes, but since unbelievers do not give me the slightest concern—they simply do not know—I shall set it down, with little comment, for what it may be worth. As for me, I "believe" it. One night I had just got into bed when I "heard" the front door being pushed open—heard it not with my ordinary ears: I sensed, that is, its opening, and then "knew" that someone was crossing the front room to my bedroom door which was also opened in the same way. Then very, very vividly the image of Mary's face, but oddly quite small, was imprinted on my mind. She seemed to want to tell me something urgently, what I could not make out; there was an impression she desired to be understood more clearly for what she had done (or not done?) in life, a regret that had nothing to do with me: it was about herself. And that was really all. I will only add that I was neither drowsy nor envisioning anything, nor was I thinking of Mary at the time, and my eyes were not closed. (Whatever else, this was no hypnogogic phenomenon.) Remember, I had only just gone to bed. I must insist on the reliability of these facts which are not written from memory that cannot, of course, be wholly trustworthy. The experience was so real, not to say startling, that I got out of bed and wrote all of it down. And I take from those notes alone in telling it here.

Naturally, it was not this that made me want to do for Mary. I had been longing to see every justice done her. In this respect the next episode has its melancholy interest. I wish to say here too that it is taken from notes written at the time, with a view to making a short story out of it one day.

There came a time for Angus, on whom had devolved more than the tasks of a literary executor, to arrange for Mary's gravestone. One day we drove to a quarry to inspect a great slab—was it not of reddish granite?—that had been cut. Heavy, heavy for her, I thought, and suddenly remembered that she had written about stones, something about getting a stone instead of the heart's desire? At home I found what I was looking for in *Death of Felicity Taverner:*

> "Truth is the heart's desire;
> There is a stone instead of the heart's desire....
> Be comforted."

We had been searching for an epitaph for her—in the Bible, in "Lycidas," and Shakespeare—without coming to any conclusion; and this—the second line omitted—how perfect this was for her! (Today I feel that even the last line would have been enough, perhaps better?) It seemed to express at once Mary's knowledge, her longing, her tenderness. Angus in all honesty (and he is the most honest of men) could not find it absolutely just, and pointed out to me what we were often discussing: Mary's sometime disregard for the conventional truth. I, nevertheless, was fired to show her ideal side, arguing it may be the far realer one, that this intrinsic message from her in perpetuity would be a most generous gesture we could make for the friend who herself made many, and Angus thoroughly agreed. Accordingly, he prepared a drawing of the stone, including the two-line quotation, and sent it for approval to her mother, with completely negative results. Mrs. Colville-Hyde's response was a "She was my daughter, and I shall not speak against her now, *but*" kind of letter that went on to offer some words from a poem on a child of wild fancies (was it from Blake? I have no note on this.) and made one or two other suggestions that would do for anyone. So in the end the design went to the stonecutter provided with nothing but Mary's name and her dates. I was even more disappointed than before, having discovered in the meantime the unquestionably sincere and deeply felt words of Mary herself (and to herself) on the pages of an unpublished essay, a long treatise on the state of the Western world: "At the end of my first notes on this I wrote a prayer to the Holy Spirit that I might come upon the truth." In another place she had written: "I may be a fool, I may be a cat . . . but I seek the truth." And I had seen again among her papers and poems how many times she had tried, and retried, phrases about the truth and stones, getting stones for truths. It was, in short, one of her favorite ideas. And it comes to me that a further study and consideration of this telling theme might be extremely profitable.* "Well, Mary," I concluded, "we have given you a stone. Somewhere you seem to imply it is better to receive one, and I shall try to understand you, for your sake in this case, though it seems *too* much poetic justice. All the same I am sorry we couldn't give you *our* heart's desire. Be comforted. . . ."

The difficult matter of Mary and the truth cannot possibly be overlooked if one is to truly approach her and must be discussed before arriving at any evaluation of her personality. I maintain that her own words must stand first: "I wrote a prayer to the Holy Spirit that I might come upon the truth. . . . *I seek the truth.*" These starkly simple statements must be wholly and utterly accepted. I go so far as to say that the secret meaning of her life lies here, the deepest motivation, known to her consciously, and am certain that it was the Truth beyond opposites she wished to know, that Truth

---

*I continue to be intrigued, and plagued, by what Mary meant by stones. There are, of course, the New Testament words on asking for bread and getting a stone, but somehow I feel that she carried the meaning further and that dogged research will turn up an answer, perhaps quite simply in some work that influenced her, such as *The Golden Bough*? Then there is Hermes Trismegistus' "Emerald Tablet" of whose arcanum we know Mary was well aware and which one may call a stone that *held* the answer but was not the answer itself (which is quite inexpressible). In Hermetic Philosophy, as in alchemy, the gold philosophers' stone was the Truth to seek, but in their search philosophers found all manner of other stones, some of precious stuff. Could it be that Mary used the analogy of finding those stones that were not the truth, but—and be comforted—such is the search? And it is the search that is important. I am hampered by not having Mary's books at hand. In them there might be clues? And in the journals, clues and revelations?

of God beyond good and evil. This is not to say that she searched faultlessly or without cease. Thoroughly aware of my own shortcomings and my presumption in speaking in this way of another's inner life—though I do so with love—I believe that Mary sometimes walked instead of ran, or ran up wrong avenues in her earlier life, finding stones instead of her heart's desire. (The very last of her life may be a different story.) And when it came to *interpreting* the truth on different levels—or dare I say the Truth?—I believe she created some extraordinary intricacies both for herself and others.

Is it not those very intricacies one sees in her writing as well as in her life? To take her writing first, I can best illustrate my point by giving an excerpt from a review of the works of Ford Madox Ford in *The Times Literary Supplement* of June 15, 1962. When I read it I was reminded so strongly of the Mary I knew I must keep note of it for just such an account as this. The review went:

> Ford's habitual romancing inaccuracy ... he elevated to the level of aesthetic principle, and called Impressionism. Impressionism for Ford meant a subjective version of experience from which there could, or at least should, be no appeal to facts. (Of one of his books he said: 'This book is full of inaccuracies as to facts, but its accuracy as to impression is absolute' [*Memoirs and Impressions*], and in *The Spirit of the People* he wrote: 'It is all one whether the artist be right or wrong as to his facts: his business is to render rightly the appearance of things.') Ford seems to have regarded all facts, including the facts of his own life, as legitimate subjects to rendering and improvement by the imagination.

I do not suggest that this was Mary's total viewpoint—for one thing she could, and did, report quite factually as in her *Manchester Guardian* article on the mullet catch—but *mutatis mutandis,* there is a remarkable resemblance between Mary's and Ford's views as writers, and it is interesting to remember that Mary knew Ford and corresponded with him. (There were letters from him in the "famous writers" packet.) Surely she must have been influenced by him in the early Paris days. Research here too might yield a good deal. I by no means criticize Mary's great artistry nor her intent. It is true that living persons depicted in her novels are not usually recognizable, we know that they are neither realistic portrayals nor intended to be, but are "romanticized," or, better, "alchemized" to another essence in her inimitable manner all the way from her mother and Tony in *Ashe of Rings* to *Cleopatra.* In her novels, too, are all those qualities I saw and loved in Mary from the beginning: her fascination, magic making, generosity, lightness, grace, gaiety, *all.* This is to be understood. It is when we come to actual facts that I am not at all persuaded as to the final merits of her "impressionism," and must take exception. I remember a terse and harsh letter Tony Butts chose to write to the *London Times* directly after *The Crystal Cabinet* was published. He called attention to a passage where Mary told of their mother's burning lovely and rare, if frankly sexual, French books that had belonged to their late father, and declared that they were nothing but paperbound, pornographic trash. He was undoubtedly correct in fact, and Mary not. For her, if they had not been exquisite volumes, *they should have been,* just as red wine should have been seen passing down Mary Stuart's white throat, or a slug named after Gertrude Stein, or I should have found a Viking Stone! (When I told Mary of a clever hoax a practical joking friend of mine had perpetrated on an island off Cape Cod, actually marking a boulder in Norse letters and leaving it to become seaworn before "discovering" it at low tide, Mary later insisted I alone found an authentic stone, though I had been but shown the bogus one. My finding a stone, however, is that not significant, considering what a stone seems to have meant to her? Suddenly, after all these years, it becomes for me as a gift she wished to bestow, I too, in her mind, looking for the truth.) If all these things weren't true, they should have been, and so in fine, for Mary, they were true. In a way I love her for it and am willing to accept it superficially as her special brand of poetic license or poetic truth. It was a delight at times. But if it was her considered interpretation of a Truth beyond our dimensional truths, I cannot agree with her—not because I happen to believe, as she appa-rently did not, that expressing true facts in our dimension, as far as one can see them, is a great deal more interesting than any embellishing of them, *pace* artistry, *pace* fancy and imagination and all other things that have their rightful time and place—but because I see a human charm and weakness in this kind of interpretation, not a strength leading to the One Truth. It is too intricate, too troubling.

Angus Davidson once labored with Mary over a black and white statement she had made that simply was not true, and all he could get from her in the end were words to the effect: "I am a writer. For me it was the truth." (If this is not pure Ford, what is?) Thus she brought those very same intricacies into her life and it, above all, seems to have led to real trouble now and then, to the difficulties with her family, and to making certain enemies. I think she was more sinned against than sinning, not wary enough of smaller people who fell far short of understanding her. Nevertheless the matter cannot be passed over. I have known of those who actively disliked Mary, called her devious and worse—but Mary was not a congenital liar, never a calculating troublemaker through lies. These are too severe judgments by far. One particularly severe and vicious indictment of Mary was rendered by William Plomer in *The Case Is Altered.* I was shocked by this book which seemed to me a fantastic caricature of Mary. Of course he was a friend of Tony's and therefore hopelessly biased from the start. Might one say it was really Tony speaking? Granting Tony his grievances makes the book slightly more comprehensible. On the other hand, even Tony should have had no use for so low an order of meanness. Plomer gave Mary no quarter down to her very shoes! He depicted as a silly affectation Mary admiring a new pair of shoes. (Poor darling Mary: I'm sure she was uncomfortable with him and tried to cover it by playful comment on the nice appearance of her feet.) I knew those shoes and Mary's innocent delight in them, she who could afford so few good things. They were a gentle-woman's brown walking shoes, narrow, of fine leather, of plain elegance. There is something in Plomer here of the monkey picking for fleas in the mane of the dead lion. He judged her past all reasoning without a care to finding any good in her. And judged Mary whom we know truly prayed for the truth!—though that was a secret he never could have approached (and we know it only because she chanced to write it marginally to herself).

To appeal to the Holy Spirit for the truth! It is of shining beauty, no small person knows this secret and its validity, its simplicity beyond all intricacies. Perhaps it was Mary's greatest secret? For now I wonder, in spite of what I felt needful to say of her interpretation of it, if the truth that Mary sought, her heart's desire, was not the Truth that only the best know, the saints and sages of the Philosophia Perennis? And I wonder if in her last phase, given her strong religious leanings, she did not consciously crave their Illumination. It is not an impossible thought, and would have been her greatest secret indeed.

I come to stress her secrets at the last—or, rather, that she had them—because now I realize it is a most important clue toward understanding what she was "really like." I have called it her "reticence," and when impatient, her "secretiveness," but I think it was more than those: she kept secrets to herself, inviolable. I had no good conception of this in the Villefranche days with her when she threw herself so vigorously, boisterously like a little girl, into having fun, laughing hard. *Everything* seemed shared. Even in the far maturer relationship of Sennen I had not fully understood—it was her constant generosity that put one off—that she did not give *all* of herself to anyone, didn't let one approach quite as near as one would have allowed in the same circumstances, making the common mistake of attributing one's own inclinations to another. Mary *couldn't* do that; I think it was not a holding back for any set reason, but a trait of character—that actually her last words to me in person, how there were things she could share only with a lover, are to be taken with complete seriousness.

Then what of her lovers? Yes, it is a legitimate question, although I can speak of it only parenthetically by asking if she ever met her match in love. Certainly she did not find lasting love in her marriages, should she have been looking for it there, and I am inclined to think, not with any lover, Sandy Maitland a possible exception. She always spoke of him with feeling, though even here—I don't know why, and I may wrong her—I felt I detected imperfection, that she had "alchemized" his memory. Once she said to me: "If he had not died young I would have been his countess," romancing, I feared, since I was told his chance of coming into an earldom was so remote as to be practically nonexistent. But I can speak with no authority whatever on Mary and the man she may have loved the most and to whom she may have disclosed the most. Only a persistent impression lingers that she was ill-fated here, that too her secret.

Again and again, Mary had her secrets from us all, and to seek to lay bare her whole personality is to find she has a way of escaping us a little. One can never know all about her because she never told all, guarding herself well. But I think I have discovered one of the great secrets of her personality, another key—her greatest attribute? It was her *gaiety*. Those who loved her knew and loved it; she projected gaiety, we bathed in it. It is true I had seen her sad. If she temporarily chose sorrow in defeat, as I had thought, it did not last. Sorrow was not at all of her basic essence. And I may have been wholly wrong in imagining her lonely in the street that day in London. Even in Cornwall when she told me of walking alone on the cliffs in the moonlight with Paddy Paws, her big tomcat, gambolling beside her, I pictured her as being all too lonely and was touched. But perhaps she was not lonely in the least. (It was of the cat she had spoken and his unusual habit of remaining with her all the way.) Perhaps au fond she was almost entirely self-sufficient? It is true that she said she was tired at times, but she kept the reason for it to herself; she did not impart to Angus, the only close friend near, how ill she must have been just before she died. I say she was gallant and courageous about this too, as about her comparative poverty. It is true she had great disappointments—but then she had great strengths to meet them. Think of the powerful new burst of work at the end. (This to me is especially noteworthy.) And where she was "ill-fated," did she not quite well realize it was partly her fault in how she had managed situations? I cannot but suppose she had regrets, yet I wonder if she did not know that for inscrutable deep, deep reasons she had had to lead the life she did.

I return perforce to her gaiety, to "East of the sun, west of the moon," to "Pink soup! Pink soup!" and all the rest, to her magic touch, the lovely lightness and brightness and all the bird images in her speech and in her books—bird names, bird gods: "the woodpecker who was Zeus," bird flight, "flash of feathers." "My bird," I have heard her say, "best and brightest." No one else has ever talked to me like that, and no one else ever will. Once I asked Mary what she thought about life after death, and she said: "Oh, we'll go on talking and laughing and walking together. We'll meet our friends and go to some heavenly pub. And we'll all be 'copains.'" Gaiety: I think this is the best of Mary, and therefore Mary. I think it is the way she saw herself, the way she wanted to be—"gaiety in the end," as Yeats concluded, or, better, something of the illuminated Teresa of Avila with her gay, babbling little songs about God. That is of Mary too. And it means, as she wrote to me: *Everything is right and shall be right—because we love.*

CAMILLA BAGG

Another View of Mary Butts

THE MARY BUTTS OF LEGEND is remembered as a great-granddaughter of the Thomas Butts who was Blake's patron and whose ancestry perhaps went back to the royal Tudors. She is associated with an extravagantly dramatic style of life, and a number of memoirs of the period contain glimpses of the gorgeous redhead living it up at that great party known as Paris in the Twenties. But Mary Butts had another side, less well-known, one of excellent practicality, the sort of thing associated with north-country backbone and no nonsense, inherited from her less illustrious ancestors, the Briggs.

It was her brother, Anthony, who was said by William Plomer, in his *Curious Relations,* to have referred to the Briggs as those "solid and by no means uninteresting people." They came from Manchester and its environs. Thomas Briggs, born in 1799, married Mary Robinson and had three children. It was the eldest of these, James, who became the maternal grandfather of Mary Butts. Thomas Briggs had been a jute merchant, owning ships in the East India trade and, having made enough money to see him out, he gave the rest of his life to a grand passion, Free Trade. For many years he was Secretary of the Free Trade League, and out of his years of research, correspondence and public speaking, he published two books on better ways of managing the country's economic and commercial affairs. I do not know if Thomas Briggs's opinions were respected or if he was considered an amiable crank; perhaps he was a great bore, with an obsession. His style of writing is, of course, Victorian, richly ornamented and majestically flowing, yet there are many flashes of good fun as he flays the politicians or mocks the follies he saw all round him. Against injustice he was ferocious. When I was younger I could not raise the interest or patience to read him. Today I find him irresistable.

James Briggs entered the church. Brilliant at Cambridge and later a university in Germany, as an ordinand he was considered to hold extraordinary promise; but, as they used to say, he was "not strong." In 1874, summoned to a deathbed in dreadful weather, he stayed for hours in soaking clothes, caught a cold, developed pneumonia, and did not recover. He was forty-four and he left a widow with five daughters. The widowed mother seems to have left a great deal to the eldest, Ada, fourteen at the time of the father's death, but somehow the girls became educated and, better than merely that, cultivated. Ada was devoted to literature and hoped to become a writer. She wrote several novels, one of which was published. She began to take part in local affairs and, in 1919, became the first woman alderman on the Poole Borough Council, at that time an impressive achievement. Irlam became a painter of considerable stature. Agnes was an excellent violinist and miniaturist. Monica had a lovely singing voice but she died young, in mysterious circumstances. If any of these gifted, energetic, young women could be said to be less interested in things of the mind, it was the second sister, Mary, but she was known as the prettiest, and practical with it. In 1888 her mother received a letter, a proposal of marriage for Mary, from the middle-aged but distinguished Captain Butts. As a very young man he had been a hero of the Crimean War, but on leaving the Army had settled nearby in the old house of Salterns. Recently he had lost his grown-up son, his only child, who died from the effects of a sailing accident—pneumonia again. Not long after, Mrs. Butts died from a heart attack on a visit abroad. That was how Mary Briggs came to marry a man thirty years older than herself, a contemporary, within three years, of her long dead father.

This story can be found in *The Crystal Cabinet* and, at a remove, fictionalized, in *Curious Relations,* and I go through it only because, as motherhood was not Mary Butts's forte and as I was in need of a home, I was taken back to the place from which she had set out and to some of the people who had surrounded her as a child. I was even sent to the same school. Thus I came to know my mother's aunts, who had, I believe, an influence on Mary Butts the writer as well as on the Mary Butts I remember.

She had a great interest in gardening. At the end of her life, in Cornwall, she managed, alone among the dwellers on the top of the cliff at Sennen Cove, to get a garden of sorts in the teeth of the Atlantic gales which swept over the coast. She achieved her remarkable results by chopping up wooden market boxes and making little protective walls for her seedlings. Fragile plants like godetia, clarkia and eschscholtzia flowered among the vegetables, and the total effect displayed some of the charm of a cottage garden far inland.

She was a good cook, when the fancy took her, and she was the first person who talked to me about food, lamenting the ruin which was the usual fate of the excellent produce available in England. The years in France had given her contempt for the British joint of meat smothered in blanket gravy. Her leg of lamb came with a crisp skin and aromas of herbs.

She was perhaps at her very best when there was the immediate need to look after someone who was ill, hurt, or in emotional distress. This has been testified by Stella Bowen in *Drawn from Life*. Your troubles mattered—for there was no one better able than Mary Butts to appreciate their drama. At the same time, she energetically took measures to alleviate the pain. Assuming that she could have controlled her enthusiasm for drama, I have sometimes thought that had she not been a writer, Mary Butts might have made a splendid nurse, or even a hospital matron. She wrote a number of suggestions for making more comfortable, and much more hygienic, Aleister Crowley's squalid Abbey of Thelema!

Gardening, cooking, nursing; she was a practical woman.

When *The Crystal Cabinet* came out in 1937 I had spent ten years in the district to which, after leaving me there, she never went again. She could not bear it—it made her feel ill—the long, creeping process of suburbanisation of a landscape which had been sacred. She found a substitute when she settled in Cornwall and, after four years' separation, we met again there, for part of the school holidays. Sea, sky, closeness to the changes in the weather, and the land with its bones showing—these surroundings she needed.

At that time I did not know how my mother felt about the places of her childhood but, independently, I had developed for myself an attitude about them, not so much of passionate despair as resigned depression. I could see for myself how beautiful the district of Parkstone and Poole Harbour must once have been, and that already it was too late. Everything natural was disappearing because so many people wanted to live in that mild, sunny climate with two kinds of sea conveniently near: Poole Bay, off the English Channel, on one side of the Sandbanks, and on the other, the quieter waters of the Harbour. It was said to be the largest in the world: from its narrow entrance, with all its inlets and promontories, a hundred miles round. On the Parkstone side there was just enough left of the past to make the scene all the more sad.

There were still some unmade roads where as you walked you could scuff the sandy soil. There were still bits of heath and woodland remaining between the building plots. Pine trees shed their slippery bright-brown needles or lay fallen in the sun, intoxicatingly resinous. There was a long country lane going past a disused sandpit which I was warned was dangerous. There were patches of derelict land covered by bramble which masked the pools of milky water where once had been thriving clay workings and pottery kilns. The last vestiges of what Parkstone must once have been came through to me without any influences from Mary Butts.

Across the waters of the Harbour could be seen the extraordinary Isle of Purbeck, not a real island but a large part of Dorset isolated by the indentations of the Harbour. It lay long, low, and not in the least like "a naked god laid down asleep," as she was to write in *The Crystal Cabinet.* More like a pair of sofa-backs. At such a distance, against the westering sun (for I was never free to see it early in the day), it was impossible to pick out detail, but the sofa-backs ran straight for miles along the dim horizon, and then curved down towards each other. Where they would have met on the plain up rose a mound. And on it there was something sticking up. A castle! What was it doing there, wedged in between those soaring downs?

On the rare occasions when I went to Corfe, the outing went to my head and added to my discontent. To be there was so glorious, and so free. The grassy slopes rose above the ruined castle; they were steep and slippery because the grass was short and dry. Auntie said I should be careful not to fall and squash the bee-orchids. At the top of the long climbs, sitting in the brilliant light, cooled by light winds off the sea and surrounded by small bright blue butterflies, I wished I did not have to return through the boring streets to the shut-in house in Upper Parkstone.

Discontented schoolgirl that I was, I despised my great-aunt's modest home, a long way from the sea and the handsome houses set in large, wooded gardens. Salterns was rarely mentioned. I was never taken to see it or encouraged to find it. My grandfather, Captain Butts, had died in 1905; Granny's second husband was dead; she and Uncle Tony moved to London after the First World War. I was born in 1920 and arrived in Parkstone in 1928. The great days were over, and my great-aunt Ada was determined that I should grow up without illusions of grandeur.

The same process of suburbanisation, though on a much smaller scale, was beginning to repeat itself in Cornwall. Mary Butts, settled in Sennen Cove and driven by the need to earn, began to do a good deal of reviewing. As one looks through her articles, it is noticeable that she was sent an increasing number of books about the English countryside. Few people at that time bothered about conservation, but she whose love had forever been given to Dorset had much to say about the insidious destruction of that county and of many other places of wild beauty. She foresaw that easy access by mechanical transport of all kinds would herald the end of remote and sacred places, and that people roaming wherever they wished, with their many needs requiring to be satisfied, would eventually destroy the beauty they had come to see. She once vigorously scolded a local builder for having run up a set of four, well-separated boxes of white concrete houses; they descended the hill to the cove and were visible miles out at sea.

Although the Council for the Protection of Rural England had been founded in 1926, showing that there existed the first stirrings of alarm, it was not until after the War that the government produced the Town and Country Planning Act of 1947 and public opinion began to change. There is today a planning principle that new buildings are not to be allowed to stand on the skyline and ruin the magnificent sweep of coastline. Such places are now bureaucratically designated Areas of Outstanding Natural Beauty; yet one has only to read Mary Butts's prophetic pamphlet, *Warning to Hikers* (1932), to learn that Mary Butts had been their defender at a time when there were no reinforcements.

No matter what she had done with her life, she must be honoured finally as a hard worker. She wrote steadily and to a routine, leaving a considerable body of work. The habit of work—surely an example had been set by her aunts. The hours spent by Ada at her desk, by Irlam in her studio, by Agnes practising the violin and the viola; also by her mother stitching her superb embroidery.

From the age of eight, when I lived with Ada for ten years (Irlam five minutes' walk away), it was in a household which had become becalmed in a way of life long out of date. In the nineteen-thirties we were still in the eighteen-eighties of their young womanhood. Morning prayers after breakfast, evening prayers after tea when the maid went home, grace before and after every meal, church every Sunday and sometimes twice, *no* excuses, church on all feast days. Kneel up straight and never rest against the seat behind you. Always the enormous attention paid to right behavior, even in the most trivial ways, not just as a matter of etiquette, or even the importance of behaving agreeably, but for the sake of "Our dear Lord, who died upon the Cross, for thee."

The young Mary Butts must have experienced much of this atmosphere even though things were a little more worldly in the Butts household. She chucked it overboard, as prodigals usually have, only to find that such a heritage will not sink and disappear. For her, particularly, a poet in the making, the beauty of the cadences of the Authorised Version of the Bible and the Book of Common Prayer would have sunk into her innermost being, if only because of their beauty. The message could be ignored.

But in the end, when she knew she must return to the fold, the prodigal daughter and the poet in her were able to meet on common ground. It was the respect for words, the falling in love with language, a powerful inheritance derived from two sources. One was the romantic which had been nurtured in her infancy and youth by the atmosphere of enchanted Salterns; her devoted father had helped her by providing just the right books for her growing imaginative powers, and always present was the unique tradition of the Butts association with William Blake embodied in those mysterious pictures of his hanging on the dining-room walls: *Nebuchadnezzar, Newton, Pity* and *The Lazar-House,* to name but a few among many others.

The other source was the down-to-earth Briggs family, who for generations had carried on official correspondence, kept minutes, written reports, made speeches, preached sermons, and exchanged vast numbers of letters.

Could the middle-aged Mary Butts have found anything more plainly stated than "Him that cometh unto Me I will in no wise cast out"? It offered a haven of unsurpassed comfort, startlingly expressed in a few simple words of dignity, and I believe she would have found it almost unbearably beautiful, even as just a sentence, standing alone, mere words. But form and meaning had at last come together, and Mary Butts would return to her Christian heritage.

Bradfield, Berkshire
1984, 1994

With Camilla, Paris, ca. 1924–25.

LOUIS ADEANE

An Appraisal of Mary Butts

MARY FRANCIS BUTTS died on 5 March 1937. She left behind her a small flurry of regret in the reviewers' columns and ten books which, when the flurry had fallen away, were revealed as being out of print. She flits elusively through most of the memoirs of the period and escapes with a single scratch from the pages of *The Apes of God;* the pattern of her life is interesting, not merely because it includes her work, but because of its deviations from a larger pattern, the literary life of her time. Ford Madox Ford thought she had genius, and indeed her writing is brilliant enough to prompt an inquiry concerning its value and its long neglect.

She reviewed her early years in *The Crystal Cabinet,* a vivid, unshapely book whose accuracy as to detail has since been questioned. Her family had come originally from Norfolk (a Robert Butts was Bishop of Ely in the eighteenth century), but her father bought a small country-house on the shore of Poole Harbour, Dorset, and as an elderly man he settled there. Salterns had little architectural distinction, but it was of some account in the neighbourhood and had extensive gardens. His daughter was born on 13 December 1890, and the place gave a quality of further estrangement to her rather lonely childhood. She says that in the pinewood she was possessed by "panic" fear; in the Lavender Walk she saw an unexplained Lady dressed in black. One is given an impression of her glancing figure, red-haired, among the trees of the orchard, or pausing to peer into one of the fourteen wells; or halted at a window, her stature like that of "a small

---

Originally published under the title "Mary Butts" in *World Review,* New Series, November 1951, pp. 23–27, this essay was virtually the only serious treatment of Butts's work in the decades of the 1940s and 1950s.

archaic statue," where she might watch a Channel storm whip the water and pour up through the woods to turn the grasses on the hills behind the house. On dark days the rooms were lit by tall candles, the hall, with its staircase on three sides, by a pendant candelabrum. There were many objects of indefinite value but illimitable fascination: "Silver and musical instruments and little old pictures of battles on copper, and brass polished to the colour of pale gold . . ."; mirrors, toys of ivory, watches, ebony boxes, miniatures, seals of cornelian and beryl and amethyst. There were some early Ming vases, rose and white, contributed by the Bishop of Ely, and there were thirteen chiming clocks. Unhappily, only Captain Butts understood the keys of these clocks, so that, at his death, they all ran down.

Apparently he was scholarly and stern, a friend of Rossetti, with a reticence which was "his form of pride. His desire was to omit, until, through omission itself, something appeared that had classic line and distinction." In his later years he had little to do with his children, but earlier he taught his daughter Greek and told her stories from Homer, and thus the emotional complexity and richness of her life was taken up and expressed systematically. From the first she interpreted the world in terms of Gods, demons and heroes, and this view, together with a concurrent attempt at proportion and formal simplicity, conditioned all her work. At this period also, her intense apprehension of alien but living forces within and without herself was formalised in terms of the occult, and her interest in magic and witchcraft received its first impetus. She was impressed by the ideal of chivalry, though she found it in a somewhat debased form: *The Three Musketeers* was a significant addition to her early reading.

Captain Butts's grandfather had been that Thomas Butts to whom Blake's letter begins:

> To my Friend Butts I write
> My first Vision of Light . . .

the patron to whom a collection of sketches, engravings, works in tempera and watercolour, even Blake's engraving cabinet, had passed. The Blake Room at Salterns housed those things (later they were bought by the Tate Gallery), and their presence contributed to the saturation of the child's mind with arcane imagery; at the age of seven she had expressed a preference for the book of Revelation in the Bible, saying that she understood it perfectly. Later on in Shelley, Spenser and Milton she found a language of symbol which she felt was in some way her own.

Soon after her father's death she was sent to school at St. Andrews on the coast of Fife. She did not adapt herself very happily to school life, but by reaction, her decision to become a writer was confirmed. So was her facility for self-dramatisation. The veil of dreams hardened into armour, and once the knight's habiliment had been assumed, it was necessary to have an opponent and a cause. A misapplied missionary fervour, occasioned by her prolonged squabbles with her relatives, often had an unfortunate effect on her work.

She studied for three years at London University, and the outbreak of war found her working for a Children's Care Committee at Hackney. She wrote her first novel, *Ashe of Rings*. She married and had a daughter, but a little later she left her husband and child in England and went to France, where she was to remain, intermittently, for the next ten years. Though she pursued the contemporary "good time" with contemporary zest, by the beginning of the 'twenties she had formed attitudes in opposition to at least three of its main trends. Her hostility to surrealism (dadaism, as she describes it) and psychoanalysis sprang from a feeling that they reflected a split between parts of the self within, and the natural order of the world without. Her view that the universe has intrinsic meaning is implied in the novel just mentioned:

> Christianity is a way, a set of symbols, in part to explain and to make men endure, the unutterable pain that is in the world. There are other sets, like chessmen. But only one game.

She found a number of friends in the shifting world of the Parisian exiles, and became attracted by two circles whose orbits often overlapped. It is possible that she had first met Ford Madox Ford in England during the war; in Paris she was rapidly drawn into his entourage, and she sometimes took her work to him for criticism. She said later that Ford had taught her to write short stories. She was also strongly influenced by the personality of Jean Cocteau, and she was acquainted with many eminent writers and artists who were in France at that time.

She also mixed with people who were more truly called the Lost Generation. It was the fashion, as Romer Wilson remarks, for everyone to be young, masculine and square, but though Mary Butts conformed to some extent to these requirements, they did not handicap either her emotional munificence or her physical beauty which, alternating between the gorgeous and the stilted, seems to have been remarkable in its power, as if for moments she had become her own goddess-ideal. Flaring with enthusiasm, her pale face lit by her red-gold hair, she moved from party to party, gathering round her a changing group of Russian emigrés, decayed aristocrats, college boys and cosmopolitan queers, to all of whom she radiated maternal sympathy and with all of whom she intrigued, quarrelled and was reconciled with more than customary conviction. Though she considered dadaism an evil thing, she was not averse to taking drugs and dabbling in "black magic." Indeed she appears to have tried almost every method of heightening or distorting consciousness, partly for its own sake but chiefly for her purposes as a writer. She had to be in the swim, having been born on the bank. If sometimes she seemed a bit bedraggled, this at least bore witness to her courage and generosity. The background to her stage was the "other Paris" of whose silence and horror Poe speaks, and which is evoked with mastery in her own story, "Mappa Mundi."

During these years she had been working hard and was achieving a reputation with her short stories. She visited Austria, Germany and Italy, and spent some time at Villefranche. The south of France lends a background to some of her work, notably her most memorable story, "The Houseparty." In 1928 she returned to England and set up a kind of salon near Regent's Park; after a further period in Montparnasse she married for the second time and in 1932 retired to Sennen Cove in Cornwall, where she was to live until her sudden death at the age of forty-six.

Mary Butts began by writing poetry. It was never collected, and its main importance for us is that the technical discipline involved clearly affected her prose to a great degree. When in 1929 the *Little Review* asked a number of writers what they looked forward to, Mary Butts replied: "A poet's success." She had something of this success: the first thing to impress the reader of her work is the pointed, exact and concentrated style, with its strongly marked rhythms and its frequent use of poetic allusion. It is brilliant with visual imagery, and if at first sight it seems obscure, this is because it is dazzling; dazzling the senses, it traps the intellect into close attention. Descriptive passages, in which a prose writer usually becomes discursive, are taut and purposeful; and as separable stretches of writing, they are rare. Disconnected scenes are knitted rapidly into the reader's single awareness, so creating a continuously changing "situation"; each paragraph, like each line of a poem, is the centre of a web whose threads reach out through the whole work. This method is the fitting expression of her narrow, deeply felt and coherent vision of life. The style of her nonfictional writing seems to have been influenced superficially by that of Charles Williams, with whose outlook and temperament she had something in common.

The world she describes is the nomadic world she knew,

the shifting underground life of every big city, a population moving uneasily across Europe, carrying with it the professional emigré, the political agent, the corrupted artist, the precious and the betrayed—in brief, the world of the lost. There is an affinity between her characters and Mr. Norris. During the 'twenties a crack or heave in the social structure enabled the writer to meet the nomads; ten years later a novelist had to go out and find these once-fashionable figures; after another decade the real exiles were to come the same way, giving significance to their predecessors. Edwin Muir once deprecated the effect of the fashionable in Mary Butts's first novel. Certainly it is damaging to find young men in another powdering their faces before descending to dinner; it is irritating to meet a girl who "came into breakfast like a pale glass cup with a nasturtium in it." But these are extreme instances of the fashionable, which is served elsewhere in a less precious, if cheaper, manner. "The cocktails tasted as if they they had been shaken in terror"; or: "Over the house, through the sparkling air, the bronze note of a clock rang, like a body falling bound into deep water." Such phrases have felicity of a kind, and often the very transitoriness of this surface view, the world described, increases by contrast the permanence of the world evoked.

The world evoked, the other level of meanings, provides the real background in most of what she wrote. She thought that "we are spectators of a situation which is the mask for another situation, that existed perhaps in some remote age, or in a world that is outside time." By various means—by a stylisation of form, in *Armed with Madness,* by the intrusion of the occult in her first novel, by a heightening of the sense of place, race, tradition, in *Death of Felicity Taverner*—the presence of that other world is implied. Appearances, for her, are copies of reality; life is a dome of many-coloured glass. The structure and movement of nearly all her work depends on this dichotomy: the characters are usually divided—sometimes too neatly—between the sheep and the goats; there is conflict between them or between truth and error in the mind of a single character. Her theme gave her the opportunity to make her unique contribution to literature, the near communication in words of an occult experience, the evocation of abnormal states of mind. For moments when reading her work, one's life seems twisted out of focus. The effect is achieved cumulatively; the process by which a shadow becomes alive and malignant, or a tree differentiates itself from a wood, is a delicate but convincing one. It is convincing partly because the experience of reading this tense allusive prose is itself a preparation for such alchemy; the mind is gradually set on fire, made aware; disbelief is suspended.

In an essay on Huxley, Mary Butts points out that his novels are really masques; to a lesser degree, this is true of her own three novels. Though in a letter she calls *Ashe of Rings* a ragged, passionate book, these qualities do not disturb the reader; the fault lies in that woodenness which attends most novels of a didactic kind, in which the characters become figures in a dance arranged from the outside by the author. *Ashe of Rings* is about a house and a piece of land, fixed points dominating the characters, whose actions thus become a projection of the past into the present. The house and family history exert an almost magical influence upon the heirs. Actual witchcraft is used by one person against another, but more impressive is the sustained atmosphere of evil and the evocation of the wartime wasteland in which the characters live. (Incidentally, this is one of the first modern novels to deal with persons "on the run" from military service.) In saying that the book treats with an evil mother, a gentlemanly seducer, a brother-sister relationship on the edge of incest, and so on, one is confessing that it is really a sophisticated melodrama. The writer fails to realise her intention completely, and the book remains, as she says, a kind of grim fairy story.

It is disappointing to find that in *Armed with Madness* the didactic device has been exchanged for one of an even more rigid kind. Here a number of young people in a countryhouse find a cup which represents for them the Sanc Grail. The cup is lost, the group searches, splits up, and some of the members return to the starting-point. This story, in which every figure is invested with definite single qualities—worldliness, courtesy, kindness—is intended to be a modern recapitulation of the Grail legend, with each character a knight. The deliberate movement of the book sometimes suggests a page-by-page translation of the legend into the writer's terms; but some arbitrary departures from convention help to cause confusion, as does the author's obvious struggle to deploy more characters than she can handle. As an attempt to integrate the Grail myth into modern literature, it is a failure.

Probably this was recognised by Mary Butts, who in her third novel employed the same characters and setting in a much more subtle play on the Grail theme. To her purpose she adapted as much as she could of the detective-story technique; but though the book is "an intellectual shocker of the first order," as a reviewer said, it is also a great deal more. Here the earlier battle between good and evil is fought again, this time with a more convincing armoury and with knights more mature. In this case the "truth," or the Grail, is represented by Felicity Taverner, who has died in mysterious circumstances abroad. The task of her friends is to find out how and why she died. When this question is answered, emphasis shifts from Felicity's death to her life, and it becomes necessary to protect her reputation and interests. Finally the stress falls on the preservation of these interests in their material projection—the house and land where Felicity had lived. Thus, as the seekers advance, and the Grail recedes, the figure of the dead woman lives with increasing intensity; the ideal Felicity, whom the reader never meets, is the dominating and most memorable influence in the book. The forces of evil are represented by Kralin, who opposes the seekers at every step, attempting finally to blackmail them into selling the land for cheap building; though vulgarised by his attachment to the Russian secret service (a deplorable intrusion of fashion), Kralin is a convincing and even subtly drawn figure, equal to his position as foil to Felicity. In frustrating him, the seekers find the Grail—but only within a material category, the land and the local pattern of culture which is preserved being merely a representation of Felicity herself. One does not meet Felicity undisguised. This description of the story is too neat to convey properly the subtlety and depths of implication it has to offer. *Death of Felicity Taverner* has superficial faults of the kind noticed in Mary Butts's other work, but as a whole it is satisfying and valuable.

Most of her short stories deal with aspects of the world she presents in her novels. Within this small vivid sphere she made mistakes, and many stories are marred by the high colouring given to personal feeling and fugitively "period" elements. It was inevitable that she should have admired the work of M. R. James, and one of her ghost stories, "With and Without Buttons" (*Last Stories*) is equal to almost anything written by the master himself. Other pieces in the same volume deal admirably with the gently corrupt and with the more pitiful aspects of the 'twenties wasteland. "The House-party" (*Several Occasions*) has received from time a dimension of satirical cruelty probably not intended by its author, but within its own terms it is the most detached and best balanced of her stories, a hard and beautiful piece of work.

The Macedonian and *Scenes from the Life of Cleopatra* are interpretations of the mental climate of the classical world, and of an ideal of human greatness. Alexander and Cleopatra are cast, perhaps, in too heroic a mould, but the metal itself is not cheapened. If the writing is less sensuous than in the earlier books, it is apt to its end, and there are some adroit pieces of construction and several powerful climactic scenes.

Mary Butts's intention as a creative writer was to present, on the one hand, a view of the contemporary wasteland, and to suggest, on the other, the presence of a supernatural order. Her achievement was slightly different. The value of her fiction lies in the momentary evocations of the abnormal, the insights into character, and the allusive wit. Her attempt to translate a traditional view of life more largely into contemporary terms was partially successful and must take a lesser place.

The reasons for the neglect of her writing will now be obvious. A "personality" of the early 'twenties, she matured later as a novelist, and her expressions of belief in the validity of mystical experience (which had led her to Anglo-Catholicism) and of a preference for an aristocratic social order, were not likely to seem acceptable to the following generation. She died before she had completely overcome those defects mentioned previously, and probably before she had fully realised her powers; she was too individual a writer to influence others, unless perhaps Elizabeth Bowen learned something from her tone of voice. She was given to emotional sophistry and struck attitudes which even to her contemporaries must have seemed odd, but she also had a sort of innocence which, though it required these elaborate and exasperating self-defences, frequently made itself known with intense and singular clarity, so that her best work still merits serious attention. Perhaps for some readers her mystical vision will seem the most valuable point of her life and writing, as she would have wished.

II

EXHIBITS

Pencil drawing by Jean Cocteau, ca. 1929.

MARY BUTTS

Angèle au Couvent

I

THEIR SCHOOL WAS BUILT inside the ruins of a monastery on the coast of Fife. The playing fields were enclosed with huge walls. Among them were a few garden-plots and a thin line of trees. On one side of the wall the sea went roaring night and day. At the intersection of the walls there was sometimes a tower. One was a pigeon-tower, full of holes. The trees, that were a row of whistles for the wind, grew small out of the bright grass. Outside the wall there was a ruin and a saint's tower. The school-tower, ill-proportioned and built of the same stone, overlooked the square. There was never anything but wind in the town whose pride was to grow in spite of nature and also to outdo nature and laugh at nature.

The girls went about the country in solitary couples, trudging, chatting. At night they were shut up under the towers, inside the walls. Those who loved the school rarely went outside. They were girl-athletes, running like deer inside the walls, leaping, turning, charging in a group, scattering to reassemble, passing slowly, cowled like young monks, into lit, stone houses at dusk. They were young monks, vowed to obedience, labour, chastely ignorant of chastity, rewarded by authority and power. The model was a god-centred word, and sometime the god had been lost, and his place taken by rules and ranks, and by great cold, and at night by the voices of the sea.

They were girls grown as boys and turned, occasionally,

From *Speed the Plough and Other Stories* (London, Chapman & Hall, Ltd., 1923), pp. 125–55.

into animals who had lost their sex. There was to be found in them a cynicism and a true accidia that they sweated out running in the wind.

A girl walked on a path cut off from the wind, under young lime trees, on soaked gravel. The sun splintered on the top of the wall, bright, cold gold. It would soon rain-in the March night.

She pulled on her hood lined with bright silk and enjoyed its touch, and out of her serge tunic pocket, over one small breast, took out a rosary she had made of nutmegs and peach-stones, spaced with red beans and finished with a cross. She was taught that it was wrong to pray to the Virgin, so it might be true. "Hail, Mary," she said, also the *sursum corda* and a psalm of penitence, going from bead to bead till she had had enough of it and there were seven beads left. She tried to make up a prayer. The sun had sunk behind the wall into wet, gold air. At supper, because it was Saturday, there would be richer food. She paced back, her eyes watching inside her hood, contemplative, up-and-sideways-looking, underscored with blue on a milky skin. Her head went up, safe inside her hood she was all attention, calling to any daimon to come and play, at anything, in a darkening garden, in Scotland, at the beginning of night.

God is a spirit. The cold wind rose.

God is the helping of man by man. Who helps me with my algebra? A mouse ran across her path, a gull cried over her.

God is a gentleman. No, that's the devil. The devil's a part of God. I always thought that myself. Lord, give me something to play with. Make my Cicero translate right. Forgive the devil and comfort him. Let Doris be my friend. Make to-morrow all right. I must finish my beads. A poem will do. She went on and looking at the dark grass said, *Round the Stem of the Fairy Tree.*

A house-mistress with a lantern overtook her.

"Are you out so early from the Confirmation Class?"

"I do not go, Miss Mackail; I have been confirmed."

"I see." She went on. The girl stepped out into the dark and trudged in her round snow-boots after the swinging light circle, and the powerful idol travelling on its edge. She wanted her to be a jolly old lady, who would call her and give her buttered toast and ask her what she thought about life. There was supposed to be a house-mistress who did that, who let her girls stay over when they had colds.

The night arrived. The clock-tower struck half-past six. The old tower sank into the night's iron sky. Her head was cooled and rested from the school-room's noise. Her colt's legs ached. Dry wires of hair rubbed her forehead under her hood.

In the school-room, on her desk, she found her sewing returned for the blood-stitched buttons to be taken off and put on again. The spread of calico had knocked over her flowers. "That woman's a beast," she said, and put a head of cotton through a darning-needle and tied the ends. The child's infinite capacity for leisure was being introduced to another kind of time, full of ends and beginnings and things which had to be done.

The Saturday night crowd, rested and expansive, saw her.

"Crazy Terry in from the playground so early," they sang and jerked the back of her chair.

Her only chance was to amuse them, to be a little crazy. A small, chlorotic matron interrupted them to say that her sewing was disgraceful. She sucked a finger rough with threads of skin. . . .

"That's right," said a girl, "go on. You like being called Crazy Terry because you think you're different. But you aren't. You're just like everyone else. Ruth's going to give you a prefect's jaw about trying to be different." The tribal life whooped off.

"Silence," called a prefect. "Why?" said a girl who knew a great many boys and wore her hair all the holidays in a white ribbon, and lived near London, in a large red house and grounds and went up to London in a car.

"Fifty lines by to-morrow morning to anyone who speaks again."

In the silence the cold could be felt passing in at every window of the long room. Terry noticed that the low sky looked as if it were dark blue and was glad to be quiet.

"It's because of the people who're going to be confirmed," whispered the girl and put out her tongue.

The new kind of time stopped. Terry had ruled off the end of her Latin dictionary into squares which were the days of the term, and she now had a square to fill in with a design for the kind of day it had been. The day before had a crescent inside a smaller square, which meant the new moon seen through glass, and accounted for the return of the buttons. A coarse darner makes a large hole in a linen button. She looked through it at a piece of the room. The gas whistled in the hazy air.

I saw a tree with gold fruit. It didn't mean anything. I was top in English, that's a Solomon's Seal. If I score off Rachel I'll draw a swastika on Monday because she's a Jewess.

She practised swastikas and counted up the days to the term's end.

There was a girl who had asked Terry to explain the Faerie Queen. She had interesting square bones and a blonde skin that tanned. Terry with dark spiral curls admired her, but she belonged to another girl, the daughter of an Indian Colonel, whose life was on a pert convention. Terry did not understand. She had thought until lately that there was a god who gave things it was good for people to have. She had asked him for Doris. There had been delicious scraps. She understood she was no match for the girl who had Doris, but did not understand why.

The Sunday was brilliantly cold. At the end of the afternoon walk their shins were sore through their wool stockings. The schoolroom fire roared. The prefects had tea in the house-mistresses' warm drawing-room. Time, that all the week hummed like a taut rope, moved into a slow beat, and Terry, at her ease, made her own time.

Doris and her friend had been confirmed the night before. Unexpectedly Doris came over to her and said:

"Will you come out into the playground, Terry? I want to talk. . . . You can't come out like that. Go and get a sweater or something."

Terry ran, and at the foot of the stairs stood still, glowing and in pain that there should be someone to tell her to put on a sweater when it was so cold.

In the Blue Dormitory Doris' friend was in her cubicle as Terry passed, putting up a sickly head of Christ, by Dolci, on the wall.

Terry knew that that sort of picture was not a good picture. It did not help her at all to think of a man like that. Old maids liked him and people called Pale Virgins in the old song. The child did not identify herself and correctly. She intended that Doris should not think like that.

The girl saw her.

"Do you like my picture, Terry Vane?"

"Well, not very much. Stiff plain Christs I like better." She was busy giving the girl a sensibility equal to her own.

"I don't suppose you would see what's in it," said the girl, who was overwrought and whom Doris had told that Terry had a wonderful mind and whom a little daring would have sent whim-pering to another friend.

Then Terry would have been protected and Doris sensitised, but Terry thinking only of the playground, ran away from her into her cubicle and snatched a sweater and with her cloak unfastened, walked her friend out and away.

Doris unhooded her bold, intelligent head. Terry seldom wore her hood because, as the house suspected, she loved her own hair. They shook off other strollers and reached a wide drive that commanded the sea.

"Well?" said the child.

"Look here, Terry, for three weeks I've been to the parson's lectures and all I remember is that there was a council at Nicaea where somebody decided that the Son was one substance with the Father. There's one thing, and what has it to do with my duty to my neighbours and what have either of them to do with eating bread and wine in church? I was so nervous this morning I might have been sick. My sister used to have tea and a biscuit before she went, but she doesn't go now. What is one to believe? Or do, once one believes?"

Terry said: "We can chuck the council of Nicaea, anyhow."

"Then the catechism?"

"That's just how people would like us to believe."

Doris grinned.

"But, Terry, who cares if we believe? That's what I want to know. Is there a God at all that we've any reliable information about? I mean is the Bible true? There's something called the higher criticism that says the Bible didn't happen."

"My bishop talked about that and told us to ignore it. So I asked. It's about the flood. All those animals couldn't have got into the ark."

The blue-pearl-coloured sea hammered on the reefs that are the coast of Fife. *Black rock and skerry* ravelling the pure water that comes from the pole into a mantling for the sea. The bitter air was cold gold, the smoke of the Scots town enchanted it. A star came out. Terry looked at it and a white ivy leaf on the wall and at the texture of old stone. The sky was green in the South. She smiled, passing into those beauties.

"What would God say, Terry, to my brother? He likes horses and he drinks, and knows about life, and when he comes into the room it goes with a swing and father's friends look small, and father gets mad and Dick just laughs. On all accounts Dick's damned. But if God isn't decent to Dick—"

"God's got to be—"

"Well, if the parson's God isn't true, is there anything? Muriel says it's Christ that matters. I can't see there's anything so wonderful there. Would you mind a few years' bad time if you knew you were going to be taken off directly it was over by millions of angels to have a good time for ever. Besides, He was never married and books are about being in love."

"Her picture is awful."

"Good for you, Terry. She got mad when I didn't like it. Now you've said so."

Terry's cheek was like milk and wine.

"Doris, I know there is a God. But the point about God is that parsons and churches spoil Him. He exists only when you are by yourself and see that things are beautiful."

"Yes," said Doris, "go on."

"He writes His name everywhere for us to see. Look at those purple cabbages. Think of an ice. That's God being friendly. Like your brother's horses. They said Christ ate and drank."

"Never too much, Terry."

"Wine and things he liked, if He was God at all."

"Wasn't He God? You don't think He was God?"

More stars came out. Terry saw a feather-moon turn into a gold knife. They were out in the centre of a great playing-field. The whole sky was over them. She put up her face for it to kiss.

"No. I understand. It is not a man or a woman. It's more like the bird they call the Holy Ghost."

"It is every beautiful thing."

It is the stars coming out and the orange square of those windows. Where we must go back.

It is every good thing.

It is especially love.

It is us when we see it. We are God.

There, that is all I know. Will that do?"

"I am going to try and believe it. Oh, Terry, you've said everything."

"Remember, if it isn't true, we've got to go to hell with the people who wanted it to be true."

"Heaven for climate, hell for company. I'm with you, Terry."

Terry thought: Will she stay with me now?

Across the brightness of her suddenly simplified conception, the question wrote itself in black. She was breathless with pleasure, but she understood that the answer was not yes.

"Still thinking, Terry?"

"Yes."

"Well?"

"Only that what I have seen is good enough. I mean that it is all that I shall have."

Doris looked aside.

"It seems to me that you have everything. Do you mind if we go back? I promised Muriel to make toast and go through to-morrow's prose."

"Will you go through my prose, too?"

"Yes, if there's time."

And Muriel does not mind,—Terry thought and had not the courage to say, and this understanding lay, like a bitter almond she would afterwards learn to appreciate, in the honey of the child's mind.

II

A girl blew a whistle. On a remote playing field they put on their cloaks and sorted out, two and two, to return. Terry under a tree saw them coming and turned back over squeaking wet turf. The even rollers of the sea ran up the beaches. She looked to see if the sun had coloured them. There were birds in the gold air behind the leaves whose turnings made her sick, and no colour in the grey water she could hear all day and all night, except when she was in school.

She imagined that she was ill and would not go over to school, but sit out there all night under a small tree and watch the uncoloured sea till it could only be heard. She was afraid of the people of the place. She was not ill and they would find her, they would ask her questions and punish her. It did not occur to her that they could be right in anything they did, or that she could defy them. She ignored them because she could not do anything else but—she was at their mercy and in fear. The wind was cold, the ground was wet—she went in at the tail of the cloaked girls.

"Where have you been, Terry? Mooning about the courts. We saw you."

"Who cares if you did?"

Anyone could see I care. God how I hate them.

In half-an-hour there would be the hour's preparation, food, then another hour's work, then bed in the icy whistling dormitories. She did not understand the work. She did not always listen when they explained. They said she could do it if she liked. This morning she had not listened. She had forgotten to attend to the beginning and there was no one who would tell her. There was a lesson to be done about Hebrew prophets. "One hour a week at that and five at algebra," she said, and drank a mug of weak tea. The tiny stimulus acted. In the hall she hung about and looked at the curve of the old stairs.

The house-mistress came out of her room. "Isn't it time you went over to school?"

"Not for five minutes," said Terry simply, and went away. She did not know that the sight of her, all sizes and none adjusted, exasperated the athletic woman.

"She is not wholesome," she said, and thought of the splendid machine she captained, also of the kind of girl she liked, neat, sturdy, predictable, smart. These were her pride. There was her technique .

Terry went back and drank some tea from the bottom of the pot. She began to see night coming, light ebbing and replaced by light. Between their pools she could he lost. She threw a Spenser into her satchel and ran across into school.

High up there was a varnished hall where the lower school did its preparation. From the roof, enormous lights threw a just-sufficient glow on to the desks. On the platform one of the sixth form kept the room, doing her almost grown-up work, writing with a fountain-pen. From time to time a girl left her place, walked up the steps, asked permission from her and went away. That was all that would happen for two hours. Terry would not have to go away. She slid sideways into her seat, curled down and looked about her. The tea worked. She thought of the fast waters of the burn bubbling, and of a girl she admired and had seen throwing up a ball and jumping to meet it and of her beautiful legs. That she was called clumsy Terry and that she could describe what they did and that it did not count. "Writing is my only joy," and that was like a song. Songs were literature. She could do literature better than them all. She knew things in a flash, out of nowhere. She spoke when no one else could. There was silence and she felt warm for days. But it was not possible to trade the flesh with the grown-up women for the algebra and the arithmetic. They would only be paid in their own coin and she could not earn it. Not if all day and through her sleep she tried to find their pennies. She could not pay them. She did not know what they wanted. The others all spoke together, "Yes, yes," they said and handed in clean competent pages and grumbled for swank. She never pretended not to understand a lesson when she did. Oh, yes, I do unless they call me conceited. On the days I can't stand them I pretend not to understand. The things they can do they won't help me with. No one ever told me how they began, why you have to take a and b away from each other. Mother says she had no education, and if I make such a fuss about it, I can look out for myself. Mother is not like the mothers in books.

She did her algebra wrong, and comforted herself preparing a poem, satisfied her sense of justice, quieted her fear of the next day. She got word and sense perfect, she rested, she lived, she began to be hungry.

Next day the algebra was returned to her to be done again, alone, that afternoon, when the others were out in the fields, the headmistress to be told, the house-mistress, the captain of the house. Terry could not see. Sweat broke out of the milk-bright skin, on to the rough wood. Cold followed sweat. Lead crept in her veins. Before her the heavy disgusted face of the mistress sucked the corners of its mouth. Horrible tears rushed up her and were held, bolted back by her teeth. *They shall not pass the barrier of my teeth.* She went into the literature class, where now her back was broken she could still speak. She knew it all, and she could not make a mistake; she was praised. It counted for nothing. Like quiet it half restored her. Like a little cup of wine it heartened her for something that she could not bear. Her isolation among the insatiable women became a state she had entered.

She reported after school to the headmistress and was contemptuously dismissed. "You here again, Terry Vane." It banged in her head, a dance-step trodden by great beasts. She was all small in a wood. A baby terror woke.

Hark, hark,
The dogs do bark,
The beggars are coming to town.

Enemies were singing towards her. She went over to the house, too sick to eat.

After lunch she had to sit and sew. The other girls had seen her outside the headmistress's door. She wanted them to say things. A prefect whispered to another, and a girl she did not like joined them.

Her house-mistress was more explicit.

"I wish you to understand, Terry, that your conduct is disgraceful. It is utterly unsatisfactory. Until I have evidence of improvement I shall recommend that you do no more literature."

At first she could have stunned herself with crying; wailing, imploring, have dropped before the woman. She had not the courage of abandon. She looked stupidly out of the window, lived a long time, forgot.

She was outside. "Devils," said the child. "Devils. No God." She thought of God as quite helpless too, and went clumsily downstairs.

"I'm sorry, Ruth, I can't play till half-time, I have to go to a detention."

"Really, Terry, I call that carrying slackness rather far. You won't work and you won't play except at things you think you are good at."

A monster that would not work and would not play formed in her mind. She remembered that at night it was dark. Then her mind ran out into a place where people were free and pranced along with grapes in their hair. It was either silly, or too good to be true. She wanted to be out and moving in the cold. In the passage they were fighting to be ready for play. She took her books and went back again into school.

Now it was empty, the great skeleton house that rushed with life and murmured with classes, quite empty. She could not hide in it. One or two others, also sent back, passed her without speaking. She could have smiled, but thought they despised her and acquiesced. She thought of an impudent game they might have played before the mistress came, and imagined it played, went into an empty class-room, opened a clean page and waited.

No one came. She was cold. She had been six terms in the place. The end would be in two years. She had been driven up north. She had only asked to be taught like a boy. She would go back south, from one failure to another, into dusty gold out of grey wind.

"I did not think I could not do anything. They are making me so that I can't do anything at all." A band outside began.

O ye take the high road
And I'll take the low road
And I'll be in Scotland afore ye.

The tune rose in her head, it was good to be alone, high

up in a room all windows, and hear music. She began to walk about, singing quietly, not in tune, swinging her curls. She warmed, tune followed tune. The mistress, coming along the passage, saw her through the glass door, saw her come back again and again to the window, and sit on it, looking down into the town and up into the sky.

"I told you to wait for me in B. This is D."

"I'm sorry, Miss Keith, I thought you said in here."

"Your work is disgraceful. I don't know what to do with you. You have ability."

The tune had drawn the child into a pattern. Terry said: "I can do one thing well. I can understand the value of words and quantities. The words in this stuff are just made up. It doesn't interest me. It might—"

The woman was astonished into attention.

"It might if what—?"

The music stopped. Terry looked round the dull walls.

"I don't know. It doesn't matter." If I could tell the woman. If I could ask her to explain from the beginning. It isn't worth it. She wouldn't. They like to bully. I can't say it. I must get it over. I must get away. She saw herself running, first against the woman beating her with her hands, then past her crying till the need for steady breath stopped her, and she was out of the place, out and out on the Fifeshire roads, till she met a man on a horse, who picked her up. She wondered how long she had taken thinking. She opened the textbook.

"It was seven and eight I got wrong."

"I set from six to ten."

"I got six right."

"I returned your work for gross inaccuracy in the eighth example."

The man was with Terry, waiting for her at the classroom door. She shrugged her shoulders.

"Shew me what I did wrong, please."

"Terry, that is not the way to speak."

She sighed into herself. The woman looked at her. She

was white and she had been red. She shewed her exactly what she had done.

"Don't let it happen again. I am sure you could do better work if you liked."

Better. She could do it perfectly or not at all. She withdrew herself. The band began again. *Turn ye to me* it played, and a point was touched to bliss like sexual pleasure in a little star. Never listen to anything but that sound. "May I stay a moment?" she said cunningly. "I should like to go through it again while I remember to understand." The pretty appeal worked. Pleased, she put out her tongue as the mistress went through the door, and sat behind her desk listening.

The tune was new. She waited for the repeats and sucked them in. "Ai, ai," she sighed in exquisite desolation.

She remembered that she was not to be allowed to learn literature any more. There would not be a band every day. Bands were not verses. Her nerves, plucked by the music, resolved into active passion. She was strong and went into agony. She leapt up and ran, down the stairs, into the playground. Scotch mist was brimming the air softly. Balls were clicking through it, all the school was playing. She could not be alone. She did not want the old kind man on the horse.

"*Turn ye to me,* it's called. *Turn ye to me,*" she said to the great wall. A bird flew out of it and the haar curled. "*Turn ye to me,*" she said evoking the girls of the house and gave a little shriek of pain walking up and down, up and down the cinder track, drenched and wild. The rain increased. There were hooded figures coming up the path. She turned back, the rain driving through her coarse stockings. She ran up to her cubicle. In the old green passage the lights were lit. She was afraid of colds and tore off her stockings and tunic, put on a white frock and her evening shoes.

"Turn to me. Oh, something turn to me. There is nothing. If I am not to learn literature I shall die."

"Die," said the wind rising out of the inaudible sea. In the dormitories the white enamelled walls glittered like ice.

The old, green passage had deep windows. She sprang on to a sill and played that she was lying in the arms of the sea.

The tune ebbed in her brain. She noticed that it was not so important now if she did not learn literature. She could teach herself. She could not help learning it. She would certainly learn nothing else. The deprivation was a mask, the house-mistress pushed up to be a paste-board cow for the enemy that would stalk her all her life. The enemy moved in every person. It was not a person but a reaction in persons from her yet uncrystallised sensibility.

"*Look out, my lovely one.*" A charming young man was speaking to her. Nicer than the old man on the horse.

"Good luck to you," he said and vanished. She sighed and came to herself.

"God is a beast. Perhaps He is miserable like me."

She thought that the young man on the screen of her imagination was sad. A girl passed her, a stock-broker's daughter, with leering eyes and a rich frock.

"I suppose you're ashamed to go down."

"No."

"Well, I should have some tea if I was you and get it over."

"Thanks."

That's June. Insult one and pat. I must have something that lasts in this world.

She went downstairs and found that she could not pass the schoolroom door. She remembered scented woods by the sea. The house-mistress called down the bannisters.

"I wonder if you would go over to school and fetch me my purse? I left it on the table in the mistress's room."

Terry heard the drawing-room door shut. As if nothing had happened. It was their bluff to pretend to mind what one did. She went out by the forbidden front door, across the quadrangle, running delicately in her thin shoes. She was going somewhere interesting. In the mistress's room there might be curious things that explained what went on there and the secret ideas that govern the regiment of women. Half-way up the stairs she felt very tired. The place was enormous now it was dark. She had heard of a ghost. She hurried, sighed and cooled her forehead against the door. She knocked. There was no answer. She went in, saw a bead of gas in the dusk, pulled the little chain, saw the purse and looked round. The room was full of shabby papers, but there was a fire and a deep empty chair. She lay down on it. There was nothing interesting. Only a re-statement of some of the poorer girls grown up. The chair only was good, and the fire. She wanted to lie there the rest of the day, in the heart of the enemies' country, be found lounging in a chair. It was like playing Indians.

She could not move. She must not. She must not rest. She thought of the school getting darker, that would not he filled for an hour.

The men were lighting up the place into a blaze. She did not remember. She lay before the rich fire. She saw the purse on the table, struggled up and fell back. Then she forgot what she was doing.

She saw a young man on the wall. He was Hermes with a child on his arm. She had gone out of life and he was taking notice of her.

She saw that it was a large print of a statue, unwound off a roller, and hung on a wall and she began to remember who Hermes was.

That's a great statue. That's beautiful. I suppose men's bodies are like that.

Oh, the old woman's purse.

She dropped off the wheel of her environment and saw the feelings of the day in a pattern unrelated to the pain of her small pains. They interested her, and there passed into her curiosity, elation, power. She saw the image of Hermes and that it was outside the time in which she was living and the people to whom she was subject, and that through her pleasure in him, she could live in his time and turn round in it and come out again. The old woman wanted her purse.

I shall see things in the world where Hermes is, and when I come out these people will leave me alone.

She chewed on the prospect of alarming the mistresses. She annihilated the years to her maturity and remembered them.

Divine Hermes, don't let me forget you. The old woman wants her purse.

Hermes, Hermes, before I saw you here, you were the boy who came and talked to me this afternoon instead of the old man.

I must take the old woman her purse.

MARY BUTTS

Questionnaire

1. What should you most like to do, to know, to be? (In case you are not satisfied.)

a) Live in a very old house in the country: ride: have all the books I want and the friends: play chess at night and dance.

b) What the odes of Pindar sounded like when first produced: if they were sung to a syncopated notation like jazz.

c) A person with a perfect historic imagination, able to reconstruct the past and live in it—or in the future—like the present.

2. Why wouldn't you change places with any other human being?

For fear of losing what is inside my head, memories and information it has taken my life to collect and arrange. One feels it would be intolerable to leave the collection unfinished, and what should finally become a view of the world incomplete.

3. What do you look forward to?

A poet's success.

4. What do you fear most from the future?

"Envy, hatred, malice and all uncharitableness" become a new morality.

5. What has been the happiest moment of your life? The unhappiest? (if you care to tell).

These questions were posed by *The Little Review* to a number of writers and artists whose answers originally appeared in the magazine's Spring Number, May 1929.

When a person should have been dead and was not. When that person died.

6. What do you consider your weakest characteristics? Your strongest? What do you like most about yourself? Dislike most?

a) Sympathy with the things my friends do.

b) The same.

c) A faculty for seeing, as a whole, as one sees a work of art, the best in people.

d) Lyrical rage when they don't keep it up all the time.

7. What things do you really like? Dislike? (Nature, people, ideas, objects, etc. Answer in a phrase or a page, as you will.)

a) The weather, beautiful people, a generalization which unifies a number of apparently unrelated things. Substances like jade, coral or ivory, objects out of the past. Everything, living and growing or static, which is "according to its kind," a bad kind or a good, but "good" in relation to what it is.

b) The pretentious and the faked.

8. What is your attitude toward art today?

Sympathetic, not often enthusiastic, deeply interested. It seems to me to be in a transition state, evolving forms and new tricks of the trade which have not yet been put to their proper use.

9. What is your world view? (Are you a reasonable being in a reasonable scheme?)

In moments of depression count myself a reasonable being in an unreasonable world. Am sure that in default of a "miracle"—which I don't consider impossible—the worst is coming to the worst with our civilization. Have a private view of the universe which does not seem to be reasonable, or "scientifically true," but which works for me, refreshes and delights me. I go by that, watch events and try not to twist them to fit. Am in the middle of a book which is supposed to show that my "hunch" about the universe is as likely to be true as any other and much more interesting that most. Also that it is of most imposing antiquity.

10. Why do you go on living?

Mainly out of good and extreme curiosity, on which depends a wish to see if the "miracle" referred to above will come in my time, or is susceptible at all to human encouragement.

MARY BUTTS

From the Journals

London, September 18, 1917. Notes for *Ashe.* Take for the central theme the hatred of age for youth, of the old for the new, of yesterday's "rose" for today's, expressed in a cruelty, part intuitive, part consciousness. This for the larger stage, implied throughout, war and its consequent *repression* and destruction.

London, October 3, 1917. The Showing Up of Ezra Pound. At last my most intimate convictions have been focused and justified, neither scholar, nor poet, nor philosopher, but a *most* kindly romantic, and competent sometimes witty critic. Then dull, all dull he and his set, dull because they have nothing to say.

London, December 7, 1918. Idleness—since flu's, should do reviewing if only to keep me to it. None to do though. Will keep this then.

In object d'art I first began to understand "significant forms" (Forms—shape plus colour plus everything else) from R[oger]. F[ry].

He showed me form in painting which I now half see in letters. Form is basic to all art. If a painting is not meant to be literary, then writing must not be literary either.

Cefalù, June, 1921. Went down to Cefalù—mixed drinks at the Inn— looked again at the "Sedia Regis" in the Cathedral. The town hummed, the landlady said I was "molto bella

---

Mary Butts regularly kept a journal from 1916 until her death in 1937. The following entries are adapted from "Selections from the Journal of Mary Butts," edited by Robert H. Byington and Glen E. Morgan and originally published in *Art and Literature* 7, Winter 1965.

Signora" (in distinction to the other Signore). I loved it all—digged into common life again, shook off the Abbey—wanted more of it, and harder and sharper.

Coming down the hill—I saw the fishing fleet—each vessel with its sail full, careened over on its side, and one saw the shape of the wind in relation to the floor of the sea.

Talked about last astral journey with A[leister]. C[rowley]. The idea is to find an authentic means of inducing the mystic state.

Cefalù, August 1, 1921. Part of the trouble here is a complex about complexes, i.e., our artificial inhibitions are cleared up, certain things will remain good and bad, pleasant and unpleasant.

This is not realised, yet the silly people imply it all to him [Aleister Crowley]—when it suits them. It is right to promulgate his law. It is wrong to criticise it—if you do, you have a complex.

C[ecil]. M[aitland]. said last night: they are making a sacrifice of personality to personality. He said that it makes A[leister] C[rowley] tragic because he is a kind, wise, honorable man crucified by his belief in his own teaching.

Cefalù, August 7, 1921. Some days ago the Beast [Crowley] attacked me—I had an unsolved "complex" that was baulking me. This is true. I have known it for a year and partly realise its nature. I faced it again here and he began to nag me about it.

Cefalù, August 16, 1921. This place is good for me. My nature is to become indignant. Here one *lâcheté*—one absurdity follows the other, and one is forced to observe infamy and idiocy and insanity, as if "good and bad" were not yet invented (except in relation to one's stomach. I want food.)

London, September 30, 1921. Back here—such windy, cold autumns. The rain comes back in brief gusts, but now the house is seen to, I shall have time to teach myself to enjoy pleasant things again.

Cefalù has given me quite a different outlook. Once it was a *blind* discomfort; now I know what caused the discomfort, my various fears. I was and am troubled by them instead.

Villefranche, Fall, 1925. [Of Paul Robeson] Remember the veins on his hand. Like a smooth, perfect, prehistoric tree.

August 4, 1926. Remember: What he [Jean Guérin] said about Cocteau—that he had never learned friendship or how to pull together—giving richly with one hand and taking away with the other—agonized at the least betrayal, yet willing to betray. It was wisely observed.

To this one might add his intellectual insufficiencies. He says himself that he is "inculte"—out in Paris' salons at fourteen, the young genius, Europe's greatest beauty and chief wit. And the result of this—that Europe's shepherd by right has done nothing better than to scuttle back to the church at a moment of general despair, when we were all waiting for his lead. He knew of nowhere else to go but to the traditional depository of spiritual comfort. Was it ignorance or fear that did not allow him to look into his own heart?

January 14, 1927. It is this splitting up of events into an irregular, inconvenient, positively demented time sequence that bitches things up. Why can't the relative things happen together, simultaneously or in close sequence? Instead, we live like jugglers, keeping a dozen balls in air.

Paris, Spring, 1927. Shall I ever make a poem out of this spring day with the sun shifting in through the shutters, the warm coolness, Paris humming at a distance, and tears because there are fairy tales in which the pain stops, a miraculous right-about-turn of misery into accomplishment that never hapens . . . and William James' "adorable genius" calling me to order?

Paris, May 2, 1927. UN RAPPEL A L'ORDRE: What I believe, after ten years, I am coming to see: up to now I am an unsuccessful writer, lover, dubious mother, of no social distinction. Well liked, but my looks are going, and to a certain extent, my health. Well, I can write and I want to, should never *want* to do much else. What for? To paint reality under ideal forms. Just for the art's sake? Yes and no. In the old cant phrase I want to show people beauty—soundness. Now the best work cannot be made up wholly from the ugly and the unsound. And our world is both. I begin to understand several things labelled bolshevism, surréalisme, eccentricities of pederasty, the Paris *Daily Mail,* my husband . . . the decline of good will, charity, friendship, the bankruptcy of religion.

What apart from the specific work of writing is what interests me?

Nothing but spiritual development, the soul living at its fullest capacity. That is the lever, the new synthesis, or vision or faith. I have not got it yet, but I am beginning to know what is wrong with the times. And many of the things we do are not wrong, it is our way of doing them. They are very good things—pederasty and jazz and opium and research.

What do I love, outside writing and clothes and opium and the weather and my friends? I have always had since I can remember an incomparable pleasure in finding someone psychically sick, and learning about it, and seeing if there is a way out. This feeling very much mixed up with sex—bed not necessary, but it makes things work better. That is, any power I have seems to work better in that relation. I've always wanted to make my lovers well, sense powers liberated in them, fears in the dustbin, raw life taken in and coming out translated.

Pramousquier, Summer, 1927. Lawrence Vail's mother's husband said when the family decided that it was time she had a lover: "I can't hear of it. It would be bad for my nerves."

Summer, 1927. The sea at Pramousquier: in bed at night the water on the open rocks below makes several sounds. Glass music. Knocking, very imperative and broken. A sound like talking. A drone that rises to a roar, almost a train noise of, I think, pebbles drawn under and back.

Paris, September, 1927. THE NEW BOOK: Carry on from the last, *Armed With Madness*—which might well have been called "The Wasteland." Eliot always anticipates my titles.... Eliot and I are working on a parallel.... Eliot only writes of my quality, dislikes me and my work, I think. But what is interesting is that he is working on the Sans Grail, on its negative side, the Waste Land. Up to now he has been before me with my titles, *The Sacred Wood* and *The Waste Land*.... What me me after years "see through" T. S. Eliot (not to lose an ounce of my admiration for his poetry).... He said: "that—in some such a way—the mandarins who went to M. Bergson's lectures at the Sorbonne may have been said to have been using their minds." The *provincialism* of that, at last understood, decided me ... Virgil [Thomson] said of T.S.E.

"between the idea and the creation
falls the shadow,
of his education."

Also

"If he would place the creation before the idea, no shadow would fall between—"

November 10, 1927. Mary [Reynolds] said: "The worst thing I know about the Surréalistes and their flirtings with Bolshevism is what Louis Aragon said to me about little

Pierre de Massot. I was tight and I asked him what they wanted with Pierre, poor boy; and he said, with a look I shan't forget—'But he is our tool.' "

October 4, 1928. The New Boeuf: glamorously beautiful, lit like some lovely futurist stage, smoke veils apple-jade lights in oblong glass globes—scarlet, sea-blue, gold, crimson, purple—mirror upon mirror upon mirror, even the doors disguised in looking glass—A good dancing floor, the bar high on the right up black steps.

But where is the little side bar for the family-party? Where the comfortable, shabby old beauties? Where is the Boeuf that was *our* party place? It was beautifully decorated, none the worse for being a little old and worn. *And* people came out of the street and *disappeared* in a sea of black bodies and grey faces, all alike. It was difficult to recognize one's nearest and dearest, all colour stripped off them: quite *too tenebrous.* I painted my face like a Petrouchka doll and carried myself straight up and I was only one degree less spectral than the rest.

Our Boeuf is dead.

Paris, December, 1928. [Suffering from a sore throat] Strange: I still feel that if I made up in the morning in a room which is not icy with the night air, I have done some action, some immorality, a compound of self poison and self indulgence. Although my throat is better after a night's warm air.

September, 23, 1929. The days pass. I have hardly seen the sun this summer, and now the exquisite autumn has come. It is as exquisite as it is painful not to share it. Never has there been such work, knowlege, desolation, vision, joy and sorrow as in these last two months. I am the same woman, but re-crystallized: something has been added to me and fused—or is fusing. I wonder sometimes if I shall live it out.

October 15, 1929. Coming up on the train on the 14th I watched as beautiful a day as I have ever seen from the long *open* french carriage window. There was Le Mans, and its cathedral, the high-pitched lower wall—apple-trees hung with enamel balls, scarlet to cold green, enameled turf under each—At Chartres the moon waxing, smoke mist in the meads—There were little lakes, and first it was red rock and apples, then slowly the great french landscape with its sense of "vast horizons." Slowly rising land, forest-arms and single poplars. Chateaux with high-pitched roofs, and occasional modern reconstructions with a tendency to break out into mosaic dragons and general heraldry set into slates.

All the way up, single magpies—all but one flight of 5 or 7. I sang "Waiting for the Moon to Rise" out of the window, and I blessed the Power which has filled my life with poetry.

Paris, December 10, 1929. Since tonight I feel capable of writing, le me put it down while I may. The black curtain that hangs across the way I must go, receding with my step but *then,* is a little transparent this night.

Think of a corridor, a passage white-wood panelled with a green carpet strip as at Salterns. My passage in life is down one of these, and I have passed many windows, some with pleasant views out onto several different lands: some onto courts squaring a wall or fountain, or a heap of tin cans. And there have been some, cob-webbed at the corner of their panels, and in the cob-webs dead bees. While very few were of stained glass so as to obscure what was without.— I remember only the one with my house's blazon and quarterings, and there the colours were transparent: though there may have been others which I never took for windows at all.

I have passed doors also, some of which I have been allowed to open. Though I walk rapidly down my corridor I can without retracing still enter the rooms I have made my own. As the windows are on the side of the sun, so they are on the side of the stairs.

And between the doors and the windows set in the white panels there are pictures. Also I know when I come to the end of the corridor, what door I shall come to. At least, I know one, its noble panels, the perfect conclusion for that corridor, warm, white wood and bright steel. I am not so sure now. It is one of the fears that I shall have lived with that black curtains overcast my mind.

The veil however is thinner tonight, as it recedes before me between the white walls.

December 11, 1929. Long night. Walter [Shaw] here. Up at J[ean]. C[octeau].'s, alone with him and P[ierre] de M[assot]. The fire. The Select. The long walk home along the Rue de Grenelle, architectural Paris in profound sleep; a cold, black and white moon night.... Four o'clock on a December morning. Lost a lover whom I love. Don't want the rest.

Anthony Butts, 1933.

Sergei Maslenikof, ca. 1927.

MARY BUTTS

Reviews

THE DARK TOWER

AS BY NOW PEOPLE have realized, between the years A.D. 1914 to 1917 something was done to the new generation of men that had never been done before. One can think of no parallel to that unique war and that peace that was no peace, coming at a time when the rational spirit had evoked a science to break down faith, and let loose forces in nature only too capable of destroying our race. These facts go on staring us in the face, and as a result we are living in a spiritual chaos for which again there is no parallel.

Now a number of men and women of that generation which the French call quite simply *la génération perdue* have taken to composing spiritual receipt books, records of trial and error in an attempt to nourish their shattered inner life.

Never was man in such need of counsel, description and analysis of the appalling situation we are in, the dreadful place to which we have come. For we are all Childe Rolands, each at a Dark Tower—and we are all one Being at the same Tower. At the door, or on its stairs; and some are coming out alive, and some are gone in and will never come out; and some are running away from it insane; and others are walking eternally round and round it and dare not go in.

While some say there is no Tower; and others that the Tower, seen in the right light is habitable; and some that the Tower is not there.

Review of *A Modern Prelude* by Hugh I'Anson Fausset, originally published in *Time and Tide,* September 30, 1933, Vol. XIV, No. 39. Some of Mary Butts's most speculative and enduringly fresh reviews appeared in this journal during 1933 and 1934.

Results of this pilgrimage are appearing everywhere, and most noticeably in the Arts. For if it had not been for the Dark Tower there would be no Surréalisme. (Nor in politics Communism.) Surréalisme, which would persuade us that the place only needs a little arrangement to turn it into a desirable residence; that the Waste Land surrounding it is preferable to any garden.

People who cannot be stampeded into that kind of belief have thought lately that the key to reality at its purest lies in religious reality, and that reality in the experiences of the great mystics. They notice at the same time, that whatever their faith—in or outside Christianity—the mystics' accounts of their experience are essentially the same. And this without loss, but to the great gain of their essential selves. The same things happened to Swedenborg and Boehme, to Hafiz; to the Indian mystics, to Clark Maxwell and to St. John of the Cross. While in telling it, each seemed to perfect their separate natures and gifts. (J.W.N. Sullivan, admitting as a scientist that here was something that could not be explained away, speculates on a future "science of mysticism"; and Aldous Huxley writes of first, second and third class mystics, comparable with the artist, but in touch with an actuality more valid than reason, and in which might lie a hope for man.)

So lately, D.H. Lawrence, Mr. Murray, Miss Brittain and others, and now Mr. Fausset have all written accounts of *their* inner lives, their search, which is in essence the search for God, and for a re-definition of His Nature, in accordance with man's new needs and his old. While today, and this again is unique, such an inquiry has to begin by asking whether God exists at all.

One criticism of some of these books is, I think, this. The great mystics—Mr. Huxley's first class—brought to their telling one of the secrets of art—that, to say what they meant, to make a supernatural experience *carry,* not as a bare statement but with a touch of its quality, the approach must not be direct but oblique, a turn something like the knight's move in chess.

... Calling the lapséd soul
And weeping in the evening dew....

The second line, with its significant irrelevance, gives an idea of it. Like

Among the lilies and forgetting them.

Somewhere Emerson says that "when you have life in yourself" you will not be able to express it straightforwardly, "the way, the speech, the thought shall be wholly strange to you."

It is this quality that this and other books lack. Mr. Fausset tells us his life-history, and his effort, the effort of all men who live the spiritual life, to lose his partial egoistic self and discover the harmonised, the delivered self. As the Founder of our religion told us we must all do. As the great mystics, independent of creed, have insisted. The ancient Way. He does not claim to have succeeded.

It is not the theory that matters. The rational description of these experiences is almost boring in its similarity. It is in the personal uniqueness of each one that the secret lies and the delight. As in a work of art. Think of the same landscape painted by Claude Lorrain, by Constable, by Van Gogh and by Cézanne.

As again in the arts, one would give a pound of theory for a pinch of practice, a backbone of dogma to stiffen the sentiment.

It is when practice fails that one hears so much about theory. This makes the first part of the book the best, the sufferings of the author's boyhood and young manhood; and later, where he puts his finger very neatly on the inadequacy of other men's solutions. D. H. Lawrence and his surrender to the primitive; the superficiality of Freud, and of Bertrand Russell's stoic optimism. For they treat sin as a cow to be looked in the face and stared out of the way. But suppose—like a bull on whose horns you are impaled—that it *is* sin.

Mr. Fausset is most adequate here. Not so later, when one is sure that his reason has let me *forget* too much. One feels that the terrors and agonies of his father's oppression of others—and of himself—are not so lightly to be put in their place. There is something superficial about it. While in a chapter, "The Creed of My Fathers," he runs through the structure of Christianity, its mysteries and sacraments, has fun with its admitted inconsistencies, pats it on the head, and passes on—something in the spirit of H.G. Wells, who seems to think the worse of the Mass and of man, because other and even primitive men have partaken of the body and blood of their God.

While, like others to whom European experiences and solutions seem inadequate, he has fallen for current optimism about the superior spirituality of the East. That's as may be; in an age when the civilization of the West is in for a most deserved scrutiny, and the easiest way is to enlarge the only too visible holes in it.

His book is about the truest things in life—the very source of truth. All—or nearly all—of what he tells us, on one level or another, is true. Yet, has he wrested truth out of it, truth for himself, truth to let others out of the Dark Tower? The Sanc Grail that will turn the Waste Land into a garden again? One is not quite sure.

VISION OF ASIA

THIS IS A very wise book, wise and good and of extraordinary interest. It is an account—with references and

Review of *The Vision of Asia: An Interpretation of Chinese Art and Culture* by L. Cranmer-Byng, originally published in *The Bookman,* Christmas Number 1932, pp. 223–225.

comparisons drawn from European classics, modern poetry and developments in physics—of the teachings of Lao Tzu, the contemporary of Confucius, of the history of the mystical secret of China.

The teachings of these two men, sometimes working in most fruitful accord, sometimes with fatal division, have shared or divided the allegiance of the Chinese mind. Out of their influences her artists or her statesmen—names which in the great epochs have often meant the same thing—her scholars or farmers, her hermits—or the Son of Heaven himself, have shaped her civilisation.

In the West we have heard more about Confucius. It is easy to understand what he was about. The figure of him rises up as an almost physical summary of what we have been taught to think of as "Chinese." The self-control, the restraint, the moral ceremoniousness, the humour, the devastating common sense: one has wondered how a philosophy which seemed to be no more than a quintessence of the matter-of-fact and a shrewd knowledge of human infirmities, could have become the final satisfaction of a deeply-imaginative race. But Mr. Cranmer-Byng says: "Confucius failed . . . because he became afraid . . . in his desire to escape from elementals, to shut down the creative fire that burns in every form of creation. . . . A purely ethical system is like flesh and bones without the blood. . . ." It is what Confucius left unsaid, that Lao Tzu supplied; and considering the two together, it becomes possible to understand more about China than one had ever hoped to before.

There were the Three Vinegar Tasters. They stood before a jar. Their names were the Lord Buddha, the Lord Confucius and the Lord Lao Tzu. Each tasted what was in the jar. The Lord Buddha called it bitter; the Lord Confucius, sour. Only Lao Tzu called it sweet. The jar held the brew of life, and the third taster came to call men, not to the ultimate despair which, when all is explained away, must be the final interpretation of Buddhism; not to the hard sense of Confucius, but to the way which is called Tao, whose understanding is the joy that is in Dionysus and the joy that is in Christ—perhaps the most satisfying statement of ultimate values man has yet made.

It is a system dependent on philosophy, and on the sharpest attention to common reality, a restatement and an explanation of that saying of Christ's which men have found hardest to understand: that he who would save his life must first lose it. But what Lao Tzu made clear was that life really *is* saved, saved in its richness and beauty and adventure, saved for action and enjoyment and above all for creation; and for a final conscious participation, outside the universe as we conceive it, in the whole being of God.

Buddha is essentially an Indian. So is Confucius a Chinaman. But Lao Tzu—though the Tao, his "Way," has been little known outside China; though, as Confucius saw, it could and did become corrupted by primitive superstition—is a figure who belongs everywhere, east or west, wherever there is a civilisation to influence, or an imaginative person in need of the purest understanding and love. A shadow more substantial than a mountain, at once friendly and exquisite and all-powerful.

Mr. Cranmer-Byng's book is to make the West aware of this. He has seen how the spiritual teaching of the East is usually presented to the West in ultimate terms with which, intuitively and sensibly, the West will have nothing to do. For Buddhism offers no more in the long run than an escape. Its last word is blissful extinction; its intermediate paradises no more than the harps and gold of our own New Jerusalem. It is here he tells the story, unfortunately too long to quote, of the man who found his way into one of the Buddhist paradises, whose inhabitants, all once great men of the world, were seeking to escape by an undiscoverable suicide.

With all the hard-headedness of the mystic—"the man who is all altruism from dawn to sunset is either a bore or a bogy"—the writer has looked at the schemes of salvation men have devised for themselves, to find failure after failure.

Only in the farthest East he has found what he is looking for, which our world is dying for want of, a *restatement* of final realities, serviceable both to the heart and head of every man of good-will. In China, in a nation renowned for its common sense and its commerce, for speculation and art, in her greatest epochs, the Taoist, the follower of the Way of Lao Tzu, was the artist, and the artist the administrator, the ruler of provinces, and more than the entertainer, the companion of kings.

It is necessary to ask how, supplemented by the *terre á terre* discipline of Confucius, so flawless a way of life, did not save, once and for ever, the whole situation. Confucius saw that answer himself. Lao Tzu's teaching, like Christ's, was above race, based on the mysticism common to all mankind; an intuition he shared with Christ and Plato, and the supreme mystics from Glastonbury to Persia. There are classes of mystics as there are of artists, or in any of the great intuitive faculties in man. The third and fourth class mystic can be a man of very nasty or of very silly mind. The first thing he does is to drop into incorrect translations of his perceptions, in terms of any folly that may be about. In China, Lao Tzu's teachings gave fresh life to the primitive animism of the common people, revitalised swarms of bogies, ghosts and demons. The salt and sap went out of it. The Tao, with intervals of re-vision corresponding to great epochs in the national life, became a glorious memory which had somehow got mixed up with a fairy-story. Confucius triumphed, with a triumph that was necessarily incomplete.

This gives some idea of the substance of Mr. Byng's book. It would seem, would it not, to be of first-rate importance; to contain, with something of the shock and delight of revelation, exactly the help that our world is in particular and desperate need of to-day? For Lao Tzu has something new to say, or rather, his mystical vision, though in itself the quintessence of what the great mystics of the past have told as their personal experience, comes with the shock of something new. Of course there is nothing "new" about it, but in its simplicity and loveliness there comes the effect, the surprise of a release of vital force. It is as though the earth, with its passions and griefs and strains and delights, is shifted, by some minute adjustment, into focus. (The reviewer is writing this, with interruptions, against time, and with the Tao in mind can take nothing but pleasure in it all.) The Tao is simple and delightful and sensible and infinitely various. Mercy and Truth *are* met together: Righteousness and Peace *have* kissed each other.

Life is unfair. Much admirable art is being done in the world to-day, whose essence is a hope too harsh for full human nourishment, or one variety or another of despair. The point is that only these things, as it used to be said, "inspire the artist" to-day. While we are all wearying of a "de profundis" chorus addressed to no possible conception of any Lord. The question is—when will a book of this kind and of this value be written by a great creative user of words? For it is no disrespect to Mr. Cranmer-Byng to say that he is not that. It is when he interrupts his account and tries to convince us more of his master's meaning by passages of "fine writing," that he ceases to hold our attention. If he were a man who could have given to his book "the deathless consecration of art," fewer men would read it at first because of the necessary strangeness that attends such things. But in time, and in not so short a time, considering our age's aesthetic sensibility and desperate need, it would be in every man's hands. Which is where the author would wish to see it. As yet, his pure intentions, his profound understanding, have not been enough. When will this happen? For it must happen.

MARY BUTTS

Three Letters

I

St. Eglistan Cottage
Kimmeridge
Corfe Castle
Dorset

My dear Glenway—

I have come here to recover my invalid.... It is a good plan—no one was ever known to die here except through drowning or old age, but none of our friends will follow us. I wonder if you would—or if you would say that towns may be very bad places, but that even the country should be decently modified. This isn't. It's my native place and I worship it, but its isolation affects most people's nerves.... To begin with, it is ten miles from a station, and that station is a wayside halt outside a tiny, medieval town, Corfe Castle. Then a flinty lane turns off a series of dangerous angles down a valley—the hills are green sheep-walks we call 'downs,' with barrows on them and neolithic grass-forts. The lane turns and climbs one of them slowly in a long white line. At the top of the down it drops like a stone, over the side into Kimmeridge—from the top you see the sea, the downs break off into huge cliffs, there are headlands and reefs. The country is empty—only turf and sea and sky—but here and there in the valleys, set very close like precious

---

These letters first appeared in *Northern Lights: Studies in Creativity,* No. 2, 1985–86. The letter to Glenway Wescott was written while Butts was vacationing in 1923, while the letters to Hugh Ross Williamson are from 1932–34.

stones, are very old stone houses, buried in flowers, a copse, a wood, a patch of bright grass like enamel. Kimmeridge is like that, but we don't live there.

There is no road to us from the top of Kimmeridge hill, but two miles of turf and a track down to a place where a wood shaped like a narrow fan runs up from the sea. That's called the Sacred Wood. Most people are afraid of it and say it is full of ghosts, and it is, if there are such things. I should worry. That's a vulgar phrase, but one can afford it here. Anyhow, hidden in the top of the Sacred Wood are three houses. The manor, which is shut up, and is a piece of perfect XVII century stonework, a shepherd's cottage which grows out of the ground, and ours. Ours has a verandah and a wall against the sea-wind 'that rests not night or day,' and over it is the great hill, Tyneham Cap, and from the garden the Sacred Wood runs down to a reef called Broad Bench and the open sea. The world really ends at Corfe Castle—here a new world has begun and pushes out the life man knows that he lives. Here is everything man once made into Gods in the state in which he made them, the crude potency.

I can only repeat what one panic-struck man said at tea. 'There's a bit of that hedge comes into the house when you aren't looking, and I don't like it.'

I do. You wouldn't recognise me—towseled hair all over my face and a sort of grubby tan over the rest of me. I walk all day and at night, when the Sacred Wood dances, I dance too. And all the while, the wild life passes in.

I have hardly any personal news. I hope this letter reaches you. Send me yours.

Cecil says—'Tell Glenway. What do they know of England who only Tony Know?' and sends his love. With all mine.

Ever yours,
Mary Butts

II

Tebel Vos
Sennen Cove
Cornwall

My dear Ross-Williamson—

Somehow we got here. It's all blue, a return not to the earth but the air. The house is perched on the top of Sennen cliffs, and you can only see the sea and the sky full of gulls. It's as though we were hanging in a balloon. I'm beginning to be incredibly happy. And Gabriel is getting strong again. And I can cook all the things they eat in France. Pray heaven I resist the temptation to write a book about Cornwall.

Do you know—there is a most remote village here, inland, called Sancreed; where there is a holy well and the ruins of a hermit's chapel. And in the churchyard a keltic cross, ten feet high, with a device carved down one side of it, a spear coming out of a cup, which must be the Sanc-Grail. This is its part of the world. Truly you ought to come and see this place. I'm only just beginning to find out how strange it all is. Round us there are untouched miles of primitive moor which have never been reclaimed, full of hollows and stones with histories and plants and birds.

I hope you had a good Christmas. We did. My small daughter came, to make her home here, for the first time, in the holidays. And it's being a great success. She *is* rather a splendid child, with a head beyond her years; and she will be good to look at. And she's like a colt out at grass in this country, tramping it from end to end with an Alsatian we borrowed. I'm a real mother with a real child again.

All sorts of gay things happened. Some fishermen came on Christmas day and cracked a bottle of wine and sang us carols. It's the only place I've found where the 'Curly Bride' is still a tradition. They sang that and brought us presents—sea-urchin shells, and the glass floats off submarine nets.

And we'd all the Christmas things to eat and several friends. The weather was cloudless blue and April-warm. A good passage. Oh, yes, lots of things happen in Sennen. I found a boy who can produce [indecipherable]; and found out a great deal more about Sancreed where the Grail happened once, and it wouldn't surprise me if it appeared again.

Last night I came in in the dark, the starry-sea-filled dark of these cliffs, and the air smelling autumn, and gorse fires down the coast. A fisherman had left a gift on the kitchen floor, 3 live crabs, one 18 inches from claw to claw, and it got me round the ankle. It felt like—well, I didn't know *what* it was and can't think of a simile.

Ever yours—
M.B.

III

[Excerpt from another letter to Ross Williamson:]

Does the question of what is called 'mystical experience' interest you? It means almost everything to me—I mean as a thing separate from any practice, from love or the arts or work of any kind, the pure quiet sudden thing, like a fire —no, a light. I believe that however diluted or partial or rare, however translated into its *practices*—that is in *everything* we love to do and do well—it is the thing, the only thing, men live by—(you can't or shouldn't live for it?)—the source of any kind of life worth having, the one way of finding out what things are. One instant of it will determine a lifetime. J.W.N. Sullivan wrote once that it was time it was really looked into, as an experience, an objective fact. He asked for a 'science of mysticism,' as though it might become the science of all sciences. While Huxley—(Aldous) pointed out that, like artists or generals, there were first, second and third class mystics. And Desmond McCarthy said what I know is true, that a mystic—the first-class kind, entendu, was a hard-hearted man. (By God, he'd better be.) Yet it is extraordinarily hard to write about, to examine and describe. Language wasn't invented to deal with it; so it mostly gets out by indirections, obliquely, something like the knights's move in chess.

What I do believe with everything that's in me is that people like us have to wait in some sort of a wilderness; and then, slowly or quickly, we'll see. See what? Well, the right way for the world to go, no just ourselves, but for man. A series of ideas, re-statements, which will put life or validity or kick into our spirits and so into our institutions again. (The 'bad patch' is affecting my prose, but if I mean anything, I mean this.) It's egoistic to talk about oneself in so great a matter, but it's the handiest example. For years I've felt it coming on me, a 'seeing' which will be serviceable to people in the state we're all in. It's as though I was lit by it, but opaquely, couldn't see its forms, only its light and that intermittently. But the wall between it and me is getting thinner, very slowly. It may never vanish, but I do know that all that's best in my work is a transcription of the light and of the forms I've guessed at behind it.

I believe something that really will save the bacon is trying to get born, a 'spiritual' or 'magical,' a mystical thing. A re-statement in living terms of something infinitely old, of course; and that's why you can't marry or just *only* be a very successful man in office; or either of us be anything but exceedingly alone.

MARY BUTTS

Pythian Ode

WHEN I think of you, Delphi, I am reminded of a fair young man smiling:
And an old woman goddess:
And an old woman goddess:
And a cluster of women pretending to be bees.

Affairs for which Dictynna was responsible, the Twins and the Erinyes, the Thriae and the Thyiades.

A city of hotel-keepers; keeping hotels, keeping brothels, keeping prize-rings. On a mountain, under a mountain and a mountain. By a spring and a spring.
Expecting an earthquake and a rich Syracusan lord.

The mind of the priests of the oracle. A delicious enquiry into the next event but one.
A game of chance, a game of chess, a guess-game.

First published in *The Transatlantic Review,* Vol. II, No. 3, 1924, pp. 235–39. Like Charles Olson's picturing of the early demise of the American republic in his *Maximus Poems,* "Pythian Ode" evokes and addresses the sacred shrine of Delphi, meditating on its history and transition from the place where the Pythia uttered holy prophesies to a "little old town with a too large cathedral," and on the displacement of Dionysus by Apollo, "the good policeman with the sun for flash-lamp." Although noting the gradual profanation/corruption of the oracle because of human venality and the desire for "a policy, a ritual, a decree," the poem suggests an answer in the appearing of an ever-existent truth, a mean between extremes, the springs of an impersonal good in place of the dominance of personality. The ode ends with a statement of the unity of heaven and earth, "Quod inferius sicut superius est"—What is below is like that which is above.

The thing-in-itself is represented by the pairs of opposites. To be weighed, to be divided, to be chosen. To be represented by the possibilities of cities and the notable vagaries of Oriental kings.

There were the iron spits:
Cold water:
Mice.
They called you the mixing bowl of Hellas because of the bowl Croesus gave. It stood by the spirits and the pretty gold statue, filled for the public beano, when the adyton hummed oracles, and the Pythias worked in shifts, and all the world had a dip into the future, and on the little thrill of wine mounted.

Grey comb of no earthly bees, lime crags-where-the-sun-goes.
The wine lifted their eyes above the temenos.
So we're round again. Thyiades, bees, metaphorical rock-comb high up Parnassos and the metaphysical bees of the soul.
For their souls were improved no doubt of it in that cunning old Lourdes.

They filled the bowl with wine.
Wine is not Apollo's drink.
We are to observe the transition
From fact to reality.

In. In. In. There are things which to display is the only way to hide. That ambiguous hint especially we call the divine mind.
It drifted up through a crack in a stone, and out from the mouth of a woman.
The wind that blows and blows crooked.
There was the Pythia, and under her a three-legged stool,
a lid on the earth's mystery.

A stone wreathed in raw wool
Not a portrait statue of the god.

Behind these was the grave of Dionysos.
There they buried mystery, put mystery of mysteries to sleep with itself
Where it doubled, added six, was halved, divided, and the three may have gone to make up the Trinity.

In the adyton Dionysos' grave.
A stone box for an explanation of the truth.

Truth is the heart's desire.
A stone instead of the heart's desire
Is given you for truth.
Truth is a mean between extremes.
Be comforted.

From the nine months called 'satiety' to the three months called 'craving' they rang the change from paean to dithyramb.
The white bees swarmed on Parnassos' cap
Yellow Apollo went through them to the back of the north wind
Dionysos was king in Delphi
They shouted on the hills.

Cunning old Lourdes kept mascots, kept women, kept detectives, kept accounts, and rising and falling stock in the possibilities of cities when the sap was rising in the world.
Choosing the Pythia
Who must not be raped.
Who must (finally) be old.
Who must be dressed as a girl.

Put it on the Pythia!
Who took bribes?
Who sold the Spartans?
Who medized?
Put it on the Pythia!
Who got it wrong again?
Who made it scan? . . .

The earth is a black pill turning.
Apollo gilt the pill.
Took it from a woman.
Took over—
Blood and onions,
Beans and honey,
And occasionally the untrodden stair to the door does not shut to the empty room. Lights and wings, and blood, and tides where there is no more sequence, and the hellenic formulae are lost.

Not for such things did he collect your ancient thrones, the good policeman with the sun for flash-lamp turning turning on a turning world.
He gilt the earth, but on its navel the Pythia turned, sick with laurel, sick with ecstacy.

The ecstacy you ordered, O Apollo, to, make men better in their cities!

Men were made better in their cities, and the old
Sun was caught medizing and from the tripod came a noise.
To be made sense, to be made significance, to be made nonsense:
To become a gnome, a policy, a ritual, a decree:
An alliance, a monopoly in fish:
A man bleeding down an empty stair.

Back again to Delphi for another series.
Where they rehearsed the Roman Curia.
In 'the western world.'

So you became
A little old town with a too large cathedral.
A ruin, a quarry:
Fouilles de Delphe.
There are the extremes of action, the extremes of passion.
Truth is a new creation out of these
Be comforted.

We have observed a transition
From fact to reality
From fact to reality.

Quod inferius sicut superius est.
Be comforted.

III

REAPPRAISALS

With Cecil Maitland (ctr.) and Douglas Goldring, Paris, 1922.

ROBERT DUNCAN

Re Mary Butts

SEON GIVENS, who in those early days edited a collection of essays on Joyce, was near my age, came to be a friend and confidant, but more—and that in the midst of our Bohemian dedications—a spiritual mentor. She was the first, as I remember, who talked of gnosticism and of early Christian eros and agape, who directed me to Barth's uncompromising *Epistle to the Romans,* and who plied me with Mary Butts's *Ashe of Rings* and *Armed with Madness.* So Mary Butts was in 1941, when I was twenty-two, an essential part of an initiation. Seon Givens had struck upon an affinity that ran deep.

There was the clarity and force of her prose. And there was the fact that she too lived in the marginal world we knew, having no remittance and only infrequent and minimal wages, finding our refuge in miserable rooms where what art we knew, whatever "find" for color or for form, had to work its magic. Stories like "In Bayswater" or "Scylla and Charybdis" were like our story; London-Manhattan. And the warp of sexuality was secretive in those days, relegated to another magic of compulsion and obsession, as it operates in the lure of Mary Butts's world.

But the important revelation was that intense personal experience suffered was more than psychodrama: it sought its realization as ritual and a threshold of the sacred: to admit the fearful. In Mary Butts's telling the psychological is but a mask; it is the hidden "face" or "glance" behind that we are brought to.

From *The Writings and the World of Mary Butts,* a brochure issued at a conference on Butts at The University of California at Davis, held February 24-25, 1984.

In the two essays in historical perspective of 1932—*Warning to Hikers* and *Traps for Unbelievers*—we see specifically how far-reaching her understanding of what is at issue can go. "Rites and sacraments are a kind of drama, a ritual play taken from universal natural events. They are about the health and ill-health of the soul." In the fabric of contemporary consciousness she seeks to come to terms with Nature and with the pagan (native) gods. The daimonic haunts her romances and poetry.

"Traps" and "Warning": the ill-health of the soul is initiatory. All the more striking in this existential anguish is her sense of the sanctuary of the house and of the countryside for the health of the soul. The protective magic of her women is to form an alliance with Nature.

ROBIN BLASER

"Here Lies the Woodpecker Who was Zeus"

THIS ESSAY on Mary Butts's *Armed with Madness* (1928) will, I fear, appear to be more an anthology than a commentary. My reasons are that her work is little known, few libraries have her twelve published volumes, and even the little that is written about her is hard to come by and confusing. I have chosen, therefore, to quote extensively and carefully. Her work belongs to the youth of twentieth-century writing, and the creative energy of it helps in the imagination of ourselves. An essay-story, then.

Mary Butts's reputation began with the publication of a volume of stories, *Speed the Plough,* in 1923. Her curious sense of the magic of personal meaning—the game of the possibility of a meaningful life—was there at the centre of those first stories. Ford Madox Ford's "Purposes," announcing the *Transatlantic Review* in 1923, included Mary Butts along with H. G. Wells, Conrad, Joyce, cummings, Pound, Eliot, Mina Loy, and Robert McAlmon. Among these, she is striking and remains so. In the history of the magazine *Pagany* (Boston, 1929–1933), put together by its original editor, Richard Johns, and Stephen Halpert in 1969, I find this statement with its strange lack of any sense of the passage of time:

> Johns' original intention was to limit his contributors to those who, whatever their ethnic background, were essentially Americans. One dictionary definition of native, "belonging to, or natural to, by reason of the circumstances of one's birth," would certainly include such writers as Ezra Pound, Gertrude Stein, Mary Butts, and Emanuel Carnevali, who despite their present expatriate status were born and bred in this country.[1]

Doubtless, this is simply confused writing—the point being the original intention. (Mary Butts died in 1937, and Gertrude Stein in 1946.) Here, the editor of *Pagany: A Native Quarterly,* taking its start and title from William Carlos Williams' *A Voyage to Pagany* (1928, but also a reminiscence of 1924)—joined by his collaborator—manages thirty-six years after the demise of his famous journal still to consider the quintessentially English Mary Butts of London, Dorset and Cornwall an American. This seems to have been part of her fate, for, as far as I can tell, it is in America that her reputation continued, avant-garde—now, I suppose the word is underground—and firm. Nevertheless, that original view, reflected upon by Johns and Halpert in *A Return to Pagany,* gives us a measure of her reputation in the 'twenties. Kenneth Rexroth wrote in his introduction to that volume:

> Many of them are now unjustly forgotten. They believed and hoped that the arts would be the instrument of a fundamental revolution of the human sensibility as such. They believed that the word or the pictorial image could be used to subvert the dead syntax by which human self-alienation had been grafted into the very structure of the brain and nervous system. They believed that The Revolution of the Word would liberate a new life meaning for man and sweep away dead shells from which meaning had been exhausted or had turned malignant.[2]

In preparation for that introduction, dated April 21, 1969, Rexroth read through a complete file of *Pagany:* "As I looked through it, it was just like Proust's madeleine." This youth of the twentieth-century literary effort included Mary Butts.

Williams' narrative of his year in Pagany—a tricky name for all of Europe—spent there at the behest of Pound, brings him back to America to search, as the New Directions book-blurb puts it, for "what is genuinely poetic at home."[3] What followed was, of course, *In the American Grain* (1925). It is useful to remember the final scene in *A Voyage to Pagany:*

America, he began again haltingly, is hard to know.

Yes, she answered, because she had made him serious so that he must speak his mind or say nothing.

I think it is useful to us, he continued, because it is near savagery. In Europe, you are so far from it that maybe you will have to die first before you will live again.—But Dev was not such a fool.—Europe, I do not know, he corrected himself, I am seeing a few superficial moments only.

But he had a quick pupil.—That is enough, replied Fräulein von J. I see now what I saw at the beginning. You are a savage, not quite civilized—you have America and we have not. You have that, yes, it is something.

It is very difficult, said Dev. I am not a typical American. We have few natives left but they would not know me—

You are holding on to something, she said.

It is very difficult, Dev went on—something very likely to be lost, this is what—So he took out the flint arrowhead he had in his pocket and showed it to her.

She was impressed. She held it hard in her hand as if to keep its impression there, felt the point, the edge, tried it, turned it over.

Yes, she said, I have seen the same thing from our own fields, more finished work—but it is very far, very far. No one believes it is real. But this you carry in your coat? It is very strange. Where did you find it?

In a corn-field in Virginia, there are many of them there.

. . . .

Moving to rejoin Frau M. they saw that it was getting on into the afternoon and that they must be stepping along if they would be back in Rome by nightfall.

You believe in America like a church, mused Fräulein von J. almost to herself.

Dev did not think so.

Do you believe then that the church is an enemy to your belief?

Yes.

She looked away.

Oh come on, said Dev, let's get out of this.[4]

I have quoted so much in order to set Williams' "nativist" position which *Pagany* adopted, never, rightly, excluding the expatriates. Williams' quarrel with the "Europeanism" of Pound and Eliot became fundamental to his imagination. His insistence upon the return of language to a sense of place and to the rhythm and imagery of that place—which is a ground rather than a sky for being—defines the major effort of the modern writer and is a triumph of twentieth-century writing. And this gives us a clue to Mary Butts's place among these writers: the rhythm, imagery, and magic of her Dorset and Cornwall are dazzling—another grounding of imagination.

A "Manifesto" by William Carlos Williams appears in the first issue of *Pagany:*

> "The ghosts so confidently laid by Francis Bacon and his followers are again walking in the laboratory as well as beside the man in the street" [Scott Buchanan, *Poetry and Mathematics,* p. 18], the scientific age is drawing to a close. Bizarre derivations multiply about us, mystifying and untrue as—an automatic revolver. To what shall the mind turn for that with which to rehabilitate our thought and our lives? To the word, a meaning hardly distinguishable from that of place, in whose great, virtuous and at present little realized potency we hereby manifest our belief.[5]

The statement reflects Williams' profound interest in modern science, particularly in relativity theory and its implications for a relational imagination. His intention here is not anti-scientific, but rather he means to pick up the changed relation to an objective reality, which is implied, and Williams early recognized the fact. A relational imagination then, rightly, turns to language "to rehabilitate our thought and our lives." As Robert Duncan puts it in another context, "Most importantly it is the word that carries with it the life-consciousness to be, the adventuring biological reality."[6] Immediately following Williams' manifesto in the original issue of *Pagany,* is Mary Butts's story, "The House-party," dedicated to Jean Cocteau. This is a finely subtle, "politely sensual"—in the manner of the time—story about homosexual young men, accurate with a Jamesian kind of suggestiveness. But in Halpert-Johns's history of Pagany, this story is said to "Epitomize the amoral living of some of the wealthy English and American expatriates on the Continent." "In contrast," they continue, "Margery Latimer ... searched the souls of simple-living Midwest American characters."[7] The problem of Mary Butts's reputation may well begin with this kind of careless, fearful comparison:

> Throughout the first two years of *Pagany* Johns had given Mary Butts' decadent sparkle a full display. By the time the fourth issue was ready to be printed, Johns knew he would no longer accept further contributions from her so that space might be available for newer and lesser-known writers, who, in his opinion, had something more vital to say. Somehow in her shorter than usual story, "Green," there seemed to blow a tempering wind through one of the untypically English country houses which generally housed an amorous imbroglio. Now Mary Butts was writing with tartness, almost as if she felt there might be a healthy future for a young couple in the heterosexuality of marriage, cleansed of the emotional friendships of other young men for the husband and the influence of a conniving, mantic mother....
>
> Mary Butts was always brilliant, and Johns was pleased to have had the opportunity to publish her works.... But this sign of good health on a generally fevered cheek was new and promising. One of her stories finally looked forward toward a balanced living, ... an apt swan song for Mary Butts.[8]

One should not, perhaps, be too harsh in retrospect, but it is disappointing to find this stated in this way in 1969. The charge of decadence involves a moral imperative which defines life by exclusion, and I hasten to add, it has the effect of denying the search for a poetics of life that was the fundamental concern of many of *Pagany*'s writers.

This denial and the editorial changes consequent upon it are reflected in *Pagany* after the October-December, 1931 issue:

> The phasing out of Mary Butts and the introduction of John Cheever indicated that *Pagany*'s fourth issue for 1931 was one of transition, a final encore for a number of writers, yet far too subtle for the reader to notice.[9]

Faulkner's homosexual story, "Divorce in Naples," was rejected as "commonplace." "Twittering birds" such as Charles Henri Ford and Parker Tyler were out. Gertrude Stein's "nonsensical couplets had begun to pall." Johns himself had been troubled by the reception given his own tentative, defensive exploration (all fiction!) of a homosexual theme in his story "Solstice" (vol. 1, no. 4), which was clearly influenced by Mary Butts in its handling of unstated relations and in one instance, by her archetypal use of classical divinities to describe character—"a Cybele for young men to learn from." Pound himself was not making sense to Johns.[10] Pound's essay "The First Year of 'Pagany' and The Possibility of Criteria" (vol. 1, no. 1, 1931) with its instructions and its remarks on "Mr. Eliot's fatigue" and "M. Cocteau's adventures" had not apparently instructed Richard Johns. The remaining three issues of *Pagany* are memorable for, among other things, Cocteau's "The Laic Mystery" translated by Olga Rudge, Katherine Anne Porter's "Banquet for October," parts of Williams' *White Mule,* and Zukofsky's "'A'—First Movement," but the adventure of the magazine was over. It began to follow another direction in modern American letters. Still, one notices that H. D. sent "Electra-Orestes" for the April-June, 1932, issue, accompanied by a letter in praise of the magazine, which closes: "You have been fortunate too, to have Mary Butts's exquisite stories."[11]

The turn in Mary Butts's reputation is nearly incomprehensible. In America, it is tied to a "decadence" already spotted in Richard Johns. Elsewhere, I've taken note of the false note in her British reputation as that is reflected in the spite and meanness of spirit of Douglas Goldring in his autobiographical *South Lodge* (1943), published six years after her death.[12] The tale of that relationship is the business of a biographer—one can only hope for a competent one with a mind as subtle and charmed as Mary Butts's. Her finest collection of short stories, *Several Occasions* (1932), is dedicated to Goldring. Suspicion begins there. The dedication tells us that he had once recognized something, and he tells us as much in an earlier autobiography, *Odd Man Out* (1935). But his own art could not openly praise the beauty of men as hers did, nor could he approach the adventure of the sacred which is her greatest concern. Biographical interest in Mary Butts will be trapped by the merely reductive if the sacred is not traced—tracked—in her work. That vitality I call the sacred begins with her childhood memories of Blake's paintings on the wall and his illuminated books on the shelves of a wondrous library that had come to the family through Blake's friend Thomas Butts. I suggest that Mary Butts's reputation, like that of H. D., suffered because of the complexity of the sacred in her twentieth-century mind, heart, and work.

* * * * *

The adventure of the sacred is then the large issue in Mary Butts's work to which I wish to call attention. The realism of many of her stories is a record of the way lives flow into and out of this adventure. But it was the adventure itself which drew Mary Butts's attention in her most important works. And that adventure is entirely marked by the condition of the sacred in the modern world. It is this, I think, that drew, in turn, the attention of Pound and H. D.—her careful probing of the problem of it. This does not contradict her stand alongside Williams' "Manifesto." Nor is she contradictory, if we read her carefully, to Williams' interest in Einstein—"St. Francis Einstein of the Daffodils, *On the first visit of Professor Einstein to the United States in the spring of 1921"*—or to his fascination with Alfred North Whitehead's *Science and the Modern World* after first reading it in 1927. Both are concerned with the elemental, the ultimate, and the cosmos, which have to do with ground and place—so we are taught first by Hesiod, Oedipus at Colonus, and Lucretius. Theirs are two different ways of writing to a similar condition. Where Williams looked to science—post-Baconian and Newtonian—where he found the ghosts and so settled on the word and a newly posed language, a writer like Mary Butts sets up the contemporary with all its dazzle, free sexuality, sense and nonsense, and finding the ghosts also, she turns to the archaic. And so it is, I assume, with one writer after another that the loosened, embattled relation to meaning, as that condition informs any meaningful life, turns up the ghosts—.

I want now to turn to Mary Butts's *Armed with Madness:*

> In the house, in which they could not afford to live, it was unpleasantly quiet. Marvelously noisy, but the noises let through silence. The noises were jays, bustling and screeching in the wood, a hay-cutter, clattering and sending up waves of scent, substantial as sea-waves, filling the long rooms as the tide fills a blow-hole, but without roar or release. The third noise was the light wind, rising off the diamond-blue sea. The sea lay three parts round the house, invisible because of the wood. The wood rose from its cliff-point in a single tree, and spread out inland, in a fan to enclose the house. Outside the verandah, a small lawn had been hollowed, from which the wood could be seen as it swept up, hurrying with squirrels, into a group of immense ilex, beech and oak. The lawn was stuck with yuccas and tree-fuchsias, dripping season in, season out, with bells the colour of blood.
>
> Once the house was passed, the wood gave it up, enclosed it decently, fenced a paddock, and the slip of dark life melted into the endless turf-miles which ran up a great down into the sky.
>
> The silence let through by the jays, the hay-cutter, and

> the breeze, was a complicated production of stone rooms, the natural silence of empty grass, and the equivocal, personal silence of the wood. Not many nerves could stand it. People who had come for a week had been known to leave next day. The people who had the house were interested in the wood and its silence. When it got worse, after dark or at mid-day, they said it was tuning-up. When a gale came up-Channel shrieking like a mad harp, they said they were watching a visible fight with the silence in the wood.
>
> A large gramophone stood with its mouth open on the verandah flags. They had been playing to the wood after lunch, to appease it and to keep their dancing in hand.[13]

Most striking in this passage which opens *Armed with Madness* is the silence, mysterious and unexplained. Its "tuning-up" proposes a primordial relation of sound and silence, even as the wit and magic of the gramophone stops us, first with laughter, then with a sense of the lives of those who play out the story to come. It is characteristic of Mary Butts's fiction that she adapts an older principle of narrative—somewhat akin to Greek drama in which the character is there for the sake of the action and not *vice versa,* or so Aristotle insisted that we understand the fact of the event in tragedy, which even in his time, following upon Plato's insistence that meaning was transcendent and abstract, needed to be straightened out.[14] Mary Butts's sense that a tale is told of human characters inside an action both older and other than themselves challenges that other sense of the novel in which character is interesting in and for itself. As a result of this different narrative technique, each character in a Butts novel remains a sketch poised within a realism of the elemental and mysterious. (That there is such a realism—that we are capable of it—Keats taught us long ago.) The expected psychological centre is displaced in such a way that, as in *Armed with Madness,* one is not always sure who is in charge of the narration which slips from one to another—the author included—allowing motivation and insight to wander.

The wood surrounding the house is old and sacred—that is to say, nurturing life-sanctities—very like the sacred wood of Butts's poem "Corfe" (addressed to Corfe Castle in Dorset), which Louis Zukofsky published in *An "Objectivist" Anthology* in 1932:

> But when I remember you Corfe, I remember Delphi
> Because your history also is a mystery of God.
> . . . .
> Very sweet is the Sacred Wood
> In the gold clearing, in the mustard patch;
> But at night comes a change
> Like a gold ball thrown out
> And a black ball thrown in
> (Not sunset behind Tyneham Cap
> On a night without a moon.)
> But a shift of potencies
> Like a black ball thrown in
> And a gold ball thrown out
> And the players are princes
> Of the turf and the weed
> And the wind-moulded trees
> And the hazel thicket
> And the red blackberry thorn.
>
> Never trust a hemlock
> An inch above your mouth.
> An ice-green hemlock
> Is a lover
> In the wood.
> Now every way the wind blows this sweetie goes
> In the south
> Where goes the leaf of the rose
> And the evergreen tree.

The poem gives us a concentrated image of the magic of the wood that is a recurring interest in Mary Butts's work—here the night brings a "shift of potencies" represented by the reversed imagery of the gold and black balls, as though one could catch the potencies in a game, all leading to the storied and threatening hemlock become a lover.

Then, in the house, we meet the main characters: first Scylla and her brother Felix, and a strong, down-to-earth fellow, Ross, "a rare plant," who shares the house with them. An American, Dudley Carston, comes for a visit, the outsider to be tested. These four are joined by Clarence and Picus, two men who share a cottage some distance away and who have come to stay in the house because, we are told, their well is low and polluted. One woman, five men, and Scylla's and Felix' old nurse who acts as house-keeper and general comforter. Nothing is ever told in the novel about the sexual relationship between Clarence and Picus, but we come to see the anguish and care of it as it falls apart, incapable of withstanding the test of the game that is played out in their lives. Scylla in the end wins the love of Picus. Clarence ends in madness and defeat, carving a punch bowl for Scylla. Felix escapes to Paris where he discovers Boris, a young, penniless, White-Russian prince whom he brings back to the house in the woods. Again, nothing is said about their relationship, though we understand enough. (Incidentally, it is Boris who prepares the plot for Butts's novel to follow *Armed with Madness, Death of Felicity Taverner,* 1932.)

Stated thus baldly, everything is lost except the tension, the possibilities, and a suggestiveness. These are not decadent, but serious and complex young lives. In Mary Butts's world, for whatever reason, male homosexuality is not a matter of decadence, but, rather, of the way lives turn. Boris, who appears near the end of *Armed with Madness* and whose first appearance in her work is in *Imaginary Letters* (dated 1924, published in 1928) is a case in point. *Imaginary Letters* begins Mary Butts's major work in fiction, though it appears very close to her life, and may be autobiographical. Here we meet Boris who will not stay still. Goldring tells us that Mary Butts had a special sympathy for these Russians, princes who had lost a world and were down and out in Paris. Boris is beautiful, underhanded, unstable, lost, homosexual, and unavailable. It is Boris, more fully imagined, who commits murder—mind you, as a gift—to save the land from a real estate development, parking lots and tourists in *Felicity Taverner.* In *Imaginary Letters,* we find the first care that brought him into her art, and there also we find anger that is womanly, direct and puzzled. He somehow starts the imaginary process. Boris, she writes, leads us "a pretty dance." "Capricious, selfish, insensitive." "Lecherous, drunken, bold, and chaste." The qualities build in the first pages—someone shapeless and changing. "He arouses equally unconquerable affection and despair." "A monster of vanity and pride." "He is cruel, devoted, jealous . . . ," this "black and green boy." The words create this figure, whom, in kind, most of us meet sometime in our lives. Protean love. He or she may be only ourselves, a desire, or perhaps that figure is out there, as Mary Butts says, "the cause of art in others."[15]

But, to return to *Armed with Madness,* the plot is not as simple as an outline of its interpersonal relations suggests. Picus and Clarence bring with them to the house in the wood a cup which they have discovered in their well—Felix, trying to help them, fished it out with a spear. The Grail, we guess immediately—"that mirage, symbol, archetype of unity and integrity that appeared to seers of the Middle Ages"—"around 1180, when the Latin Kingdom of Jerusalem was seen to totter," first with alarm and then spiritual defeat "in 1187, when Jerusalem fell."[16] In Mary Butts, the Grail is stunningly there and not there simultaneously, symbolic of a possible meaning and of a meaninglessness, neither of which conditions is privileged in the characters' lives. This profound symbol of spiritual fulfillment has returned again and again to modern letters, most brilliantly, I think, in Jack Spicer's *The Holy Grail,* but, then, Spicer was himself indebted to Mary Butts. Later in the novel, we find out that Picus has stolen the cup from his father, an antiquarian of some reputation, and that he planted it in the well and arranged for Felix to use a spear when trying to clear the well. The characters are, all of them, then caught up in an enactment of an old pattern. The interplay—the magic that meaning is, when it is love and a task of lives—among one woman and five men is a tale of a possible Grail. We never know whether the cup is simply a jade cup, an old altar vessel, an ashtray as it is once used in the novel, a spitting-cup, so used by Picus' father's mistress before her death, as the old man cruelly tells us, a poison-cup out of the East—jade is said to detect poison—or the Sanc-Grail. It is, of course, all of these in one way or another. In this way, Mary Butts tests the symbol and pursues her imaginative investigation of the condition of the sacred in our century.

The lives of Scylla and the five men around her shape a spiritual condition that is both frightening and, in the words of the novel, an "enormous lark"—like our own lives. "There was," she wrote, "something in their lives spoiled and inconclusive like the Grail story" (91). And this remark by the youngest of the characters, Felix, which he addresses to Ross, seems especially harsh:

> You're looking for something. I'm not. And I hope when you get it, you'll like it. Looking for the Sanc-Grail. It's always the same story. The Golden Fleece or the philosopher's stone, or perpetual motion, or Atlantis or the lost tribes or God. All ways of walking into the same trap (121).

Certainly, this is a very modern attitude toward the old unicity, but the trap is also sexuality, and Felix speaks his own young fear, confusion, and innocence. What he is looking for he does not yet know. The "trap" in Mary Butts is inchoate and personal, and it always leads to the puzzle of larger meaning.

Early in the novel, when Scylla and Ross are discussing the arrival of their American visitor, the narrator comments:

> "Give him a good time and see what happens." That was her part of their hospitality, whose rewards were varied and irregular. None of them, with perhaps the exception

> of Felix, could understand a good time that was not based on flashes of illumination, exercises of the senses....
>
> Something long and white came up behind them out of the sea. An extra wave washed Felix a ledge higher. "Thank you," he said and skipped across.

A "pleasant memory" unites them, and

> they became a triple figure, like Hecate the witch, amused, imaginative. They put on their things: Felix' pretty clothes, Ross' rough ones, the girl, her delicate strong dress. With their arms round her shoulders, they crossed the rocks and went up the cliff-path, and through the wood to the house (5, 6).

The deft touches, the careful realism—all coloured by the sudden simile of the witch, Hecate—begins a strange suggestiveness that will take us into the magic and witchery of their lives.

Strange suggestions accumulate throughout the novel. Early on, the reader stops over the name Scylla:

> They called her Scylla from her name Drusilla, altering it because they said she was sometimes a witch and sometimes a bitch (4).

Exactly, but the name also returns us to Greek lore—initially, to *The Odyssey* (12. 235) where we find this mighty daughter of Crataeïs, who lived in a cavern along the straits of Sicily, the rending, mangling, troubling face of the sea. Drusilla, on the other hand, returns us to the *Acts of the Apostles* (24) wherein St. Paul defends himself and his belief in Christ so strongly that he frightens the procurator Felix and his wife Drusilla, the daughter of Herod Agrippa I and sister of Herod Agrippa II. This curious method sets up layers in Butts's story of some very ordinary characters who are to become extraordinary through the serious game of their lives. The novelist appears to work by association and she expects us to. Here, the point is a lightly brushed blend of ancient and Christian heritage carried by contemporary people, if only in their names. Later in the novel, she will call this "the Freud game"—what do you remember of this or that. We need only let our minds play over the elements which the story brings together by association—ancient, Christian, and modern, noting especially the easily and almost sportively associated Scylla and Hecate, leading finally to a further association of love with violence and madness. Only at the end of the novel will we realize that we have been warned from the outset of a possible violence in this pursuit of the love-game which in Mary Butts is always an aspect of the sacred.

This is, perhaps, because the sacred, however we define it, is a power over one, such as love is. One may fail in entering upon the sacred or one may come through into an intelligence. At the beginning of the novel we have seen Poseidon momentarily, or perhaps we missed him: "Something long and white came up behind them out of the sea." A good source book, such as Morford's and Lenardon's *Classical Mythology,* will help me to summarize the depth of association that, I believe, Mary Butts wishes us to have. We should remember that Poseidon, god of the sea, is "violent in his loves." The god

> made advances to Scylla, the daughter of Phorcys and Hecate. Amphitrite was jealous and threw magic herbs into Scylla's bathing place. Thus Scylla was transformed into a terrifying monster, encircled with a ring of dogs' heads....

They remind us that

> Ovid (*Met.* 13. 917–68; 14. 1–71) tells us this same story about Glaucus, a mortal who was transformed into a sea-god. It was he who fell in love with Scylla; when he was rejected, he turned to the sorceress Circe for help. But Circe fell in love with him and in her jealousy poisoned the waters of Scylla's bathing place.

And Hecate, the triple-figured—here amused and imaginative—descended from the Titans, who has her house in the depths of things

> is a goddess of roads in general and crossroads in particular, the latter being considered the center of ghostly activities, particularly in the dead of night. Thus the goddess developed a terrifying aspect; triple-faced statues depicted the three manifestations of her multiple character as a deity of the moon—Selene in heaven, Artemis on earth, and Hecate in the realm of Hades. . . . How different is the usual depiction of Artemis, young, vigorous, wholesome, and beautiful!

We also remember that Circe, a daughter of the Sun, is the aunt of Medea. So, the associations play around Mary Butts's novel. Violence, sexual frustration, and sexual transformation all lie in wait in this book. Irradiative associations inform the realism of the characters' young lives.

Throughout the novel there are introspective moments in which the narrator of the moment mulls his or her personal stake in this. Here, for example, Scylla goes to meet their American visitor in Starn, while Ross and Felix go picking mushrooms.

> It was all very well. She had told Felix to collect mushrooms and not allow Ross to experiment. He could get them in Ogham meads—What was she worried about? Money, of course, and love affairs; the important, unimportant things. Hitherto God had fed his sparrows, and as good fish had come out of the sea. But everywhere there was a sense of broken continuity, a dis-ease. The end of an age, the beginning of another. Revaluation of values. Phrases that meant something if you could mean them. The meaning of meaning? Discovery of a new value, a different way of apprehending everything. She wished the earth would not suddenly look fragile, as if it was going to start shifting about. . . . There was something wrong with all of them, or with their world. A moment missed, a

> moment to come. Or not coming. Or either or both. Shove it off on the war; but that did not help.
>
> Only Ross was all right—He never wanted anything that he did not get. Life had given it up and paid over Ross' stakes, because once his strong appetites were satisfied, he did not want anything in human life at all. It was something to eat and drink, to embrace and paint. Apart from that, he knew something that she was only growing conscious of. And wouldn't tell. Not he—laughed at her for not knowing, and for wanting to know.
>
> Felix was quite different. Felix was scared. Fear made him brittle and angry and unjust. Without faith.
>
> Faith was necessary for the knowledge of God. Only, there were fifty good reasons for supporting the non-existence of God. Besides, no one wanted to believe that any more. That was the point. And it was a shame for those two men to make her go all that way through a valley, while they were grubbing about in the wind (10–11).

This haunted passage, ending in the strictly personal, is exact in its description of the modern predicament—the missed meaning of tradition, the loss and the change.

Scylla meets the American, Carston, rents a car and brings him back to the house in the woods. Meanwhile, Ross and Felix have interrupted their mushroom hunting to visit Clarence and Picus, which, as we have already noted, brings all four back to the house in the wood. The following passage allows us to watch the visitor size up the main characters.

> That was the situation for him, as he listened, translating, to the story Felix had to tell. Felix said that Ross and he had been to a place called Gault, and he'd sung to it. Presumably a dangerous place. They had then decided to call on distant friends, who might or might not be inhabiting a cottage on a place called Tollerdown. Anyhow, supposing they were not there, a rare species of hawk known as a honey-buzzard might be observed in the vicinity. On arriving they had found their friends (Scylla seemed to

be the only woman in the group, a point for reflection) in difficulties owing to their well, shrunk by the drought, yielding nothing but dead hedgehogs. A digression on the use of soda-water to make tea. An excursion down the well to clean out the hedgehogs had led to a discovery. An odd cup of some greenish stone had been found, rather like pea-soup carnelian. The state of the well had necessitated the transfer of Picus and Clarence for an indefinite stay. "You're done in this country if your well gives out. Wait till ours does." Carston was not interested. This might interfere with his making love to Scylla, which he had decided was to be his expression of a successful visit. Unless he found out how to use it.

Then Ross produced the cup suddenly, out of his pocket, and handed it round. Carston said:

"That means nothing to me."

"Been cut by hand," said Felix. "Is there a kind of opaque flint glass? Keltic twiddles, I think, very worn round the rim."

A good deal was told Carston, casually, about Kelts and Saxons and Romans and early Christianity; things completely over so far as he knew—Not that they talked about what he hadn't heard. Only they talked as if there was no time, no progress, no morality. He knew, of course, that there was no progress, and no morality.

Then Ross said, roughly and softly, as though he was loving something:

"The thing was that we fished it out with a spear."

Scylla said: "Ross, that's odd."

Clarence fidgeted attentively. Felix stared, and Carston saw the boy's tricky brilliant eyes light up. Picus was grave, a man so tall and thin he seemed to go on for ever. Unnaturally supple, he had seen him pick up something behind him as if it had been in front. He tried to think what a spear had to do with it.

Felix said, sharply:

"Good old Freud."

"Idiot!" said Ross, and turned away furious and contemptuous.

"It seems to me," said Scylla, "that people had to start some way of thinking of things. What they saw once they'd learned to think might be quite different from the things they'd learned on."

Then, to Carston, she said that odd things were always happening, and old patterns repeated themselves. That it was sometimes alarming when they did, and Freud very useful in the case of irrational fear. Very true, too, when there had been a row, and no one could feel what was just or what was not. Always look out for the suppressed wish that's taken the wrong turning. But that what had happened to-day was objective and odd.

Carston said:

"I think I'll have to ask you to explain a little more than that."

But Ross had turned round again. "I'm awfully sorry," he said. The insolent insincerity was not meant to be lost on Carston, but it was. "Put it down to the solstice or the heat."

"Tell us the news," said Felix. "We couldn't get back without our tea. Ross believes in perspiration. I don't."

Carston had come with elaborations of the best gossip. They listened to him—rather too attentively, he thought. At the same time there was something that spoiled his effects. It was the place, the faintly lit room mixing with the starlight outside. A shallow little green dish was lying among the glasses. Might have been made out of star-material. The woman had called it a diversion, but they weren't going to let him play. He began to dislike them, wish to humiliate them. Far too troubled to think how to do it.

Even Ross saw there was something wrong when he left them and went up to bed.

But this Carston had seen. Four ways of saying the woman good-night. Ross nodded to her. Felix embraced her. Clarence kissed her gallantly, with a flourish indicating affectionate indifference to their difference of sex. Picus, busy with a syphon, crooked his fore-finger at her across the room (19–22).

The next day, following up on this astonishing and annoying event of the cup and the confusing responses to it, Carston turns to Felix for information:

> "Tell me more about your friends."
>
> "Picus is Clarence' 'old man of the sea' only he's young. Clarence doesn't know it. Scylla says I'm hers. He only does one or two small things like whistling, but he does them perfectly. Riding and blowing birds' eggs. You saw how powerful his body is, but he's like a bird. Off in a flash. Hence the name. Picus was the Woodpecker.
>
> "Clarence fights for him and with him. What he fights for, I don't know. Clarence is quite all right. A bit insincere, because he's afraid. And what he's afraid of, I don't know" (24–25).

The passage tells the reader a great deal in spite of its being limited by Felix' innocence. We need to remember the "old man of the sea" in the *Arabian Nights* and that he climbed on Sinbad's back and, then, refused to get off after having been carried across a stream. Finally, Sinbad made him drunk and shook him off. In *Armed with Madness,* Scylla breaks the pattern of dependence which holds the two men together.

> Carston could only say: "Tell me more."
>
> "Scylla's a different egg. If there is anything wrong about my sister, it's everything. I've said the word 'fear' at least ten times lately. This time it's my own." He horrified Carston—he was like a desperate butterfly, angry, petulant and white.—"It's she at one end, and Picus at the other, who get me going. It's because she wants everything to happen to its last possibility. That's how she gets kick out of life. Once a thing's got going, she'll understand it and manage it. And enjoy it. She'll never tone it down. Sort of woman who'd have mothered the house of Atreus, and though I owe her everything, it's wasted on me. She'll enjoy—"
>
> "What will she enjoy?"
>
> "What will happen out of what happened yesterday.

> Don't you see? That infernal Picus is a psychic if there ever was one. Or if there is such a thing."
>
> "Does she believe in that?"
>
> "Believing doesn't trouble her. Only what is going to happen. She doesn't create situations. She broods them and they hatch. And the birds come home to roost. Some mighty queer birds. Truth isn't everyone's breakfast egg. She isn't happy till it's hatched. Calls it knowing where you are. I wish I knew where I was—" (25–26).

I have stopped over the associative nature of Mary Butts's use of names, and it is necessary to do so again: "Picus was the Woodpecker," as Felix has told us. This is the first mention in the novel of the peculiar provenance of this character's name. He is "like a bird"—"Off in a flash"—"Hence the name." Carston lets the matter pass. We know pīcus is one of the birds used in augury (Plautus)—a woodpecker, and we may remember Pīcus, son of Saturn, king of the aborigines of pre-Latin Italy and prophet who for spurning Circe was turned into a woodpecker (Ovid and Virgil). Such archaic elements require attention because they colour the characterization and inform the imagery.

Carston then continues to ask about Scylla whom he considers his primary interest until the Grail involves him also.

> Carston revised his ideas again about Scylla as a lover. He could only say: "But what can she and your friend Picus make out of what happened yesterday, anyhow?"
>
> "Don't you see? It was fishing it out of the well with that old spear—they always went together."
>
> "What went with what?"
>
> "The cup of the Sanc-Grail, of course. It and the spear, they always hunted in couples. You've heard of it. All sexual symbolism. I wish I hadn't."
>
> "Does sexual symbolism get you?" It would be news if it did.
>
> "I should worry. But the Sanc-Grail was a very funny thing. People used to think it was a shallow greenish dish. Those well-shafts on the downs might be any age. So

> might it. Tollerdown had a bad reputation, and I never heard of the Sanc-Grail doing anyone any good. With that moron Picus behind it, and that demon, my sister, in front of it."
>
> Carston took stock of several things: what he remembered of the Grail story, the possibility of anyone behaving as if it had happened, and what that implied in human character. Felix' youth.
>
> He said at last:
>
> "Don't tell me your sister is superstitious."
>
> "Not she. Better if she was. She'd read it up and do processions and things. It might be like that. But with her it won't get its home comforts. It will get vision."
>
> On the last four words he changed, and Carston saw the sister in the brother, in the elegant, frightened boy now explaining that what he wanted was not vision, but fashionable routine (26–27).

Such conversations not only delineate the quick changes of personality that fascinate Mary Butts—here, Felix' resistance to sexuality, his own and that of others, and Carston's slowly increasing awareness—they also forward the contemporary tension of the sacred as it belongs to imaginative life.

This tension increases as it is enacted by the characters—some of them named for ancient and archaic sanctities—and as they respond to their memories of medieval English Grail stories. Two scenes seem especially important. Ross goes up a hill to paint:

> Then he whistled as he drew, out of tune, but as though he was loving something. No nonsense about being the thing he loved, but like a lover, aware of the presence of what he loved everywhere.

Just so much is given us to suggest the special knowledge that had earlier eluded Scylla. Suddenly,

> There was a hard, explosive sound. Several mixed noises. A bird tore out of a thicket and crossed an open

> space, indirectly, frantically, and disappeared. He imitated its call and burst out laughing. "Woodpecker up to his tricks again." Then he went back to his work, straining his eyes (32).

We do not know that Picus of the novel is responsible, nor do we ever find out, but we do know that the Latin *pīcus* was a trickster. In addition, this is a kind of warning—mysteriously understood by Ross—well before we find out that Picus has tricked them all, for it is Picus who arranges to bring the spear and the cup together when Felix goes down into the well.

In the second scene, a doctor has come to check on Picus' health.

> The doctor said:
>
> "Shew me the cup you got out of the well."
>
> And when he had looked at it: "The luck of the country's with you. I'm glad to find a few roman pots. It isn't glass at all, too heavy. I think it's jade. It may have been set once. I tell you, it might have been the cup of a chalice." Intelligent interest. Carston felt quite friendly now towards the thing. The others were giving polite attention. Five people at once thinking about a spear. No, six. He was.
>
> "One has time to remember things, shooting about this country in a Ford. Do you know it makes me think of what I remember of the cup of the Sanc-Grail?"
>
> Picus said, meekly: "What was that?"
>
> Carston thought: 'How was that camp, or wasn't it? Would one of them pick up the challenge? Of course, it was a challenge.' Ross said: "That's a long story," but Scylla leaned forward, excited, and said: "The best way to get that story out is for everyone to say what he thinks or feels or remembers. The Freud game really. Start, Felix!"
>
> "Tennyson," said Felix.
>
> "Oh, my dear," said Clarence, "those awful pre-Raphaelite pictures put me off it long ago."
>
> Ross said: "A mass said at Corbenic."

"Wagner," said the doctor.

"A girl carrying it," said Carston, staring at Scylla and trying to play.

Scylla said: "*Quod inferius, sicut superius est.*"

Picus said: "You haven't told me much."

"Second round," said Scylla,—"people enlarge on what they said before."

"I said Tennyson," said Felix, "because I hate the Keltic twilight. And nearly all its works. I hate it because it's a false way of telling about something that exists. No, a messy way. Responsible for the world's worst art. Now and then it nearly comes off. Milton left it alone, and I don't blame him. Tennyson made it idiotic with his temperance knights. Fixed it, too, enough for parody. Killed the unstated thing which I don't mind telling you scares me."

Clarence said: "I agree with Felix. I can't stand bad drawing."

Ross said: "At Corbenic, wherever that was, there was a different mass. It may have been the real thing."

The doctor said: "Parsival is like a great religious service to me."

Carston, embarrassed at his turn coming, saw their pained faces. He said: "I supposed the girl who carried it was the female spirit of life."

Scylla said: "I quote again: '*Here lies the Woodpecker who was Zeus.*'"

"Thank you," said Picus (37–39).

All the elements of the narrative are brought together almost violently in this exchange, whether or not the reader thinks that Scylla has taken the part of trickster. A certain amount of confusion is the result for both the characters and the reader, but I want to point out that this is part of the operational magic of the book—a concurrence and competition of layers of meaning. The history of the modern Grail is reflected from Tennyson to Wagner. Each character, except for Picus who is slyly noncommittal, expresses some tentative relation to the original spirituality that the Grail represented. The doctor's taste is for the dramatic and ritualistic in religious matters, but we know so little about him that we can only trust his curiosity about the cup and try to measure his love of Wagner's *Parsifal.* The words "a great religious service" seem carefully chosen, though the service is hardly to be considered conventional. In contrast, Ross's suggestion that there was once a "real" mass—presumably with reference to transubstantiation—expresses contemporary loss. The doctor effectively brings the most important modern imagination of the Grail story—"like a belated inheritance," in Pierre Boulez' words—into the novel.[17] (*Parsifal* was first performed in 1882.) Again, I believe we need to stop—this time over Wagner's overwhelming presence in modern thought about the Grail. The doctor may represent the ordinary Wagnerite since he appears to hold the mistaken view that *Parsifal* is Christian. The knights of the Grail have been greatly modified when compared to those of Wagner's principal source, Wolfram von Eschenbach's thirteenth-century *Parzival,* and, as Martin Gregor-Dellin has noted, "the Grail itself has been divested of its Eucharistic function."[18] The doctor's remarks may simply reflect a modern sentiment for religion or a religious aestheticism. Still, I cannot help but think of Nietzsche's surprising recognition of the *Parsifal* Prelude: "Supreme psychological assurance with regard to what is intended to be said, expressed, *communicated*. . . . Such things exist in Dante, but nowhere else. Did ever a painter portray so melancholy a loving gaze as Wagner does with the final accents of his prelude?"[19]

Carston's view is perhaps the most twentieth-century and anthropological. Clarence, who will be driven mad in his helplessness, unlike Felix with whom he says he agrees, is attached to the merely stylish and mannered, a voice out of the 'twenties that could dismiss in the name of a newer, more geometric art, pre-Raphaelite, *art nouveau* and symbolist alike. Felix, with characteristic emotional energy, points to a profound aspect of all the Grail legends that whatever they were about was unstated—"Killed the unstated thing"—which leads to the modern arguments about Keltic sources and vegetation myths.

Scylla's responses are more gamesome and complex, in part because she has a clear motive—the winning of Picus. Her point is to push the edge, as Felix has warned us. Her first rather imperious and priestly sounding remark is a quotation from the most important of alchemical texts, the *Tabula Smaragdina,* the Emerald Table of Hermes Trismegistus. The complete quotation reads in translation:

> What is below is like that which is above, and what is above is like that which is below, to accomplish the miracles of one thing.[20]

It is striking that Scylla quotes from the Latin in which the text comes down to us—(the original text was probably Greek and may date back to the first or second centuries of the Christian era).[21] And it is remarkable that Scylla quotes only one half of this famous formula: "What is below (inferius) is like that which is above (superius)." In so doing, she does not complete the alchemical formulation of the unity of all things; instead, she leaves the other characters and the reader with a fundamental statement of correspondence, understood, so to speak, from below whatever spiritual or transcendent is above. Scylla's phrase brings into the novel the ambiance of the Hermetic tradition—"a magical attitude to life." Titus Burckhardt, an engaged scholar of this tradition, remarks:

> The perspective of Hermetism proceeds from the view that the universe (or macrocosm) and man (or the microcosm) correspond to one another as reflections; whatever there is in the one, must also in some manner be present in the other. This correspondence may best be understood by reducing it to the mutual relationship of subject and object, of knower and known. The world, as object, appears in the mirror of the human subject.[22]

In Frances Yates's words, "the famous *Emerald Table,* the bible of the alchemists . . . gives in mysteriously compact form the philosophy of the All and the One."[23] But the tradition was not originally philosophical, however we abstract it; rather, it was a perceptual practice by way of image, metaphor and symbol. With this magical attitude in mind, one begins to reread some of the characters: Ross's love, which we have already noted, for example, probably represents an aspect of this view, and we return to Felix' remark that his sister would "read up on it and do processions and things," leading to "vision"—whatever that may turn out to be. Vision in Mary Butts's work repeatedly leads to a *dynameis* of experience, conflictual, creative, and harsh, rather than comfortable.

The novelist would have been fully cognizant of the controversy surrounding the lore of the *Hermetica* and of the occult tradition that derives from it, not only alchemy, but Cabbala, Tarot, Rosicrucianism, astrology, magic, theosophy, and the various texts of the mystery religions, Egyptian, Eleusinian and gnostic. What is often considered the "muck" of "religious back-waters." This disreputation sets aside the true imaginative value of such sources. She, born in 1890, like her peers, inherited the turmoil of belief and disbelief of the nineteenth century along with its literature and scholars. One thinks immediately of A. E. Waite's *Lives of the Alchemical Philosophers* (1888) and *The Hermetic and Alchemical Writings of Aureolus Philippus Theophrastus Bombast, of Hohenheim, called Paracelsus the Great* (1894), of J. Ferguson's *Bibliotheca Chemica* (1906), and of G.R.S. Mead's *Thrice-Greatest Hermes* (1906)—perhaps also E.A. Wallis Budge's *The Gods of the Egyptians* (1904)—to name only the most obvious whose influence remains current among those whose concern is with the lore of the human mind and imagination.[24] Such studies come into the play of imagination because they represent an anthropology faced with the direct imagination of a cosmos which is not a doctrine, an objectification, or abstraction. Such thought is always by way of protest against definition and determination, whether social or religious—Robert Duncan's "unregenerate archaic subscriptions." Duncan, discussing Allen Upward, writes of a time when "religion and childhood phantasy—the Christ and the Wizard King—are seen anew in the light of comparative folklore and the new anthropology. . . ."

> Anthropology, even as it presented itself in late nineteenth-century thought as having the grown-up authority of a science, was also a development of the early nineteenth-century Romantic Vision of Man with its poetic and spiritualizing revaluations both of the Christian enthusiasms of the Seventeenth Century and of the Classical rationalism of the Eighteenth Century Enlightenment. Man—it was to be the persuasion of the new Sciences of Man—in his religions, even as in his dreams and in his romances and phantastic fictions, was everywhere at work to create at once a Self-Reality and a World -Reality.[25]

After Isaac Casaubon in 1614 dated the *Hermetica*—"though there may have been a man called Hermes Trismegistus of hoary antiquity, the *Hermetica* cannot have been written by any such person"—academic reason made the subject increasingly disreputable.[26] The battle for "reality"—first seen to be crucial in the poetry of William Blake—was given over to objectivity. Though the Hermetic tradition continued to be voiced, out of the Renaissance, well into our own century, the ability to understand this ancient and modern imagination of reality came increasingly to be more "occult"—"embarrassing," Auden said of this side of Yeats's work—until even the reputations of the scholars of it, such as Mead and Waite, were deprecated.[27] Mary Butts joins her peers in the use of this material—Yeats, Pound, and H.D. are the most obvious. (We should also, I think, recall such figures as A. R. Orage and especially Allen Upward whose work she is likely to have known.) She also had a strong interest in most things French and had lived in Paris, which suggests that she may have known the work of Sâr Péladan (1858–1918), such as his odd and cranky *Le Secret du Troubadour* which Pound had reviewed in 1906.[28] I also note that Péladan had himself established an Ordre de la Rose Croix du Temple et du Sanct Graal. Thus the combination of the Hermetic tradition with the Holy Grail was not unprecedented, but there is another precursor closer to home and to the new anthropology that we will consider shortly.

The lore of this multifarious tradition should be better known and acknowledged for what it is: a continuous activity of direct participation in the divine—the old sacred of the world that did not objectify reality or leave personal experience to a lonely, singular subjectivity. Its central concern is the activity of subject and object in the largest terms—cosmological and epistemological, which are not pretentions of art but fundamental to art. Mary Butts chooses the magical aspect of this old tradition—in personal lives to disturb and transform any singular dullness, and in a sense of the world to know that it is alive—so the gramophone plays to the wood. This "disreputable" side of Mary Butts's work is not simply nonsense. Her sense of magic is skillful at the same time that it is modernly tentative. In an essay of 1932, she writes:

> Magic has not yet been properly defined. In its *practise* it is, of course, very largely primitive science, misunderstandings by false analogy of the way things work, of natural law. But behind that there seems to remain a very peculiar kind of awareness, an awareness modified and sometimes lost by people whose life has been passed in towns. It is most difficult to describe. It has something to do with a sense of the invisible, the non-existent in a scientific sense, relations between things of a different order: the moon and a stone, the sea and a piece of wood, women and fish.[29]

In other words, the imagination and character of difference—what I have called a relational imagination which will have profound consequences in twentieth-century art.

This "awareness" is fundamental to a cultural conflict that continues into the present, involving the use and abuse of the human imagination. Blake is the first and greatest warrior of this conflict. His "mental fight" first clearly draws attention to the issue—that subject and object must meet, and it is in art that such a meeting is possible. Blake himself chose Newton to represent the contraction of reality—"Single vision and Newton's sleep." But the contraction goes back to the quarrel with the Hermetic tradition, as Frances Yates's distinguished studies inform us.

> In his eagerness to establish a purely objective view of nature as a mechanism, in his enthusiasm for pure mathematics as the only safe tool for objective enquiry, Descartes was left with the problem of mind somewhat embarrassingly on his hands. He provisionally solved the problem in a very crude way, by his so-called dualism, "one world consisting of a huge mathematical machine, extended in space; and another world consisting of unextended thinking spirits. And whatever is not mathematical or depends at all on the activity of thinking substance ... belongs to the latter." Descartes even assigns an actual place in the body, the conarium or part of the brain, to this "thinking substance" which has to deal with everything which is not part of the vast external machine. This strangely inadequate way of dealing with mind did not long remain unquestioned and since Descartes' day many philosophers and thinkers have struggled with the problem of knowledge, of epistemology, of the relation between mind and matter. Nevertheless, this bad start of the problem of knowledge has never been quite made up. About the external world, man has discovered ever more and more. About his own mind, why he can reflect nature in it and deal with nature in it in this amazing way, he has made much less progress.
>
> Why was Descartes so contemptuous, even one might

> think, so afraid of the *mens* that he wanted to park it by itself, out of the way of the mechanical universe and mathematics? Might not this be because of the struggle of his world to emerge from "Hermes Trismegistus" . . . and all that he stood for? The basic difference between the attitude of the magician to the world and the attitude of the scientist to the world is that the former wants to draw the world into himself, whilst the scientist does just the opposite, he externalises and impersonalises the world by a movement of will in an entirely opposite direction to that described in the Hermetic writings, the whole emphasis of which is precisely on the reflection of the world in the *mens*. Whether as religious experience or as magic, the Hermetic attitude to the world has this internal quality.
>
> Hence, may it not be supposed, when mechanics and mathematics took over from animism and magic, it was this internalisation, this intimate connection of the *mens* with the world, which had to be avoided at all costs. And hence, it may be suggested, through the necessity for this strong reaction, the mistake arose of showing the problem of mind to fall so completely out of step and so far behind the problem of matter in the external world and how it works. Thus, from the point of view of the history of the problem of mind and of why it has become such a problem through the neglect of it at the beginning of the modern period, "Hermes Trismegistus" and his history is important.... In any case we ought to know the history of what they discarded, if only to understand the motives which lay behind the triumph of mechanism. And that history uncovers the roots of the change which came over man when his mind was no longer integrated into the divine life of the universe. In the company of "Hermes Trismegistus" one treads the borderlands between magic and religion, magic and science, magic and art or poetry or music. It was in those elusive realms that the man of the Renaissance dwelt, and the seventeenth century lost some clue to the personality of that *magnum miraculum*.[30]

I have quoted at length this summary view both because it helps to clarify my own argument and because I believe the disreputation of this material may have tended to put Yates's work aside also.

In the four years between *Armed with Madness* and her essay *Traps for Unbelievers* (1932), it is clear that Mary Butts continued to study the magical and religious aspects of her concern, but with the new anthropology in hand. This essay is a major statement of her modern view: "The word Religion, with its vast connotations, is working its way into the category of shame-making or obscene":

> But with all this discarding, man, whether he likes it or not, whether he thinks about it or not, has been forced back (and that was the last thing he bargained for) onto the final, inescapable, and implacable question: "Is there anything there or not?" Anything at all? Or has the whole vast various structure been built out of nothing but my misunderstandings of phenomena and my suppressed wishes?[31]

One notices the characteristic, modernist concern with the loss of the old definition of being, the old metaphysical or God, but with that I wish to return to the magic of her imagination.

The "Freud game" passage in which Scylla insistently affirms the alchemical-magical tradition when faced with a possible Grail is rich in implication. In so doing, she proposes an interpretation of the Grail, that it is—in the words of the later essay, adapting a vocabulary from the new anthropology—the "Mana" or "virtus" of things:

> What a man or a woman will, if put to it, have no nonsense about, is the question of the "virtus" common and proper to both, their virility, courage, the source of each of their separate virtues. The best name for it is "Mana," the word which science has taken from the Polynesians; that which gives a man or a woman potency in every act or situation.[32]

The Grail, then, of the novel—"the unstated thing"—has to do with energy, act, and intelligence:

> Where a modern might ask: "What is it?" the medieval mind asked: "What must it have been?" No sacred object was conceivable outside of Christianity; therefore the search was for a known Christian relic with which it could be identified. By no later than 1200 two conflicting explanations had been advanced. One claimed that it was the cup with which Joseph of Arimethea caught the blood of Christ as it flowed down from His crucified body; in which case, the lance of the story was the lance of the soldier Longinus who pierced the side of the crucified Christ. The second claimed that it was the cup with which Jesus instituted the Eucharist at the Last Supper, and it was this second explanation which was to prevail among writers after 1225 or so. Meanwhile there was the confusing word "graal." Around 1200, the monk Helinandus of Beauvais sought in vain for a Christian tradition of the Grail, but his statements affirm the existence in Old French of a common noun "graal." It signified, he said, "a broad, deep dish," a kind of platter, and was derived from Latin "gradalis" or "gradale" because such dishes were "pleasing" (grata) to guests![33]

And so the unstated—even unstateable—is the issue for the modern mind. In *Armed with Madness,* Carston questions Scylla directly, rather than Felix:

> "And the new name for all this is our subconscious minds. And between Freud and Aquinas, I've managed to tell you about it completely wrong. For another of its names is intellectual beauty, and another, the peace of God."
>
> "D'you believe in God?"
>
> "I don't know. All we do know is what happens to faith based on catch-as-catch-can visions."
>
> "Weren't all religions based on that?"
>
> "They were, and look at them! But now you see why we felt we were being laughed at, dangerously, when we lifted that cup out of a well on the point of a spear?"
>
> Carston pulled himself together. "What did you mean by the other thing: '*Here lies the Woodpecker who was Zeus*'?"
>
> "A little poetry, a little witchery, a little joke. It's the

> same thing as I said before. Now I'll tell you something worse than what I said before.
>
> "Along with faith fit for people like us, and good taste which are where morals end, there is no goodwill left anywhere in the world. Which started to go first, or if they all went together, or which pushed the other out, I don't know. I've an idea that something else, a principle we haven't named yet, got rid of the lot."
>
> Beginnings for an erotic conversation (41–42).

This last sentence is, of course, Carston's wry sense of the canny conversation with Scylla. Carston, as a character, always presents a near stereotype of the American who has lost all memory of the past: he belongs to the new, the direct, the simply sexual, until late in the novel; it is he who resolves as much of the Grail trick as is possible, a true modern Grail knight in that he asks the right questions.

Though Carston asks those questions, Scylla's answers on one level merely tease—"a joke," perhaps. (I think of a quotation Butts uses elsewhere: "Mais comme tu taquines éternité.") On another level, her remarks turn about the darkness of modern meaning—God become the unstated thing. She is sharp, bitter, and troubled, much as she was in her ruminations on the way to meet Carston.

Scylla has subtly shown her understanding of the whole business in her emphasis on "below" in the quotation from the *Emerald Table.* She has, if we could only follow—and she wants that possibility to be difficult and mysterious—indicated that the high mystery of the Grail is here at work among them, dangerously and laughingly; with the erudite reference to Picus the Woodpecker, she has, while mystifying everybody except Picus, tipped him off to the fact that she knows he is the trickster. Carston continues to question her:

> "Stay a minute. Maybe it's because I have no memories, but I don't see where the fun comes in."

> "Don't you call it fun to watch how violently, strangely and in character people will behave? Watch Ross, watch Clarence. Watch me." He was watching her (43).

Seriousness and laughter interplay in Mary Butts, even cruelly. But Carston's necessary question leads back to "Here lies the Woodpecker who was Zeus." With those words, bird-magic enters the layered meaning of the novel, and such magic leads directly to a chapter in Jane Harrison's *Themis* (1912, 2nd ed. 1927), a brilliant example of the new anthropology and of the new reading of the ancient world. There the mysterious phrase, as cited in Suidas, is given and translated: ενεάδε κεῖταλ θανὼν ... Πῖκος ὁ καὶ Ζεύς.

> —*"Here lies dead the Woodpecker who also is Zeus."*[34]

Scylla's version is carefully edited, removing the word "dead" and changing the tense to the past. The original suggests an ancient mythic event in which Zeus displaces or assimilates an indigenous Pīcus. The quotation has obviously been adapted to the magic of the narrative. Picus "lies" both because he is present and, in the tradition of Pīcus, the magician and trickster, he is lying in the matter of the cup. Picus who "was" Zeus is now the Picus of their own lives, setting off the recurring pattern of the search for the Grail.

Jane Harrison's discussion of Picus occurs in the chapter on magic, and she begins with a consideration of the word itself: "The word Μαδεία from which our word magic is derived was, among the Greeks of the classical days, never really at home." Yet, she notes that "the first dialogue that bears the name of Alcibiades" contains a surprising definition of the term. Of the four Persian "Royal paedagogues" chosen for their virtues—the wisest, the most just, the most prudent, the bravest—it is the wisest who teaches the magic (Μαδείαν) of Zoroaster. And it is Socrates who surprises when he explains: "The art of the magician is the service (Θεραπεία) of the gods." Harrison remarks that "... in primitive Greece, as in Persia, magic had to do, if not with divinities (Θεοί), yet at least with things divine, with sanctities (Τὰ Θεῖα) . . . ." She reminds us of Picus in Aristophanes (*The Birds,* 480), in Vergil (*Aeneid,* VII. 170 ff), and in Ovid (*Metamorphoses,* XIV. 6 and *Fasti,* III). "Picus and Faunus are not regular *dei* like Jove, they are *numina,* spirits, genii, a bird spirit and a wood-spirit; like the Tree-King who watched over the Golden Bough, they haunt the dark groves."[35] Her argument that there existed sanctities before the anthropomorphic gods of sacrifice, suits Mary Butts's sense that we have returned to sanctities, personal and natural, unnamed things. Harrison concludes her remarks on indigenous Picus:

> Finally Picus enshrines a beautiful lost faith, the faith that birds and beasts had *mana* other and sometimes stronger than the *mana* of man. The notion that by watching a bird you can divine the weather is preceded by the far more primitive notion that the bird by his *mana* actually makes the weather, makes and brings the rain, the thunder, the sunshine and the spring. Beasts and birds in their silent, aloof, goings, in the perfection of their limited doings are mysterious still and wonderful. We speak of zoomorphic or theriomorphic or ornithomorphic *gods,* but again we misuse language. Birds are not, never were, gods: there is no definite bird-cult, but there are an infinite number of bird-sanctities.[36]

Picus, she argues, can be seen in Ovid to have been preempted by the thunderer Zeus, but the name becomes a title of Zeus. The history of the curious Greek phrase which Scylla adapts to her purposes is complex:

> Picus himself, according to the Byzantine syncretizers, knew that he was really Zeus. 'When he handed over the western part of his kingdom he died at the age of 120, and when he was dying he gave orders that his body should be deposited in the island of Crete, and that there should be an inscription:
>
> '*Here lies dead the Woodpecker who also is Zeus.*'[37]

Crete is, of course, Zeus's ancient birthplace, indicating that the Greeks had never lost their sense that their gods were born of the earth. One can hear Mary Butts's laughter and feel her delight in the wildness of this history of the divine. She then prepares it again, through Scylla, in *Armed with Madness.*

Jane Harrison's work leads us, in turn, to another great example of the new anthropology, A. B. Cook's *Zeus: A Study of Ancient Religion* (1914). Cook comments at length on the strange history of the phrase Πῖκος ὁ καὶ Ζεὺς which cannot be traced beyond the second century—a "wild farrago" of world history put together by Byzantine chroniclers. But Cook notes:

> In weighing ... various hypotheses we must not lose sight of the fact that Πῖκος ὁ καὶ Ζεὺς is consistently said to have been buried in Crete. Now the Idaean Cave has yielded a *tympanon* of the ninth or eighth century B.C., which represents the youthful Zeus or Zagreus in definitely Assyrian guise.... Moreover, we have seen reason to surmise that at *Hagia Triada* the soul of the prince embodying this deity took the form of a jay (*pica*)—a bird whose bright plumage suggested comparison with the woodpecker (picus).... It is, then, conceivable that the phrase Πῖκος ὁ καὶ Ζεὺς finds its ultimate explanation in an actual Cretan cult, and that this cult was known, at least by tradition, to the chronographer who first tacked the history of Rome on to that of Assyria. When Euelpides in Aristoph. *av.* 480 spoke of Zeus as 'soon destined to restore the sceptre to the Woodpecker,' it was no mere flight of fancy but a genuine piece of folk-belief....[38]

Indeed, it is Cook who begins the investigation of the phrase by calling attention to it in 1903, to be followed by Jane Harrison in 1912, W. R. Halliday's *Greek Divination* (1913), and J. Rendel Harris' *Picus Who Is Also Zeus* (1916). It is fascinating to trace the fun of what Mary Butts is likely to have read and then to note the serious side of her interest in archaic awareness.

The key to the violent combination of *Emerald Table,* Grail and ancient bird-magic, with which all these associations began, is, I believe, to be found in the work of still another scholar. Jessie Weston's studies of the Arthurian cycle may all have been important to Mary Butts's imagination, but it is *From Ritual to Romance* (1920) that seems particularly suggestive. This book draws upon a large range of the new scholarship, so important to twentieth-century writers, including direct reference to Sir James Frazer, Franz Cumont, Anrich, Jane Harrison, G. R. S. Mead, and Sir Gilbert Murray. Especially important is Harrison's commentary on a Cretan Hymn of the Kouretes, which is addressed to Zeus as a "full-grown youth," not to the "most unreasonable and ungovernable of the Olympians." This is, of course, "Zeus-of-the-birth-cave" whose nature seems so strange to those who know only the later strata of myth in which Kronian Zeus is an overpowering sky-deity. In Harrison, this example becomes striking evidence for an older, archaic sanctity that is part of an original relation to nature.[39] Ms. Weston's use of this to approach the "secret of the Grail" is complex in that her ultimate endeavour is to trace all mystery religions back to such archaic vitalities. In so doing, she searches out the earliest Christian material available to her, what she called the "Naassene Document"—and here she draws upon G. R. S. Mead who analyzed and translated the document in *Thrice-Greatest Hermes.* His chapter on "The Myth of Man in the Mysteries" takes up this document, which Hippolytus (c. 222 A.D.) incorporates into his *Refutation,* and argues that it is a palimpsest: "an original pagan source," a "working over by a Jewish mystic of the time of Philo" (1st century B.C.), and a "Subsequent working over by a Christian Gnostic (Naassene) in the middle of the second century A.D."—all this edited by the arch-enemy of the Gnostics, Hippolytus. Ms. Weston is especially impressed by Mead's summary remarks: "The claim of these Gnostics was practically that Christianity, or rather the Good News of the Christ, was precisely the consummation of the inner doctrine of the mystery institutions of all nations: the end of them all was the revelation of the mystery of Man."[40] Drawing from this and from Frazer and Harrison, among others who sought archaic human nature, Weston concludes her famous argument: "The Grail story is not *du fond en comble* the product of imagination, literary or popular. At its root lies the record, more or less distorted, of an ancient Ritual, having for its ultimate object the initiation into the secret of the sources of Life, physical and spiritual."[41] However much we are disinclined to turn to Weston nowadays for an "explanation" of the Grail story—she seems so unaware of the place of narrative and imagination in thought and of the sheer energy of language—her book was startling in its day for good reason. Mary Butts had only to follow her own bent in the imaginative use of this scholarship to set about a novel in which "the unstated thing" would become active in contemporary terms. "Old patterns repeat themselves," one character tells us, and we may note that they are sometimes dangerously new.

Mary Butts was twenty when Roger Fry's first post-impressionist show opened in London—that is, when modernism first came to England, of which Virginia Woolf, looking back in 1924, would say in a lecture at Cambridge: " . . . in or about December, 1910, human character changed." "Think how little we know about character—think how little we know about art."[42] Cézanne, Van Gogh, Gauguin, Matisse, Picasso, Redon, Signac, Seurat were a storm for the English mind. For Mary Butts, behind this was the commotion of Victorian and Edwardian change, held together by what Samuel Hynes calls "established orders" until 1914–1918:

> As it was, the trauma of 1914–1918 ended the garden party as swiftly and rudely as a shower of hail or a four-letter word. It did so most dramatically within the fighting forces, though only after a good deal of bloody fumbling; but it also ended the more gracious aspects of the age. After the war there was never again so much money in the hands of the wellborn.[43]

With the established orders weakened what was left to responsible minds was the inheritance of change that the Victorians had left them:

> Victoria's reign had been a triumphant Age of Science; advances in geology, biology, and physics had not only affected the way men thought about their physical environment but had altered men's ideas of their relation to that environment—had brought, that is, a new cosmology and a new conception of the nature of change. It had been a scientific revolution, and, as is often true of revolutions, the revolutionaries in their moment of victory saw only their successes and not the new problems that success had created.[44]

This revolution with its resultant new cosmology also required a new anthropology, bits and pieces of which I have been considering. Most of this anthropology goes unnoticed now by a later non-classical, more "scientific" and structuralist anthropology. And, it should be noted, cosmology, new or old—not simply a detached logic of epistemology—is a fundamental activity of art, even if it is understood as self-expression. A new cosmology was the issue and remains so for the twentieth century.

One gets a charming view of this matter from Virginia Woolf's essay "The Cosmos," a review of *The Journals of Thomas Cobden-Sanderson, 1879–1922,* which she wrote in 1926:

> "'And what is Cosmos, Mr. Sanderson?' asks Sister Edith. 'What is the meaning of the word?' And then I go off like a rocket and explode in the stars in the empyrean." These two volumes are full of the sparks that fell from that constantly recurring explosion. For Mr. Cobden-Sanderson was always trying to explain to somebody—it might be Professor Tyndall ("I gave him my own view of human destiny, namely, the ultimate coalescence of the human intellect in knowledge with its other self, the Universe"), it might be Mr. Churchill, it might be a strange lady whose motor-car had broken down on the road near Malvern—

> what the word Cosmos meant. . . . we are left asking, with Sister Edith: "But, Mr. Sanderson, how does one 'fly to the great Rhythm'? What is the extraordinary ring of harmony within harmony that encircles us; what reason is there to suppose that a mountain wishes us well or that a lake has a profound moral meaning to impart? What, in short, does the word Cosmos mean?" Whereupon the rocket explodes, and the red and gold showers descend, and we look on with sympathy, but feel a little chill about the feet and not very clear as to the direction of the road. . . ."My idea was magnificent; the act was ridiculous," he said. "Besides," he reflected, "nothing was explicable." And perhaps he was right.[45]

As Hynes observes, "Victorian science may have made metaphysics obsolete [still the work of our contemporary deconstructionists] but it had not destroyed men's metaphysical itch, and much of what one might generally call Edwardian science is concerned with the problem of restoring metaphysics to the human world."[46]

One effect of the new sciences, including the new anthropology, was that it implied and required a new psychology. We have seen Mary Butts, through Scylla and Felix, fooling around with Freud, which is not to say that she was not also serious. But the recognition of Freud came late to England, in fact, not until the War put his work to the proof.[47] Mary Butts was, thus, in the thick of the matter as she was writing. Nevertheless, she had available to her in her youth, the extraordinary work of Edward Carpenter and Havelock Ellis, which has a history of its own. As Samuel Hynes notes: "One field of scientific investigation in particular seemed to offer an escape from Darwinism—the field of mental events. Psychology . . . became in late-Victorian and Edwardian times the liberating movement in science, as the suffrage movement was in social relations, and socialism was in politics; and as such it attracted many of the same people."[48] We need to remember, in this context, that the Society for Psychical Research was founded in 1882, later to count both Freud and Jung as honorary members, and that the first English psychological journal, *The British Journal of Psychology,* begins in 1904, which, Hynes observes, withdrew from speculation "about the nature of sex"—"Edwardian England's principal contribution to modern psychology."[49] The acceptance of Freud in America came even later, and what Butts's editor Johns did not know and could not understand was the fact that something else was at work in her milieu. She may have known Carpenter's pamphlets of the 'nineties: for example, *Woman and her place in a free society* and *Homogenic Love and its place in a free society* (1896), but the influence of his *Love's Coming of Age* (1906) she can hardly have missed. The something else at work is likely, in part, to have been derived from Carpenter: "he sought human freedom, and when he wrote about sex it was about the sexual implications of the whole liberation of men."[50] His is the first voice of this in the English speaking world—except, once again, Blake. Carpenter's is also the first defense of homosexuality. There was also Havelock Ellis's great work in seven volumes, *Studies in the Psychology of Sex* (1897–1928). Ellis, with whom H. D. would work, sums up his own sense of his achievement:

> I had done mankind a service which mankind needed, and which, it seemed, I alone was fitted to do. I had helped to make the world, and to make the world in the only way that it can be made, the interior way, by liberating the human spirit.[51]

However their contribution to later psychology is judged, they were pioneers and prophets who had spoken to one part of Mary Butts's life and art.

* * * * *

In order to clarify the interplay of all these intellectual and spiritual concerns in Mary Butts's work and before I turn to the final scene of *Armed with Madness,* I want to draw attention to a few passages in the essay of 1932, *Traps for Unbelievers:*

> Jung has something to say about the value, the possibly unexhausted value, of classic religious symbolism and myth. It used to be fashionable to think that they had survived because of the motifs they supplied to the arts; we know now that it is more true to say that it was the quality of the belief which produced the works, and that each religion gets the art it deserves.
>
> What sort of religion was it? . . . Then came the rise of anthropology and the science of comparative religions, and we have learned how to take fresh stock, compare Zeus with Jehovah, Aphrodite with Ashtaroth, and the pair of them with the Virgin; re-state Athene as a "functional daimon," as a vegetation spirit, as a totem, as a Luck; as an owl, as a feminist, as a wish-fulfillment; compare Orpheus and Osiris as Saviours, and both with Christ. It was a re-examination of extraordinary possibilities and value. Its exaggeration came from a desire to be primitive at all costs, to scour the cults and ceremonies for traces of totem-worship and fetish, for cannibalism and human sacrifice, for orgies and black magic, for exogamy and endogamy, and all the "gay science" of the anthropologist.[52]

Her critical mind goes over and over these new disciplines, never sentimental and never at rest.

> So far as christian [*sic*] theology is concerned, it is all a question of date. We are still only emerging from its forms, the bones of them sticking up all about us, still dripping wet from that sea; and determined, or presumably determined, to get dry as soon as possible. Like all lately rejected things, about which we feel self-conscious, Christianity is going through a period of tabu, of being one of the things which are not done.[53]

And she continues:

> So it would seem that the Gods, who for two thousand years have survived the organised forces of Christianity, are about to descend into a final twilight with their conqueror. As we have seen, they have not, like Christianity, become tabu, merely more and more symbolic, and what is more at the moment, artistically suspect. . . .[54]

We need only note, in this regard, her sensitivity, accurately outlined, to the growing positivism of scholarly thought and intellectual tradition.

Much of her concern seems involved in an analysis of the twentieth-century's translation of Renaissance humanism into a modern humanism of closure and its escape-hatch, power. Immediately following upon the remarks above comes one of Mary Butts's most prophetic and incisive admonitions:

> But the God to look out for is the God who does not put up a fight. His successes may not be spectacular, he has no hell up his sleeve, nor even much of a heaven. He is himself, for what he is worth. Take him or leave him, he makes no protest. Takes himself off, manifests himself in other ways, is called by another name. Until one is suddenly aware of him again, that his departure has been a feint, a trick that has been played on one by oneself.[55]

This is, I repeat, 1932, and this magical mind seems capable of reading European ideologies, including what was to happen to Communist practice, in a glass darkly. (Yeats's "Second Coming" which appears to go on coming is dated 1920.)

And who or what is this trickster that turns out to be ourselves?

> These Gods, "to whom a doubtful philosopher can pray, . . . as to so many radiant and heart-searching hypotheses," are no more and no less than so many descriptions man has made of himself. Descriptions that cover the ground pretty fully, the "subtle knot" retied, thread by thread. Man as an animal, as a prince, as a saviour, as a lover, as a phallos, as a warrior, as an artist, as a "magic,"

> a flash of the hidden forces in nature. The subdivisions are often exceedingly delicate. Put together it is difficult to find one aspect of human nature or occupation or desire which is not personated. And always, as Professor Murray points out, the trivial or base, the obscene or irrational, the mysterious or the merely obscure and tiresome elements, are subordinated and kept within bounds. Which is, after all, what man likes to think about himself and do with himself.[56]

This is not exactly the euhemerism that the Sicilian came up with around 300 B.C. because it is Man who is deified in this argument, not an historical person or event, and it is the Man who burst out of the nineteenth century to find only Himself. Some few pages later, she returns to her point of departure and to the magic of the meaning she wove into her work:

> We have seen the universal discredit of christian monotheism. In an age of violent transition and discovery its old weakness has appeared again, its insufficient insistence on the wild, enchanting, incalculable force in nature, the mana of things, the non-moral, beautiful, subtle energy in man and in everything else, on which the virtue of everything depends.[57]

"We are," she concludes,

> back in the historical situation which Nietzsche described of a people "for whom God is dead, and for whom no baby-god is yet lying in his cradle." Back where we were at Alexander's death, with an instinct that is more than an instinct, a habit of life and a necessity for us, unsatisfied. Back in the blind and primitive assertion of that instinct; running after Luck and awaiting Destiny, or indulging ourselves in an orgy of mana, stripped of the morals and even of the tabus which once made it serviceable. Or, if we must specialise, back with certain people of the Hellenistic Age, in "chic" cults of the least of other men's divinities.... In common with the christian, the classic mind at its best insisted that, though it was possible

> for the divine and the human to mix, "man is not God and it is no use pretending that he is".... Something not very far off the deification of man is on us now, not, or not yet, of the kings and millionaires, but, and again, and this is primitive, of the conspicuous young men and women, our sexually desirable ones, whose nature it is to wax and wane and be replaced. Our Year-in-Year-out spirits, *eniautoi daimones,* "whose beauty is no stronger than a flower."
>
> Human nature was not meant for that strain. The star-dust at Hollywood is full of dead stars. For the potency of the human god wanes, and his end is horror; rebirth, but for their human nature, terror. That is a story told in the Gospels as well as in *The Golden Bough.*[58]

One catches the translation of Frazer and Harrison into contemporary terms without Harrison's "beautiful lost faith" and a direction of vision very different from D. H. Lawrence's discovery of "blood-knowledge" in Frazer's *Totemism and Exogamy (Letters to Russell).* Nor does she here express herself as a companion of Bloomsbury, "the formulators," as Hynes puts it, "of that religion of art, intelligence, and human relationships that was born in Edwardian London and died in the Second World War."[59] She had, however, some respect from Virginia Woolf, for, having submitted an unnamed manuscript, she was invited to tea with Mrs. Woolf on Sunday, 29 October, 1922. It is also interesting to note that Virginia Woolf apparently intended to publish what must have been *Armed with Madness,* but rejected it for financial reasons: "Novels are the great bloodsuckers." In her *Diary* from which this information comes, Woolf seems interested in Mary Butts, but her judgment is clearly coloured by William Plomer's friend and Mary's brother, Anthony Butts. The entry for March 18, 1932, quotes him: "I cannot say anything of my sister—She is a bad woman—pretentious—I can see no merit in her books—pretentious. She corrupts young men. They are always committing suicide. She now has married Gabriel Atkins—without any character. They were given 25 decanters for their wedding." And Mrs. Woolf comments: "Tony is ashamed of Mary, who thus defiles the Butts blood." Many of these details are simply repeated by Goldring in *South Lodge.*

It is also notable in these passages from *Traps for Unbelievers* that they are preparation for her last two novels, *The Macedonian* (1933) and *Scenes from the Life of Cleopatra* (1935), which begin to track that "historical situation" by way of a life of Alexander, well founded on historical sources, and a feminist defense of the personality of Cleopatra who, of course, came to her position in Egypt as one result of the Macedonian's imperialism. Without biographical information, one can't be sure which came first, the essay or *The Macedonian,* since the preface to the latter is dated August, 1931. Still, I wish to say that her work is all of a piece, a deeply probing interrogation of an historical situation, which never ignores the "fun" that is part of the answer. *The Macedonian* closes with the death of Alexander, having delicately interwoven the characteristics of the public and private man:

> And Demosthenes was soon to say: "Alexander is not dead, for if he were, the whole earth would smell his body."
>
> But in the Serapeum, a priest sang:
>
> . . . .
>
> *"I praise him for his wars and quickness:*
> *"I praise him for his patience and far-seeing:*
> *"I praise him for his solitude and beauty:*
> *"I praise him for Clitus and Hephaestion:*
> *"I praise him for the fleet and the phalanx:*
> *"I praise him for Tyre and Alexandria:*
> *"I praise him for Arbela and Gedrosia:*
> *"I praise him for the East and the West.*
> *"I praise him that he is Alexander: and more than Alexander: and less.*

> *"I praise the Earth that she has restored to herself Alexander the Macedonian, son of Philip the Macedonian—being so nobly named—*
>
> *"That on her breast lies there*
> *he of the fairest-rare-*
> *hyacinth-curled hair,*
> *of the world famed."*[60]

This finely imagined hymn is no simple praise of the heroic; instead it is addressed to Earth who receives him and ends with the deft, personal touch of the "hyacinth-curled hair" reminding us of the boy from whose blood sprang the iris of that name, marked αἰαῖ, "alas, alas!" (Mary Butts carefully credits not only Murray on Greek religion, but also Harrison's *Prolegomena to the Study of Greek Religion* and *Themis* for helping to tell this tale.) We are also to remember the long tradition that in 324, Alexander "officially" requested the Greek cities to recognize him as a god and another tradition that Alexander believed in his own divinity. The novel is a study of the man Alexander and that edge of power which we have called "gods" and which so tempted him in Persia and Egypt—a range of energy very like what Mary Butts calls the virtue of things.

Near the end of *Traps for Unbelievers,* we come upon another aspect of the intelligence of her work, which she drew from Nietzsche. This may already have been noted in *Armed with Madness* where, in Scylla's meditation as she goes to meet Carston at Starn, we come upon the phrases "Revaluation of values" and "Discovery of new value, a different way of apprehending everything." A Nietzschean concern, for Mary Butts, is not pretentious—though it might seem so to society writers such as her brother, Plomer, and Goldring—nor does it set her apart; rather, it firmly places her in the context of the most important English effort to come to terms with the change that marks the end of the nineteenth century and the beginning of the twentieth. The modern philosopher, *par excellence,* had long been a part of English literary thought during her lifetime, for, in the words of one writer at the turn of the century, Nietzsche made possible "a new habitation for the imagination of man."[61] The first English translations of Nietzsche were of aphorisms and began in New York in 1889 and in London in 1891.[62] After overcoming obstacles, machinations and delays, the editor, Oscar Levy, published *The Complete Works of Friedrich Nietzsche,* the final eighteenth volume in 1913. This important event meant that the young writers of the day had the texts at hand and would no longer be dependent upon such popular, poisonous introductions as Max Nordau's *Degeneration,* first published in English in 1895, "coincident" with Oscar Wilde's trials, and reprinted in a "Popular Ed." in 1913 and 1920—a thoroughly reactionary view which appears to have had profound consequences for both popular and literary understanding. David Thatcher's indispensible study, *Nietzsche in England, 1890–1914,* discusses this in detail for the first time. He notes that Wilde, in Nordau's book, "finds himself in the distinguished company of the pre-Raphaelites, Whitman, Gautier, Baudelaire, Maeterlinck, Tolstoy, Ibsen, Wagner, Nietzsche, and almost everybody of artistic account in the late nineteenth century, the writers, in fact, whom Havelock Ellis had praised in *The New Spirit* (1890)."[63] Behind this reaction, then, we have, as already noted, the recognitions of Havelock Ellis and Edward Carpenter—both strongly literary—who present the beginnings of a renewed, revalued literary psychology. And central to this psychology is Nietzsche whose "transvaluation of values" both implies and argues a changed psychological ground. Thatcher draws attention to the way in which this problem is slipped over in such studies as John A. Lester's *Journey Through Despair, 1880–1914: Transformations in British Literary Culture* (1968):

> This was, Lester maintains, a time of confusion and bewilderment, of disillusion and malaise; the transition from materialistic determinism to a world of chance and change involved "the urgent and pained necessity of a

> 'transvaluation of values,' to keep man's imaginative life alive under conditions which seemed unlivable."

But, for all the weight here upon that famous phrase, Nietzsche, in Lester's discussion, becomes one of the symptoms rather than harbinger and guide. That literary minds took up the imagination of an indeterminate human nature, founded in change and chance—among them Mary Butts—both before and after the meeting with Nietzsche is a major aspect of the profound meditation of twentieth-century thought. Thatcher cites two important passages from Nietzsche on this transvaluation, both of them available to the enquiring Mary Butts:

> These weeks I have employed in 'transvaluing values.'—You understand this trope?—After all, the alchemist is the most deserving kind of man there is! I mean the man who makes of what is base and despised something valuable, even gold. He alone confers wealth, the others merely give change. My problem this time is rather a curious one: I have asked myself what hitherto has been best hated, feared, despised by mankind—and of that and nothing else I have made my 'gold,' (Letter to Brandes, May 23, 1888, London, 1914),

and Nietzsche's definition of the "transvaluation of values,"

> an emancipation from all moral values, in a saying of yea, and in an attitude of trust, to all that which hitherto has been forbidden, despised, and damned (*Ecce Homo* in *Collected Works, XVII,* 92).

This issue of values, which involves a psychology, a practice and an imaginative structure, has been painful to think about for decades. Mary Butts, like many of her peers, seems to have simplified the problematic of "crossing over" inferred in the prefix "trans." The term "revaluation" is common in discussions of Nietzsche then and now. In *Traps for Unbelievers,* she, like Yeats in "The Second Coming," seems to have stopped over the moment of terror—a necessary moment, I think, in all such thought and one in which one notices the constant interweaving of cultural condition and imagination in twentieth-century art.

Having been reminded, in Thatcher's words, of "Havelock Ellis's judgment that Nietzsche was one of the greatest spiritual forces to appear since Goethe," I turn back, briefly, to brushstroke the strength of Nietzsche's presence in English literary thought. Phyllis Grosskurth's recent biography of Ellis (1980) notices that his judgement of Nietzsche is largely based on early work, which is true, but it is hardly likely, setting aside *The Will to Power* and *Ecce Homo,* that *Thus Spoke Zarathustra* "had nothing to say to him," given, as she also notices, that his "reality" is "based on a biological structure."[64] This opening, more likely through Freud than Ellis, will have an extraordinary history in modern letters by way of Charles Olson, Robert Duncan, and Michael McClure. Nietzsche has, indeed, been difficult to come to terms with, in large part because of the fascist preemption of his work, which translated what is first a psychological condition and then a problem of meaning on every level of the human structure—Mary Butts's "historical situation"—into a monstrosity—her "terror." Only recently has a new effort been made to understand his influence on the modern imagination in such studies as Otto Bohlmann's *Yeats and Nietzsche* (1982), Ofelia Schutte's *Beyond Nihilism* (1984), and fundamentally, whether one is de-constructionist or not, Gilles Deleuze's *Nietzsche and Philosophy* (French, 1962; English, 1983). Deleuze:

> The sense of Nietzsche's philosophy is that multiplicity, becoming and chance are objects of pure affirmation. The affirmation of multiplicity is the speculative proposition, just as the joy of diversity is the practical proposition.[65]

The speculative character of modern art, especially writing, is often underestimated and undervalued. For Mary Butts and many another young writer, Nietzsche, in Thatcher's words, "was the philosopher *á la mode* in England between 1909 and 1913."[66] This influence grew dramatically with the appointment of A. R. Orage as co-editor of *New Age* in 1907—a socialist journal, one notes, and a factor in the hopes of the time. He was the author then of three books which have seldom been gauged, except by Thatcher, for their place in the modern imagination: *Friedrich Nietzsche: The Dionysian Spirit of the Age* (1906); *Nietzsche in Outline and Aphorism* (1907); and *Consciousness: Animal, Human, and Superman* (1907)—this last one, for us startlingly published by the Theosophical Publishing Co. of London. With his appointment to the *New Age,* he carried these concerns into the currency of periodical publication. Thatcher adds this up: "From May, 1907, until the end of 1913—a period of five and a half years—Nietzsche's name is hardly absent from the pages of the *New Age.*"[67]

I think of the extra-ordinary range of public and private concern represented by the *New Age* and of its authors, particularly Ezra Pound. There, one finds, to name only one instance, Pound's "I Gather the Limbs of Osiris," a series of essays on his "New Method of Scholarship," a method of "luminous detail," 1911–1912. Pound's "Obituary: A. R. Orage" (1934) and "In the Wounds (Memoriam A. R. Orage)" (1935) remember the importance of *New Age* to his welfare, but his praise of Orage himself is mainly subsumed under their companionship in Douglasite economic reform. In the latter, Pound writes: "I had no interest in Orage's mysticism and am unqualified to define it. I was thankful he had it simply because it kept him in action."[68] There can be no doubt that Pound's sense of process is the contrary of Orage's "mysticism," but, though I have no time to bear it out here, a bridge can be made by way of Allen Upward's *The Divine Mystery* which Pound read as "a history of the development of human intelligence."[69] It is important, I think, to our understanding of Mary Butts's compounded elements in *Armed with Madness* to notice—Orage as our example—

the connection between hermetical beliefs and Nietzsche, especially in the proposition of "Übermensch," best translated by Thatcher's "Beyond-Man."[70] That is to say, beyond the manhood so confused, determined and despairing that the arts had undertaken, along with Nietzsche, to answer with an undetermined imagination of human nature. Thatcher tells us that Orage's interest in Nietzsche began in 1900, following a chance meeting with Holbrook Jackson, "already an avid reader of *The Eagle and the Serpent*" (1898–1903), an early English, Nietzschean journal, and he cites Jackson's memory of what followed:

> We all developed supermania. He wanted a Nietzsche circle in which Plato and Blavatsky, Fabianism and Hinduism, Shaw and Wells and Edward Carpenter should be blended, with Nietzsche as the catalytic. An exciting brew.[71]

Such syncretism can be easily criticized, but it does demonstrate both the desperation and the effort of a new meaning. It is also an unprofessional and undisciplined response to the dialectics of Kant and Hegel.

More relevant to our literary interest here is, perhaps, a passage from Orage's *Friedrich Nietzsche: The Dionysian Spirit of the Age:*

> Friedrich Nietzsche is the greatest European event since Goethe. From one end of Europe to the other, wherever his books are read, the discussion in the most intellectual and aristocratically-minded circles turns on the problems raised by him. In Germany and in France his name is the war cry of opposing factions, and before very long his name will be familiar in England. Already half a dozen well-known English writers might be named who owe, if not half their ideas, at least half the courage of their ideas to Nietzsche. Ibsen seems almost mild by the side of him. Emerson, with whom he had much in common, seems strangely cool: William Blake alone among English writers

> seems to have closely resembled Nietzsche, and he who has read the *Marriage of Heaven and Hell,* and grasped its significance, will have little to learn from the apostle of *Zarathustra.*[72]

This led in turn to the affirmation of such affinity in *New Age* by its co-editor, Holbrook Jackson.[73] It is fair to say that the ability of twentieth-century readers to read Blake begins here. Without the necessary biographical underpinnings, I can only guess and speculate, but based on Mary Butts's autobiography, *The Crystal Cabinet* (1937), covering only her childhood, I can say with some assurance that her attentive sense of the Nietzschean problematic begins with Blake in whose work the issues of becoming, consciousness, and will are given a necessary vision. From Orage and the Nietzscheans, she seems also to have caught hold of a sense of our "historical situation" that Thatcher describes as "a relativist view of history in which all phenomena were interpreted in terms of the conflict of polarities, a philosophy of man which stressed his role as the noble protagonist in the drama of tragic existence. . . ."[74] A very ancient view which is reflected in Pound's Ulysses and Malatesta and in Mary Butts's Alexander as well as in the curious trickster quest of *Armed with Madness,* packed as it is with more ordinary-extraordinary personal affairs. On the one hand, as one writer says of Hölderlin, in whose work, like Blake's, so much that we call modernism begins, "a precarious dialogue with the Other—whether this take the form of madness, revolution, or those gods of ancient Greece . . . vanished immediacies," and on the other, the "reinvention of antiquity out of the evidence of wreckage."[75] Blake and Nietzsche share a "consolidation of errors," psychological, social and religious, which "coincides with the revelation" of what they called the truth—that is to say, cultural belonging.[76] We have tended to give up this incredible compounding of theosophy, anthropology, psychology, reinvented antiquity, and Nietzsche consolidation—to leave it unstudied and unimagined—for the Freudian approach to mind, imagination and culture, also hailed by later issues of *New Age*. There are, it seems to me, good reasons to consider both Freud and Nietzsche as consolidators and "physicians of culture." For Mary Butts and many another who lived much longer facing into their work, the truth is a kind of indeterminacy of what we are. It is well to remember that Freud entered the English imagination late, and when he did, it was through this wide-spread interest in "mental events." Samuel Hynes takes note:

> Psychoanalytic ideas had spread more slowly in England than anywhere else in Europe or America. When Freud was made an honorary member of the Society for Psychical Research in 1911, he wrote to Jung that it was "the first sign of interest from dear old England"; the London Psycho-Analytical Society was not founded until two years later, in 1913, and then with only nine members, of whom only four ever practiced. Freud's methods became acceptable to the British medical world only after they had been proved in war-time treatment of shell-shock cases. . . .[77]

What is apparent and of enduring interest is, as Ellis, Carpenter, and Orage had discovered and argued publically with the considerable assistance of Nietzsche, art cannot be considered apart from the cultural condition in which it works. In this instance, a loss of cultural meaning. Mary Butts startlingly plays a game of hide-and-seek with such meaning.

* * * * *

Now, out of this labyrinth—necessarily speculative—of her heart and mind (I like her proposal of a speculative imagination), let us turn to the final scenes of *Armed with Madness*. Carston has managed to track down the source of the cup, and Picus produces a document to the effect that it was found in a church in 1881. The Rev. John Norris who could verify this is dead:

> Carston said:
>
> "Then we get nowhere."
>
> "Nowhere. Only in ghost-stories, and those not the best, do you get anywhere that way."
>
> "But what are we going to do with the damned thing? It can't lie about the house like a green eye that doesn't wink .... This has been a fool's errand—"
>
> "I have an idea," said the vicar. "Take it back to Tollerdown and replace it where you found it. If the next drought sends it up in a suspicious manner, well and good. It seems to like wells. And truth, if she prefers to talk, can return to one."
>
> Carston said: "I like that."
>
> "Good," said Picus, "learn it to be a toad" (196).

Meanwhile, Clarence has been spitefully informed by a letter from London that Scylla and Picus intend to marry, and Scylla, having found this out, goes to Tollerdown to talk with Clarence:

> Clarence had not seen her. Unshaved, half-dressed, he was trying to torture the body of Picus, the statue he had done of him in clay. He had dragged it out against the quarry wall and pierced it with arrows of sharpened wood, feathered from a gull he had shot overnight.
>
> Scylla found the door open and went softly in.
>
> "Clarence, I've come all this way. Can I have tea?"
>
> He heard the low voice, thought of the gull crying. She saw the bird's half-plucked body, bloody on the floor, and that there were papers torn in strips and little darts. She turned over a fold and saw her own body, and her cry was more like the gull. Bird-alone in the lonely room. Except for a ghost called Clarence, everything was empty. She thought:
>
> 'Run away: Can't: Where to? It's all empty, and my knees shake. And I'm curious. Curious and furious and only my body is afraid.'
>
> Clarence wanted to be sure about the bird. He came in slowly, dazed with violence and grief. Bad conscience and fear of making a fool of himself nagged his blazing

obsession. He saw Scylla at the door in silhouette, her scarf fluttering off the back of her neck, sweat-darkened curls appliquéd on her forehead, her hat thrown familiarly on a chair, her mouth open.

"Come and look," he said, and with the fingers of one hand dug into her collar-bone, led her through the kitchen into the half-circle of quarry behind.

She saw Picus in greenish clay, pricked with white feathers. Clarence had made him exactly as he was, a body she had known, for which hers ached.

"You see," he said, "I only had what I'd made of him to do it to."

There was an arrow through his throat, and his head had not fallen forward.

"You're going down the well, where the cup came—"

"Why, Clarence?"

"Best place for you, my fancy girl. If there's enough water, you'll drown. If there isn't, and I don't think there is, you'll break every bone in your body."

She could run like a lapwing, but he could run faster. She was strong as a tree-cat, but he could tear her in two.

"I came to bring you to Picus. He does not want you to be alone on Tollerdown. He is at Tambourne. Lydia sent you a silly letter because" (get his vanity if you can) "she is so in love with you that she's mad."

"And so are you, it seems. Gods! I'm a lucky chap. Unfortunately, Picus doesn't join the harem. He doesn't like me any more.

"Going to marry me, are you? You shall in a way. I mean to follow you down the well."

"Picus is at Tambourne, waiting for you."

"In time he will be here again. My body will fetch him."

"You are the most beautiful man in the world, but you won't be when they get you up out of the well."

He took her other shoulder in his fingers, thrusting them into the muscle-hollow under her neck, hurting her. She forgot him exacting, petulant; remembered him long before, beautiful, merry, inventive, good. And cruel now. Cruelty frightened her. She lied:

"Clarence, I am going to marry Carston—I teased

> "Clarence, I am going to marry Carston—I teased Lydia—" He turned her towards the well.
>
> "There will be one less of you bitches to come into our lives."
>
> "We bear you, and I am no stronger in your hands than that bird. Why did you shoot a gull? It isn't done." Time seemed very precious. Only a thimbleful left. The well very near. The sun turning a little away from them.
>
> "Woodpecker," she shrieked, and flung Clarence off, and ran to the statue. She had been careful not to say that name, and now saw Clarence hurrying to her, the mournful crazy mask splitting, the mouth turning up, the eyes shooting death at her. And Picus, pierced with arrows, smiled down his sweet equivocation. She heard: "That'll do better." He had a cord round his waist. He had cattle-ranched once: that was his lariat. She ran once round the statue. A second later he had thrown her, picked her up half stunned, and tied her against Picus. A black flint had cut her head, a patch of blood began to soak through the moon-fair hair.
>
> Clarence walked back and stood by the kitchen door, fitting an arrow to the string. It ripped the skin on her shoulder and entered the clay. She saw another fly towards her and notch her forearm. Another, and there was a tearing pain below her left breast.
>
> Three instants of pain, set in one of fear. Like a great jewel. Clarence stood by the kitchen door, sharpening an indifferent arrow. She made a supreme effort: not to scream much; not to betray herself. Then a moment of absolute contempt of Clarence. Then of pain. Then, as if she were looking out a window, into a state, a *clarté* the other side of forgiveness. Not by that route. She fainted (198–202).

Carston makes his way to Tollerdown to return the cup to the well and so interrupts this violent scene, just as Clarence is preparing another arrow. It is Clarence who is made to drop the cup in the well—"Plop went a noise a very long way below them" (205). This is no novel to bring in the police or social judgments. The next day Clarence cannot remember his actions; he only wishes to carve a punch-bowl for Scylla, but he is led, step following step by Picus, through exactly what he has done, the madness seeming to be a part of himself:

> Of Picus. Of the band he had grown up with. Of war, whose issues he had found too simple. Of their spiritual adventure he had not been equal to. Of the fool he had made of himself. The revenge his death would be. Not stay to be called Judas. *And bring our souls to His high city.*
>
> He took a step to the edge. Scylla jumped off the divan, and with her hand at her side, ran out to him.
>
> "Clarence, come in."
>
> She had hold of him as he had held her.
>
> . . . .
>
> "Look," she said, and pulled off the handkerchief that tied her shoulder—"and my head is cut and my side. It was partly my fault that Lydia wrote to you. Go on carving while we talk."
>
> He did as she told him. Carston watched them. Like an idyll: a young lover making a present for his sweetheart, sitting on her bed. A harrow of wild geese with their necks out at flight. A border of fish (218–19).

In the end, Carston takes Clarence away to rest we are not sure where or for how long. Carston himself is asked to return to the house in the wood:

> "Our house is your house," said Scylla.
>
> "Besides," said Picus, "did you ever enjoy a summer more?"
>
> "Hasn't it been better than a movie? Leave Clarence at Tambourne and come over and look at Felix' find."
>
> In his heart he knew he would not. Though there was continuity in this adventure, a circle like the design on Clarence's mazer, a ring near to a magic ring, he knew that nothing would induce him to go back to that poverty and pride, cant and candour, raw flesh and velvet; into that dateless, shiftless, shifting, stable and unstable Heartbreak House. Not for a bit. Off to Paris on his own folk-

> adventure. In his last moments with them, looking at Clarence's bowl, he saw the changes in things.
>
> There had been an apple once. There had been an apple tree. When it gave no more apples, it had made fire, and a slice of its trunk had become a bowl cut out into birds. The bowl unless it was turned into fire again, would stop growing and last for ever. Things that came out of time, and were stopped; could be made over into another sort of time (220–21).

And, of course, the novel ends with Felix's "find," Boris, the cause of art and magic in others.

This return to the magic circle in the wood, to bird-sanctities and metaphors of them that colour the characters of Scylla and Picus is youthful and indeterminate of meaning, constantly endangered by violence. In the novel to follow *Armed with Madness, Death of Felicity Taverner,* as I have already noted, Boris takes murder to be a gift, and so implicates all the characters in his lack of understanding. The only figure in *Armed with Madness* who is truly armed is mad in loss and otherwise forgetful. A curious weight in the novel falls on Carston's meditation that "Things that came out of time, and were stopped; could be made over into another sort of time": art, perhaps, but, then, there is the commotion of lives, valued because it is not determined, or, for that matter, material.

I have laboured long over what is my own fascination with Mary Butts, and I have insisted that we remember the context and stake of her art because when memory goes, it leaves so many fine things behind. In closing this essay-story, I note that the transformation from determinism to chance and change—a matter of companionship between art and science, which companionship too often goes unnoticed because our sense of what we mean by science changes—brings us into twentieth-century art. It is one of the curiosities of this century that "reality" continues to be pre-empted by objectivity, which leaves us with a loose, even more preemptive subjectivity. Needless to say, this is destructive of imagination and our understanding of it. Closer to the necessary imagination are these remarks of Octavio Paz:

> in extirpating the notion of divinity, rationalism diminished man. It frees us from God but encloses us in an even more rigorous system. The humbled imagination avenges itself, and atrocious fetishes sprout from God's corpse: in Russia and other countries, the divinization of the leader, the cult of the letter of writings, the deification of the party; among us, the idolatry of the self. To be *one's self* is to condemn oneself to mutilation because man is perpetual longing to be another.

And so it is with Clarence's defeated desire for Picus and with Scylla's successful game to be with him—true also of Carston's departure for Paris and of Felix' finding Boris. We need, somehow, to arrive at such a perspective to understand our art and in this context, to read Mary Butts. Paz continues:

> The revolt of the romantic poets and their heirs was not so much a protest against the exile from God as a search for the lost half, a descent into the region that puts us in communication with the *other.* Therefore they did not find a place in any orthodoxy, and their conversion to this or that faith was never total. Behind Christ or Orpheus, Lucifer or Mary they were seeking that reality of realities we call the divine or the *other.* The situation of the contemporary poets is radically different. Heidegger has expressed it admirably: *We were too late for the gods and too early for being;* and he adds: *whose poem, already begun, is being.* Man is that which is incomplete, although he may be complete in his very incompletion; and therefore he makes poems, images in which he realizes and completes himself without ever completing himself completely. He himself is a poem; he is being always in a perpetual possibility of being completely and thus fulfilling himself in his non-completion. But our historical situation is characterized by the *too late* and the *too early.* Too late: in the tremulous light, the gods, already disappeared, their radiant

> bodies submerged below the horizon that devours all the mythologies of the past; too early: being, the central experience coming out of our selves to the encounter of its true presence. We are lost among things, our thoughts are circular and we perceive but dimly something, as yet unnamed, that is emerging.[78]

Mary Butts's grail, Felix' "unstated thing," and so on—*

---

*Mary Butts became unknown because men didn't like women that intelligent—because "closeted" writers like Plomer, Goldring, and Anthony Butts had more style than intellect—because the editor of *Pagany* was out of touch with her real effort—because Bloomsbury was "ignorant" of Nietzsche: he was "practically ignored by almost everyone known by me in the last seventy years, and I cannot remember even a discussion about him" (letter of Leonard Woolf to Thatcher, Oct. 17, 1968, cited by him, *Nietzsche in England,* p. 267)—because literary history gave too much credit to T. E. Hulme, which made the dropping of Nietzsche the easier, and the readership could become the new criticism which often had only the shadow of our art to talk about—because English Departments go on and on in an unintelligence of our cultural situation and the task of it in art—

NOTES

1. Halpert, Stephen, ed., *A Return to Pagany: The History, Correspondence, and Selections from a Little Magazine, 1929–1932* (Boston: Beacon Press, 1969), p. 17. Later, p. 41, it is said that "the exquisite *Armed with Madness*" has "introduced her to this country."
2. Ibid., p. xiv.
3. Williams, William Carlos, *A Voyage to Pagany* (New York: New Directions, 1970), back cover.
4. Ibid., pp. 265–66.
5. Halpert, reprint, p. 50.
6. Duncan, Robert, "Introduction" to Allen Upward, *The Divine Mystery* (Santa Barbara, Calif: Ross-Erikson, 1976), p. xxviii.
7. Halpert, p. 43.
8. Ibid., pp. 335–36.
9. Ibid., p. 337.
10. Ibid., and p. 162.
11. Letter printed in ibid., p. 444.

12. My "Afterword" to Mary Butts, *Imaginary Letters* (Vancouver, B.C.: Talonbooks, 1979), pp. 64–5.
13. Butts, Mary, *Armed with Madness* (London: Wishart, 1928), pp. 1–2. Page numbers for this novel will hereafter be given in the text.
14. Brilliantly discussed in John Jones, *On Aristotle and Greek Tragedy* (London, Chatto & Windus, 1962), pp. 15 ff.
15. My "Afterword," op. cit., pp. 75–6.
16. Adolf, Helen, *Visio Pacis: Holy City and Grail* (The Pennsylvania State University Press, 1960), pp. 1 & 11.
17. Cited in Martin Gregor-Dellin, *Richard Wagner* (New York: Harcourt, Brace, Jovanovich, 1983), p. 447.
18. Ibid., p. 448.
19. Cited in ibid., p. 457.
20. This translation printed in John Read, *Prelude to Chemistry* (M.I.T. Press, 1966), p. 54. The translation is reprinted from G. F. Rodwell, *The Birth of Chemistry* (London, 1874). Mary Butts is likely to have known A. E. Waite's *The Hermetic Museum, Restored and Enlarged* (London, 1893, two vols.).
21. See John Read, ibid., pp. 51–5, for a summary discussion of the *Emerald Table,* its importance and the arguments about its age.
22. Burckhardt, Titus, *Alchemy: Science of the Cosmos, Science of the Soul* (London: Stuart and Watkins, 1967), p. 34. See also James Webb's *The Flight from Reason: The Age of the Irrational* (London, Macdonald, 1971), p. 125, perhaps useful, but spoiled throughout by an unexamined privileging of Reason and no apparent understanding of the psychology of this undertaking.
23. Yates, Frances A., *Giordano Bruno and the Hermetic Tradition* (London: Routledge and Kegan Paul, 1964), p. 150.
24. See Kenneth Rexroth's measured introductions to G. R. S. Mead's *Fragments of a Faith Forgotten* and to A. E. Waite's *The Holy Kabbala,* both reissued by University Books, 1960.
25. Duncan, op. cit., p. xv.
26. Quoted and commented on in Yates, op. cit., p. 170.
27. For the important opposition of such thought to Victorian values, see Samuel B. Hynes, *The Edwardian Turn of Mind* (Princeton University Press, 1968), especially his chapter "Science, Seers, and Sex." I am greatly indebted to this study, as will appear later in the essay.
28. See Leon Surette, *A Light from Eleusis* (Oxford University Press, 1979), pp. 34 ff, for an interesting discussion of this in relation to Pound.
29. Butts, Mary, *Traps for Unbelievers* (London: Desmond Harmsworth, 1932), p. 25.
30. Yates, op. cit., pp. 454–55.
31. Butts, *Traps,* pp. 12–13.

32. Ibid., p. 40.
33. From Helen M. Mustard's and Charles E. Passage's "Introduction" to Wolfram von Eschenbach, *Parzival* (New York: Vintage Books, 1961), pp. xl-xli.
34. Harrison, Jane Ellen, *Epilogomena to the Study of Greek Religion and Themis* (New York: University Books, 1962), p. 109.
35. Ibid., pp. 75 & 106–07.
36. Ibid., p. 110.
37. Ibid., p. 109.
38. Cook, A. B., *Zeus: A Study of Ancient Religion* (New York: Biblo and Tannen, 1965), vol. 2, p. 697 n.
39. Harrison, op. cit., p. 6 ff.
40. Cited in Jessie L. Weston, From *Ritual to Romance* (New York: Peter Smith, 1941), pp. 144–45.
41. Ibid., p. 191. For lack of space, I can here only refer the reader to Henry and Renee Kahane, *The Krater and the Grail: Hermetic Sources of the Parzival* (Univ. of Illinois, 1965).
42. Cited and the exhibition discussed in Hynes, p. 325, taken from Virginia Woolf's "Mr. Bennett and Mrs. Brown"—"a paper read to the Heretics, Cambridge, on May 18, 1924"—published in *The Captain's Death Bed and Other Essays* (London: Hogarth Press, 1950), p. 91.
43. Hynes, p. 13.
44. Ibid., pp. 132–33.
45. Woolf, "The Cosmos," in *The Captain's Death Bed,* pp. 79, 81, & 83.
46. Hynes, p. 134.
47. I wish to emphasize the usefulness of Hynes's discussion of this in the chapter already noted, "Science, Seers, and Sex," pp. 32–171.
48. Ibid., p. 138.
49. Ibid.
50. Ibid., p. 151.
51. Cited in Hynes, p. 159.
52. Butts, *Traps,* pp. 35–6.
53. Ibid., p. 33.
54. Ibid., p. 37.
55. Ibid., pp. 37–8.
56. Ibid., p. 39.
57. Ibid., p. 47.
58. Ibid., pp. 49–50 & 51.
59. Hynes, p. 154.
60. Butts, Mary, *The Macedonian* (London: William Heinemann, 1933), pp. 209–10.
61. John Davidson, cited in David S. Thatcher, *Nietzsche in England, 1890–*

1914 (University of Toronto Press, 1970), a valuable discussion, pp. 51–93.

62. Helen Watterson in *Century Magazine* (New York, May, 1889) and John Davidson in *Speaker* (London, 1891), noted and discussed by Thatcher, ibid., p. 22.

63. Thatcher, pp. 27 ff.

64. Grosskurth, Phyllis, *Havelock Ellis* (Toronto: McClelland and Stewart, 1980), pp. 200–09.

65. Deleuze, Gilles, *Nietzsche and Philosophy,* trans. by Hugh Tomlinson (Columbia University Press, 1983), p. 197.

66. Thatcher, p. 42.

67. Ibid., p. 235.

68. Both are reprinted in Pound's *Selected Prose, 1909–1965,* ed. by William Cookson (New York: New Directions, 1973)—this quotation, p. 446.

69. Pound, "The Divine Mystery" in *Selected Prose,* p. 403.

70. See Thatcher, pp. 219 ff.

71. Ibid., pp. 221–22.

72. Cited in Thatcher, pp. 230–31.

73. Noted in Thatcher, p. 234.

74. Ibid., p. 233.

75. Richard Siebuth's introduction to *Friedrich Hölderlin, Hymns and Fragments* (Princeton University Press, 1984), pp. 11 & 33, slightly adapted for my purposes.

76. The notion of the "consolidation of error," adapted here, is from Brian Wilke and M. J. Johnson, *Blake's Four Zoas* (Harvard University Press, 1978), p. 141.

77. Hynes, p. 164.

78. Paz, Octavio, *The Bow and the Lyre,* trans. by Ruth L. C. Simms (University of Texas Press, 1973), pp. 247–48.

With Duff Twysden, Paris, ca. 1925.

BARBARA O'BRIEN WAGSTAFF

The Effectual Angel in Death of Felicity Taverner

WITH THE PUBLICATION of *Death of Felicity Taverner* in 1932, Mary Butts's trilogy of novels was complete. This book brings together Boris Polteratsky and the unnamed letter writer of *Imaginary Letters* (dated 1924, first published in 1928) and Scylla, Felix and Picus of *Armed with Madness* (1928). Before this third volume opens, Felicity Taverner, the cousin of Scylla, Felix and Picus, has died mysteriously in an automobile accident; and whether it was an accident, suicide, or murder, her death, her cousins are convinced, was caused by the hatred of her mother, brother and husband. The cousins soon realize that, not content with her death, Felicity's husband, Nicholas Kralin, seeks to defame her by putting out an edition of her letters with his interpretation of them and of her and also by developing the land she loved into a resort. Felicity's mother, Julia Taverner, who cares little for her daughter though a great deal about the family name and the land, and Felicity's brother, Adrian, who cares only about himself, cannot prevent Kralin because they are too busy quarreling. Scylla, Picus and Felix do not know what to do, and, at last, it is Boris who acts, avenging Felicity by leading Kralin into a trap and drowning him.

The most traditional in style and form of her novels—almost a "romance"—and full of references to great English poets, this book is darker in outlook than her earlier novels and faces squarely the question of how to offset evil, a problem which remains unresolved. Hence, perhaps, a shift in focus, after this book, toward the divine and human interaction in history, and the emphasis on the God-man in the lives of such individuals as Alexander and Julian. It is as though Mary Butts had finally broken free from, exorcised, the demon of her personal past, and so found that historic imagination she had so long wished for. *Death of Felicity Taverner* plays a pivotal part in this liberation and discovery because it confronts the loss of the ideal self, Felicity, and the possibility of its partial recovery. What Felicity and her friends contend with largely through their devotion to each other and their land and through the alchemy of poetry will soon be grappled with in a bigger drama on a larger stage and with reinforcements.

In *Ashe of Rings,* Mary Butts's first novel, a character says, "I want to stop wickedness, and I don't know how."[1] Judy's malevolent hatred of Vanna in that book, like Kralin's of Felicity, is fierce. Judy would murder Van, but the Rings, an ancient precinct like Eleusis, protects Van who depends on the "signatures of potencies who are watching man" (174); however, she does not know how to include her friend Serge in this safety. She tells him, "When I was drawn up that night onto the Rings, and lay outstretched on the stone, I thought that I had done it for us both." "How could you save another?" he replies. "I see that now," she answers (284). In *Armed with Madness,* Scylla can not, as could Van, avert her own crucifixion, though she brings about a stronger community by feeling past her fear and Clarence's hatred to "a clarté the other side of forgiveness."[2] Then, in *Death of Felicity Taverner,* where there is no saving Felicity and where the "anti-life" menacing the characters and the land is extreme, the wickedness is stopped. Van's refuge, her reverence for Rings Hill and her "words of power" (*AR,* 280), so like Joyce's "words of silent power," is also Scylla's and Felicity's; staying in this sanctuary, they help make true, if only in part, Dante's assertion in his *Paradiso,* "There will be seen that which we hold by faith."

Like many individuals of her time, Mary Butts saw "sinister forces . . . a black cloud gathering to overwhelm us all,"[3] appearing partly in the form of "'envy, hatred, malice and all uncharitableness'"[4] threatening community on a global as well as on a personal level. This dark cloud descends on the Taverners' home, as it was descending on the world, with the presence of the comfortless, and Mary Butts, like her Scylla, felt that "we must combat it with the good, the pure, the sweet, the true."[5] The thunder at the end of T. S. Eliot's *The Waste Land,* pointing a way, says "Datta. Dayadhvam. Damyata." Van, Scylla and Felicity give and sympathize; but Shelley's awe-ful Prometheus, in whom Mary Butts finds "the meaning of human life,"[6] suggests that power, control, only comes with the spirit of charity.

Felicity never appears in the trilogy. She is not a character in *Armed with Madness,* and if she is the letter writer in *Imaginary Letters* she does not sign her name; and, by the time of *Death of Felicity Taverner,* she is a ghost, influencing and focusing the battle. What others say about her tends to reveal themselves, while what they do because of her helps reveal her. Like the grail in *Armed with Madness,* which disappears at the end of the novel, she is many things. Mrs. Taverner considers her a wanton; she cannot see her actions in any but a sexual light. Felicity climbs fences, she avers, to show off her legs. Adrian's view of his sister is colored by his mother's. Kralin, recognizing only personal gratification, calls Felicity "an erotic expert,"[7] and his relentless efforts to wipe out all trace of his wife suggests how much she disturbs him. Boris, who at first pretends not to have known Felicity, comes to see she is like the sister and mother and his own goodness destroyed in the Russian Revolution. Scylla, Felix and Picus see Felicity as Shelley did Keats. They would like to enhance her reputation and they try to incorporate what they understand of her in their lives. Called naive, repressed, loose and abnormal, Felicity suffers the artist's fate, and especially the true saint's, whose efforts to make earth a heaven are considered either immoral or unrealistic. As Scylla says of Felicity, she was "made for a particular kind of love . . . that the world at present has particularly no use for. . . . It was as good as any art to her. *'In whom alone love lives again'* and all that" (36).

"Who killed Cock Robin?" the nursery rhyme asks, and no one knows why the sparrow shot him with his bow and arrow, but all the creatures mourn. "Who kill'd John Keats?" writes Byron, continuing, "I says the Quarterly,/ So savage and Tartarly;/ 'Twas one of my feats." Scolded and berated by Mrs. Taverner, bullied by Adrian who denies the possibility of disinterested action, and hounded by Kralin who denies her very soul, Felicity, without pretension, without sufficient confidence in herself, lacks the instinct for self-preservation. Kralin speaks of her "Electra complex," and while she has no ability to get along with her mother, she cannot or will not retaliate with her knowledge of Adrian's patrimony, nor does she plead with Adrian nor try to justify herself to him; and, she will not use Felix' love for her. Instead, her hold on life weakened by the harsh judgments and misunderstanding of her family and the hatred of her husband, she dies. As Scylla sees it, "Her humility destroyed her.... She did not know her own power—her own discovery" (37). Without someone to help her, and without the disillusion to see what people are like, Felicity is helpless against the negation of Kralin whose talent is to undo what others do or would do.

Nicholas Kralin is Mary Butts's portrait of the devil in the modern world and probably also of her first husband, John Rodker, poet, translator and publisher. A Russian Jew, whom Boris, a Russian aristocrat, dubs a Red agent, a purveyor of obscene ikons (Rodker's publishing included erotica), Kralin is to Scylla and Felix the snake slithering through their Sacred Wood, a worm or slug leaving its trail of slime on their lives. He is the ultimate foreigner, alien to the honor, truth, beauty and love they value, and Boris cannot understand why Felicity's family allowed her to marry him. This picture of Kralin reflects the anti-Semitism of the period and the class-consciousness of England, but finally his evil, like that of Mary Butts's other monstrous characters, Jewish and non-Jewish alike, is his thorough denial of life, a rejection she knew from her reading of the Romantics and of myth and folklore, and also from her own experiences.

In *The Crystal Cabinet,* she describes her discovery as a young girl that "The world isn't like what people tell you. There are ugly things about like wolves running, and the Psalms are quite right" (*CC,* 114). Part of the ugliness is the contrast between the way people live and the way poetry, particularly Shelley's, describes living:

> [T]he crude world in which I found myself solitary was only a fire-bearer's apprenticeship. Perhaps only Shelley knows how I escaped the destruction of self-pity and unteachable priggishness.
>
> As to many generous children, it was the contradiction between the two worlds that bewildered as it hurt. Since goodness, loveliness, wisdom, adventure and high thoughts were so obviously preferable, why did people prefer ignorance, convention, commonness? All expressed in the unlovingness I felt around me on every side. Why didn't they listen to the men called philosophers who were there to show them? And to the painters and poets and great architects and men of learning? (*CC,* 125).

Throughout her stories, age constricts and prevents youth, ugliness attacks beauty, malice love, and spite generosity, an eternal conflict *Prometheus Unbound* depicts also, where Jupiter, the very spirit of constriction, hate, and the will-to-power endeavors to suppress the beauty, love and liberty of Prometheus. Besides the horror of Jupiter, there were the Norse myths, Odin hanging on the tree and Baldur's death, ballads and stories of bogies, and the child's awareness, in the woods especially, of "a much smaller, meaner form of supernatural life":

> Of every sort of kind and quality, in and out of doors; in patches, and often, as in the case of the great pine-tree,

> especially attached to things. God and your Angel took care of you through it—the Angel who was later to stand beside you, as his daimon by Socrates.
>
> "It" was infinitely less than God. The thought of God could send "it" scattering in an instant—if you remembered in time. Only there were bits of it, come upon suddenly round corners, so terrifying that they caught you before you could remember Him. It was awfully interesting too. Things to explore when you were grown-up. And some of the gods even were "like" it—Hecate, of course, and Loki; and because of "it," in another grander way, people died when they saw Pan.
>
> All this I found out for myself in the ancient garden at Salterns, and in the woods, in the salt-marshes and by the sea (*CC,* 139–40).

Mary Butts finds this "smaller, meaner form of supernatural life" depicted in Montague Rhodes James's ghost stories. In a review of his art of storytelling, the first published during his lifetime, she writes:

> The evidence for their [good and evil potencies'] existence is, from many angles, as strong as the evidence for their non-existence. But—it is harder to follow; common-sense or even learned incredulity is essentially easier and simpler. Also more à la mode.... Perhaps the doubt felt about Doctor James' subject is not only shallow scepticism, but sound, self-protective sense. Better not—certainly for the majority—better not enquire too closely; ask too many questions as to the existence of such things. Everyone who has lived much out of doors feels something of what he tells. Not by association with tradition, but by a direct kind of awareness, an impact on the senses—and something more than the senses. It can be a recurrent, almost an overwhelming, experience. Much ancient bogey-lore was a rationalisation of it. Today we talk of suggestion, exorcise with the magic word "unscientific." But I doubt if our ignorant scepticism is any nearer truth than our ancestors' ignorant creduity.[8]

Unlike Algernon Blackwood "who relies on suggestion, a strengthening atmosphere in which very little ever happens; or rather one is not sure whether it has happened or not," M. R. James renders the supernatural and the horrible "unspeakably real, solid, present,"[9] through careful detailed descriptions of events or facts of history, setting, places, weather, and of what the characters observe as they run up against this malignity in the course of their daily lives and work. Blackwood's deep feeling for nature, his evocations of mountains, forests, lakes and rivers, particularly of landscapes remote from men's influence, enthrall by their sheer beauty, a sublimity human nature of itself cannot withstand, whereas many of the places and settings in Arthur Machen's tales and in M. R. James's stories threaten more. In their writings, the encounters with this other dimension are experienced as incursions which few survive intact, whereas in Blackwood the crossing-over can be a blessing. *John Silence* is Blackwood's series of stories about a doctor who helps others through a process of spiritual alchemy, an unusual Sympathy involving an active psychic negation and neutralization of evil forces and an identification with the good. It is intriguing that a work of occult fiction by Dion Fortune (Violet Mary Firth), founder of The Society of the Inner Light, entitled *The Secrets of Dr. Taverner* and widely read in its day, appeared in 1926.

"Taverner" the O.E.D. says is one who keeps a tavern and also one who drinks or takes intoxicating substances. "Felicity Taverner" encompasses an earthly and a heavenly nature and suggests intoxication whether by material or spiritual means. Robert McAlmon wrote that "Mary breathed in an exalted ecstasy of being,"[10] which other descriptions of her corroborate. Intoxication, whether by drink, drugs or the "words of power" in poetry and magic—all of which she knew by experience—may lead to transformation, and in her writings such transformation has often to do with love. In the works of Éliphas Lévi on magic, with which she was familiar, love is strongly identified with woman. Lévi discusses the relation between Christianity and the ancient mysteries and magic, bringing out the importance of knowing, daring, singleness of will, and silence, all of which the Taverners practise. Scylla's silence at her crucifixion in *Armed with Madness,* her dim realization that her business is "to bring order, proportion, light into what is happening. That where there has been falsehood and muddle, there shall be knowing and clearness, conception for misconception" (*DFT,* 122), saves her; and, in *Ashe of Rings,* Van is protected because of her knowledge of Rings and her relation to it.

The experience of the supernatural, central to Mary Butts's works, involves familiarity with woods, seashore, moor, cliff, birds, turf. As in myths and legends, these are sentient; they participate in the lives of humans. Her rendition of them includes the realism, the sense of danger, the evocation of place, as well as the terrible beauty of surroundings she admires in both James and Blackwood. What might be termed "Christian" and "pagan" elements coexist in her world. Her characters know the horror of nature and the supernatural, and also the supremacy of a love and a glory born not of themselves, as it is felt in the poetry of Spenser, Milton, Wordsworth and Shelley, authors crucial to her awakening as an artist.

Like the beasts in Arthur Machen's "The Terror" who reflect the hatred raging in the world from war, Kralin looms larger than human to Felicity and her cousins and Boris. It is an old belief that at those times when humans are less than human, the powers of evil rejoice and are more active; the little people are about more, and Boris's "fairy-tale mind" sees Kralin "with cheeks drawn in" carrying a bag containing "a small iced wind" he lets out in puffs (*DFT,* 205–06). This something about him they can only refer to as "the grey thing" or "le Kralinism" is the terror Boris imagines as pockets of poisoned air and Mary Butts experienced sometimes in the woods and encountered once on the Fifeshire sands, "inimical and deadly," "a focus, a column of energy, cold and vile and hateful, spinning there" (*CC,* 204).

Worshipping Nodens, God of the Abyss, "Not-Being, Un-Meaning, Un-doing" (*DFT,* 106), which Mary Butts gained an increased knowledge of from her visit to Aleister Crowley's Abbey of Thelema at Cefalù, Kralin causes Felicity to despair. Felix tells of her "panic-fear" of anything grey, of sea-mist and grey skies, which suggests to anyone interested in magic that Felicity was a victim of what some writers call a psychic attack, and which, they contend, is far commoner than is generally realized. The fear and oppression Felicity suffers from, her nervous exhaustion, the notion of evil odors and even the association of these with slime and the color grey are characteristics of such attacks, the imposition or intrusion of one will on another. Of course, literature and history and life are full of such instances of imposition though we still tend not to explore this aspect of events, but Mary Butts's works include it. As Picus says, "You can get a first in Greats or fly round inside the crater of Vesuvius, but what you depend on for your private life is your degree in witch-doctoring. How much you can smell-out the propitious from the unpropitious" (*DFT,* 24).

Married very young and having little experience of the world, Felicity has no nose for "the unpropitious" she meets in Kralin. Though her instincts to love are in the right direction, there is no John Silence to encourage her, and her cousins are too concerned with their own affairs to heed her danger. How could any of them believe in such a dark thing as Kralin? It takes them most of six weeks as the story unfolds to realize what he is like, and even Kralin is ignorant of the horror of himself, disgusted and impatient as he is with one of M. R. James's stories. The grey thing, like Felicity herself, is larger than the particular person or thing that manifests it.

In accompanying Felicity and a lover around Paris, Boris notices what they fail to see—not just "people hating what they should love" but "people practising how to kill what they do not like. Their ill-will *works.* And among certain people I know of in Paris, they know how to *make* it work. This they do for fun, or under some compulsion; or an order. How can I convince you? It was as if it had been decided on that she was to be crucified" (*DFT,* 84). He continues, "I knew that 'le Kralinism' had bitten into [her lover], and I did nothing. I, who knew enough to know that they were the condemned and that the grey web had been thrown over them. I let myself be its instrument" (*DFT,* 86).

Felicity's "crucifixion" recalls Scylla's as well as Van's and her ancestor's. None of these individuals is saintly in the usual sense, and the attacks on them are not wholly undeserved; but, each one is searching for a deeper community than those around her comprehend, and the vilification each suffers suggests how much such community threatens the security of identity which excludes the sacred. The story "From Altar to Chimney-piece" describes a group which practises a cult of cruelty, a "subjectivity run mad." A young girl with whom the narrator of the story is in love has been singled out as a victim, and as an old woman takes her dirty handkerchief and rubs out the name of Christ on the ancient ciborium now used as a candelabra, the narrator sees that her "contempt for . . . all that . . . makes life worth living, had something enormous about it."[11]

This denial of ties not only to other people but to things supernatural and natural for the most part undetected—to gods, places, trees, stars, animals—leads to the horror of Kralin. Modern individuals as Mary Butts depicts them in her works and discusses them in two essays, *Traps for Unbelievers* and *Warning to Hikers,* is cut off from both Nature and the divine, from what lies below and what is above; and, lacking these ties, their bonds with their fellows break also. To Kralin, who only appreciates the land for the revenge it affords and the money it will yield as a tourist attraction, everything, including sacred ikons, becomes an object.

The desecration of individuals, land and things which follows this unchecked subjectivity, which she also calls a "plague, a Black Death of the spirit" (*CC,* 138), can only be offset, Mary Butts's works suggest, by recontacting what John Shorthouse called "Eternal Truth manifested in Phenomena,"[12] in nature, myth, and art. In *Traps for Unbelievers* she speaks of the "very peculiar kind of awareness ... [which has] to do with a sense of the invisible, the non-existent in a scientific sense, relations between things of a different order: the moon and a stone, the sea and a piece of wood, women and fish," an awareness which "has no more died in man than has his sight or any other of his senses; only he does not now try it out...."[13] Van, Scylla, Felicity—mostly, it seems, it is women—have cultivated such a perception; they have grown up close to the sacred resident in poetry, music, and nature, and these come to their aid. A woman in the story "Friendship's Garland" is released from fear and regenerated by a tree, and in "Green"[14] a couple is protected from a Kralin-like character by their consciousness of the Hermes and Aphrodite power surrounding them. The denial of love, imagination, beauty, freedom, is real in Mary Butts's books, and just as a bad smell tends to overpower a sweet one, there is small hope for those who of themselves try to stand up to a Kralin; but, keeping tabu and preserving carefully their mana objects may get them through, unless, like Felicity, companionless, they find themselves pitted against Nodens himself. However, Felicity triumphs when the land, her cousins and Boris become a working community to help her.

Boris, who lives off his looks and wit and who drinks and takes drugs and avoids deep friendships all because of bad memories, is slowly transformed by his contact with the Taverners. He dates the hour of his ruin from his wish to be rid of his mother and sister when the family was fleeing Russia, a ruin he feels is symbolized by his losing an ikon his mother gave him. The letter writer of *Imaginary Letters* tries to dissuade him from accepting his ruin and following the usual remedy "not to think, to scurry through life to artificial oblivion"; but, it is not until the confrontation between his friends and Kralin that Boris sees his place in this "sad little war [they're] fighting" (*DFT,* 198, 234).

Scylla, Felix and Picus are ignorant at first of the operation of Kralin's destructiveness, unsure how it has killed their cousin until they encounter it firsthand. Only Scylla senses how to face Kralin. As she begins to feel sick and cold during a visit she pays him, she instinctively starts to play his game, "mean and sharp and of the ways of the world," telling him lies to put him off her track, and to think of such lines as *'Love your enemies'* and the one about the man *'who gave his enemy his plank and plunged aside to die'* (*DFT,* 176). She begins to control her awe and fear of him and summons up the power to tell him off and bring herself away from the interview intact though shaken. Later, the thought comes to her for them to call on the Elemental Spirits, but she wonders about their ability to solicit their aid; drawing closer together, she and Picus and Felix await the movement of events.

What they do not know and only gradually become aware of is that the ghost of Felicity is about. At first only a figure of speech, "the ghost" slowly materializes from a lover's dream to a felt presence a blackbird shouts at. She is so much in the hearts and minds of her family and friends that she cannot help coming to them. "This place is somehow full of Felicity," Adrian says, adding, after the ghost leaves, driven away by her mother and brother in death as in life, "Just now I felt a kind even of physical emptiness about us—There had been a sort of presence before" (*DFT,* 217, 222). Then, as Scylla and Boris stand on a crest overlooking the land and observe its beauties and discuss Kralin's plans, Boris's past and present experience merges with that of the Taverners, and "the ghost of Felicity Taverner," so identified and named for the first time, comes and sits down by her cousin "who moved a little, as though disturbed by an unaccountable breeze" (*DFT,* 242). Finally, she whom Scylla and Picus have seen as "a shape of bright darkness, blowing out flowers" and have felt as a third often with them, because, so at one with the land she loves "that the hills were her body laid-down, and 'Felicity' was said, over and over again, in each bud and leaf," she comes to accompany Boris as a third, a "confused transparency ... as of a shadow threaded with brightness" when he leads Kralin to his death (*DFT,* 40, 256). "Ghost of Felicity, is not this what had to be? You know that, for we've felt you about us and you have not prevented us," observes Boris (*DFT,* 260).

This portrait of Felicity recalls Mary Butts's reading of M. R. James's story, "Lost Hearts," which seized her, she writes, with "terror and felicity."[15] Slowly, powerfully, this quiet land-cup with its sacred wood has been weaving its net of destiny. Its beauty has worked its magic on Scylla, Picus, Felix, and Boris, and though Kralin is insensitive to it, he is lured by his desire to use and destroy it. In James's story the ghosts of two children take revenge on their murderer and protect another child from the same fate. Mysterious figures, they present a terrifying spectacle, menacing and dreadful in a still, moonlit night. Thomas Nashe's line, "Brightness falls from the air," haunting Mary Butts's writing, not only suggests the terrible fall and loss of youth and beauty, like that of Keats and Cock Robin, but also the avenging spirit of such loss. Like the Erinyes who are also called Eumenides, Felicity is a bright darkness, which has less to do with orthodoxly Christian notions of good and evil than with the presences of places, objects, individuals and things unknown which can benefit or injure according to one's relation to them. Adrian, who is throwing away his "mana object" (*DFT,* 97), is making a wilderness of his life; and Kralin, who has no understanding of the powers of creatures and sacred objects and places and who enjoys turning gardens into deserts, becomes fish food. The land-cup with its wood, birds and cliffs towering above the sea, sacrosanct to Felicity and her cousins, is a magic ring changing Boris and drawing him in, thrusting out Kralin, protecting Scylla, Picus, Felix and itself. Like the providence Hamlet senses just before his duel with Laertes, which perhaps indicates how he is able at last to say "Let be," so the circumstance of Kralin's death has something large and inevitable about it, of which Boris's deliberation is only part. As an effectual angel, Felicity's ghost suggests such providence, the operation of divine powers coming into play when what Van calls "the art of life ... to let things come" is practised (*AR,* 212).

Mary Butts writes that the link for her between the God of her fathers and her belief in the ancient gods "was my belief in the Guardian Angel" (*CC,* 137), and in Felicity are joined the Christian idea of love and the pagan reverence for nature which derive, at least in part, from Mary Butts's reading of Celtic literature, the Bible, Spenser, Milton and the Romantics—rhythms, lines, images and ideas of which appear throughout her writing. Angels, the host of heaven, come as messengers, holy ones, watchers, spirits in Genesis, Ezekiel, Daniel, Revelation and the gospels; and attendant spirits, spirits of nature, harbingers, heralds, angels and other bright ministers abound in Milton and Shelley. In the Book of Revelation angels and the earth help the woman fleeing the red dragon, and Shelley's Prometheus, buoyed by spirits of the hour and of earth and by unseen spirits, prevails through wishing no living thing to suffer pain. As in H. D.'s poetry, these luminous beings are real, not symbolic representations. Referring to Felicity, Adrian cites the lines from "Comus" about the "thousand liveried angels" who protect "saintly chastity," while Scylla's feeling of Felicity as a presence accompanying Picus and her at sea and through the woods evokes the divine creatures peopling Shelley's poems. The animated interchange between nature and humankind found in Romantic poetry helped Mary Butts to much of her vocabulary and experience. "The first thing that I remember is a puddle of yellow mud," *The Crystal Cabinet* begins, and then she describes tasting it. The venerative, receptive, alert passivity enabling Wordsworth to hear the "things forever speaking," and to feel "A presence ... [which] rolls through all things,"[16] and to admit the blessings of all he beholds despite the dreary roar and commerce of daily life, informs Mary Butts's response to her surroundings.

> ... there were times when the trees and stones and turf were not dumb, and [Scylla] had their speech, and the ruins rose again and the sunk foundations, and copse and clearing and forest changed places, and went in and out and set to partners in their century-in, century-out dance. There were times, out on the high turf at sun-rise and set, when in the slanted light she saw their land as an exfoliation, not happening in our kind of time, a becoming of the perfected (*DFT,* 183).

This devotion to living in accord with this other is a transfiguring formula which has its counterpart in human relationships, however more difficult its terms be to apply. Though the war undermined this faith, as did most human relationships, in Mary Butts's books is felt the urgency of the need to bring the unimagined into play in the world. In a fever over Kralin's projected development of their land, Scylla invokes this Spirit, murmuring "'It will be all right only if we love each other enough'" (*DFT,* 263), almost the very words Boris's mother spoke to her family as they tried to escape and which "had dissolved the grain of his evil thought" (*DFT,* 195). Struggling to objectify Felicity's love, Scylla instinctively, increasingly cherishes what is sacred as Kralin's destruction looms ever more imminent; and, while Felicity found no Prometheus, Scylla has Boris, who rejoins community by stepping outside it.

In murdering Kralin, Boris performs an act of violence to equal his denial of others since that fatal day before a small tree outside a train station in eastern Russia when "for the first time ... there came upon him hatred of his sister and his mother.... Into that pit of the spirit he had sunk with his father" (*DFT,* 194). One day out on the moor near the Taverners' home, as he muses over their situation, he sees the same tree and that Kralin is like it. Just as there is bad human nature, so is there bad nature, like the stone at Stone's End which causes evil thoughts or stops thought altogether and which Boris dubs "Kralin's Stone." Mary Butts speaks of the humming going on in everything which can be heard in stillness, a thought similar to Blackwood's that ideas come to people from trees and flowers. Of course, such thoughts are not always healthy for human beings, as many of Machen's and Blackwood's stories show; and Boris, familiar with the effects, if not with the process of such thoughts coming both from nature and from human beings because of his experience outside the train and his life in Paris, recognizes their characteristics in the Taverners' predicament.

From a lazy, petulant dependent, Boris changes to a determined, ruthless soldier, who having seen an enemy of his community, destroys it. In the context of Mary Butts's work, his act poses a question—Is not love, of itself, sufficient to offset Kralin? Scylla, Felix and Picus have retreated to their house, and though Scylla feels helpless, she clings to their love for each other. Again and again Mary Butts comes back to this redemptive capacity of love. Is Boris the *geburah* accompanying the *hesed* of his friends? His act is a reentry into a sympathy with others and with a locale which he has lost since leaving Russia, while it also puts him altogether outside the Taverners' world. Scylla sees that she and Picus and Felix must "be for honour what they [Kralin, Mrs. Taverner, Adrian] are for dishonour; for truth what they are for lies; for charity what they are for spite; for loveliness what they are for filth"; and perhaps, at that instant of insight, the "release that felt like a glory [which] came about them, as though separate and converging paths of light lay to be walked on at their feet," suggests the bright darkness coming into action: "It was, at that moment, as though all that Kralin had done was to open a door onto a stadium set for the players of the sacred game. On which field he had his place also" (*DFT,* 160).

Begun for these characters in *Imaginary Letters,* played in *Armed with Madness,* and continued in *Death of Felicity Taverner,* the game of letting life alone, so that the divine rather than a mental machination can reach into and transform the human, is becoming more difficult. It has never been easy, and as the awareness of mental causation became more common around the turn of the century, as witness the proliferation of occult societies and literature, claims and accusations of mental manipulation and even of mental murder were not unusual. Anna Bonus Kingsford, for example, a doctor, and author with Edward Maitland of *The Perfect Way,* felt she succeeded in mentally assassinating some vivisectionists; in turn, she was herself thought to be a victim of mental murder. Mary Butts's associations, particularly in the early 'twenties, with occult groups and with practitioners of magic, such as Aleister Crowley and Cecil Maitland, surely increased her awareness of the perils of the mind unleashed, and certainly her writings indicate that to her the idea of mental malpractice was neither ridiculous nor far-fetched. Though Boris's solution to Kralin hardly seems his author's, the question of what to do about such psychic malfeasance as Kralin is guilty of, of how to do as the thundering angel in *The Waste Land* advises and Shelley's *Prometheus* does, is unresolved. Kralin must be resisted, as Boris and Scylla resist quarreling because quarreling is what Kralin wants. Nature and the supernatural come to the aid of those who resist, but what would happen without Boris's intervention and what will happen because of it, is uncertain, though it hardly could be a fulfillment of Felix's wish that "someone be born . . . who will make *'On Heaven'* true" (*DFT,* 47). In *The Crystal Cabinet* Mary Butts recalls a teacher's comment, "Jacob was sent an angel. . . . There are blessings that are fought for—and others that cannot be earned or snatched, which are given only 'without money and without price' " (227–28).

Less terse and staccato in style and manner than *Armed with Madness, Death of Felicity Taverner* presents a greater madness. The 'twenties are over. The dancing, jazz and snatches of song integral to the spirit of *Armed with Madness* are mostly gone, and in their stead are long vigils in restless rooms and lines from "Lycidas." Scylla, Felix and Picus feel they will go mad if they cannot account for Felicity's death, and they only account for it by themselves encountering another madness, Kralin, and Boris's act of war. For years Boris has "been trying to find a happy-go-lucky way to kill himself" (*DFT,* 198), but rather than such disintegration, he is compelled into thought and action by his friends and their surroundings, tree, stone, moor and sea, a community which, he discovers, includes the felicity he has lost, and which demands each member's response.

In 1932 Mary Butts retired to a fishing village in Cornwall, it may be to draw close to those potencies which alone, perhaps, could help her to meet the coming world upheaval. Her childlike communion with beloved places and objects, and her awareness of poetry as a power, were her sustenance; and "blessed," she writes in *The Crystal Cabinet,* "are the grown-up people who have not lost [such communion]—a reminder of the conditions under which we enter the Kingdom of Heaven" (84). Later in the same book (118–19) she recounts an experience born of this lifelong conversation:

> It was in London, in the last lap of the war, when the air-raids were screaming out of the high winter sky. I was alone in a Hampstead studio, my first home by myself. The high fragile roof was made of glass, and the gun on the Heath shook the earth and the engines droned overhead, and suddenly panic came over me. I dared not go out through the dropping shrapnel, and the infernal things were zooming nearer and nearer overhead; and instantly the danger of it all and the horror were made clear to me, and I ran to try and hide myself in a little out-building, a dark hole full of wood, where the roof was low, and no airy brittle roof rose above me into shadows.
>
> I can only try and tell what happened as I tried not to crouch there. Which was an infinitely clear, infinitely quiet voice repeating: *'Love and man's unconquerable mind. Love and man's unconquerable mind';* and I was suddenly charged with knowledge that, somehow, it was important that I should command myself, that, in some unrealizable way, I had it in me to preserve or to destroy the meaning of those words.

Repeating them, I went back; and inside the studio and the racket overhead there was a quiet into which I entered where both fear and death were swallowed up.

NOTES

1. Butts, Mary, *Ashe of Rings* (New York: Albert and Charles Boni, 1926), p. 294; hereafter cited parenthetically as *AR*.
2. Butts, Mary, *Armed with Madness* (New York: Albert and Charles Boni, 1928), p. 214.
3. McAlmon, Robert and Boyle, Kay, *Being Geniuses Together* (New York: Doubleday & Co., Inc., 1968), p. 124.
4. Butts, Mary, "Questionnaire," *The Little Review,* May 1929, p. 21.
5. *Being Geniuses Together,* p. 124.
6. Butts, Mary, *The Crystal Cabinet: My Childhood at Salterns* (London: Methuen & Co. Ltd., 1937), p. 116; hereafter cited parenthetically as *CC*.
7. Butts, Mary, *Death of Felicity Taverner* (London: Wishart & Co., 1932), p. 131; hereafter cited parenthetically as *DFT*.
8. Butts, Mary, "The Art of Montagu [*sic*] James," *The London Mercury,* Feb. 1934, vol. xxix, no. 172, pp. 315–17.
9. Butts, Mary, "The Art of Montagu James," p. 307.
10. *Being Geniuses Together,* p. 124.
11. Butts, Mary, *Last Stories* (London: Brendin Publishing Co., 1938), p. 166, p. 174.
12. Shorthouse, J. H., *John Inglesant* (London: MacMillan and Co., Ltd., 1881), p. x.
13. Butts, Mary, *Traps for Unbelievers* (London: Harmsworth, 1932), p. 25.
14. Butts, Mary, *Several Occasions* (London: Wishart, 1932).
15. Butts, Mary, "The Art of Montagu James," p. 306.
16. William Wordsworth, *Poems,* introd. Edwin Markham (New York and London: The Co-operative Publication Society, n.d.), pp. 236–37.

IV

DATA

With Camilla and Gabriel Atkin, Cornwall, ca. 1933.

ROBERT H. BYINGTON

Chronology

December 13, 1890
Mary Butts is born at Salterns, Parkstone, Dorset.

Fall, 1897
Begins attendance at Sandecotes School, Parkstone.

April, 1901
Anthony Butts is born at Salterns, Parkstone, Dorset.

1905
Captain Frederick Butts, Mary's father (b. 1833), dies.

1906
Publishes her first work, a poem, "The Heavenward Side," in *Outlook* (June 30, 1906).

Fall, 1906–Spring, 1909
Attends St. Leonard's School, St. Andrews, Fife, Scotland.

Fall, 1909
Enrolls as a "general student" (which meant, practically, that she was not sitting for a degree and was therefore not bound by normal curricular requirements) at Westfield College, London University.

December, 1911
Comes into her personal inheritance and begins making her way into the avant-garde literary and artistic groups dominated by Ezra Pound, Ford Madox Ford, Wyndham Lewis, and their counterparts in the other arts.

June, 1912
Meets and falls in love with Eleanor Rogers, about whom little is known, except that, according to Rebecca West, she was dark-haired and without Mary Butts's "spectacular good looks."

July, 1912
Leaves Westfield College and moves into a Westbourne Park flat

with Eleanor Rogers (5 St. Stephen's Gardens, Westbourne Grove, London W. 2).

1912–1914
Develops her associations in the literary world of London and by the beginning of World War I, according to Rebecca West, was quite well-known in avant-garde circles.

May 7, 1915
Is appointed a volunteer member of the Children's Care Committee for Homerton Row School, Hackney.

1916
Meets and falls in love with John Rodker and begins *Ashe of Rings.* Also begins her journal, which she keeps for the rest of her life.

April 1, 1917
Leaves Eleanor Rogers in Hampstead and moves with John Rodker into another London flat (1 Glenilla Studios, London, N.W.3).

1918
Marries John Rodker and publishes "Vision" in *The Egoist,* and her first book, a translation into French of H. G. Wells's *God the Invisible King.*

1918–1919
Completes *Ashe of Rings* in Cornwall.

Spring, 1919
Moves into 43 Belsize Park Gardens with John Rodker, who begins operation of the Ovid Press, which over the next two years publishes T. S. Eliot's *Ara Vus Prec* and Ezra Pound's *Hugh Selwyn Mauberley,* and other literary works.

Fall, 1919
John Rodker succeeds Ezra Pound as London editor of *The Little Review,* and MB meets Cecil Maitland, who moves into "43" to help with the Ovid Press.

1920
Journeys to Paris with John Rodker, where they turn down an opportunity to publish *Ulysses* under the Ovid Press imprint, and returns to "43;" "Speed the Plough" is published in *The Dial.*

November, 1920
A daughter, Camilla, is born.

January-March, 1921
Five chapters of *Ashe of Rings* are serialized in *The Little Review.* John Rodker, informed of MB's affair with Cecil Maitland, leaves "43." Three days later, she deposits the four-month-old Camilla with Poppaea Vanda at 25 Belsize Crescent. Poppaea Vanda was the pen-name of a ballet critic, a friend of MB, with whom Camilla lives for the next five years. Then MB goes away with Maitland to Paris.

April, 1921
Has her first experience with drugs (hashish).

Summer, 1921
Spends the summer with Maitland at Aleister Crowley's abbey in Cefalù, Sicily.

September, 1921
Returns with Maitland to "43" after a brief stay in Paris following their summer at Cefalù.

1922
Goes on a trip with Cecil Maitland to Paris, Germany (St. Anton in the Arlberg and Berlin), and Austria (Vienna).

1923
Salterns is sold. *Speed the Plough* is published, and MB meets Glenway Wescott, who reviews *Speed the Plough* in *The Dial.* Maitland is hospitalized because of an old bullet wound (a fictionalized account of which appears in the story, "A Dinner Party"), and she takes him to convalesce in Dorset. She and Maitland then go to Paris and, finally, in October-November to Italy, where they meet Bryher, Norman Douglas, and Ezra Pound; they then return to "43."

March, 1924
MB and Maitland are forced to leave "43" because of circumstances fictionalized in her story, "The House," and take rooms in Douglas Goldring's house at St. James Terrace, Regent's Park, London.

1924
MB and Maitland take occasional trips to Paris, where they stay at the Hôtel Foyot. Meets Robert McAlmon and other members of "The Crowd."

1924–1925
Meets and associates a great deal with Duff Twysden, for whom she develops "strong emotion," apparently not reciprocated by Duff; nevertheless, lends Duff £350.

Winter, 1925
McAlmon's Contact Press publishes *Ashe of Rings,* as well as "Friendship's Garland" in McAlmon's *Contact Collection of Contemporary Writers.*

Late spring, 1925
Parts with Maitland, who goes to Brittany.

Summer, 1925
Meets, falls in love with, and separates from Geoffrey Dunlop, the original of Alan Courcy in the story "A Lover."

October, 1925
Meets and takes up with Murray Goodwin, the original of Paul in the story, "The House Party."

Late fall, 1925
Although retaining a lease on the rooms at St. James Terrace until July, 1926, moves to the Welcome Hotel in Villefranche, where she meets Jean Cocteau and associates with his circle, including Georges Auric, Gene MacCown, Glenway Wescott, Monroe Wheeler, and others.

Late spring, 1926
Leaves Villefranche and moves to Paris at 14 rue de Montessuy, where she lives with Mary Reynolds and Kitty Cannell and meets Sergei Maslenikoff, the original of Boris in *Imaginary Letters.*

Summer, 1926
Spends the summer at Giverney with Camilla (who can no longer stay with Poppaea Vanda) and Sergei.

Fall, 1926
Moves back to "14" in Paris.

December, 1926
Cecil Maitland dies of alcoholism in London.

1927
Stays in Paris at "14," but departs for visits of varying length to Villefranche, Cannes, Pramousquier, and elsewhere. She meets and falls in love with Virgil Thomson in March, and they part in November.

1928
Publishes *Armed with Madness* and *Imaginary Letters.* Meets Mireille Havet, an actress in Cocteau's *Orphée,* and Harcourt Wesson Bull in Villefranche.

Late autumn, 1928—April, 1929
Is living in London. At the beginning of this period she is able to get her Aunt Ada in Parkstone to have Camilla permanently, then takes rooms in Clarges Street. This was the time of the "Wild West" and "Greek" parties recounted in Martin Green's *Children of the Sun,* Evelyn Waugh's diaries and elsewhere.

1929
MB is back at "14" in Paris, where she sinks into poverty and drug dependency with Mireille Havet.

September, 1929
Relationship with Sergei Maslenikoff ends.

October, 1929
Meets Gabriel Aitken, a watercolorist and cartoonist, at San Malo, and they begin living together.

Spring, 1930
Gabriel Aitken leaves MB and goes off with Lucille Coons. She sinks even further into poverty and despondency, some of the characteristics of which are treated in the story "In the House."

June, 1930
Is rescued from a nervous breakdown in Paris by her mother, Mary Colville-Hyde, and brought back to England.

October, 1930
Is reunited with Gabriel Aitken, and they marry.

April, 1931
MB and Gabriel take a trip to Switzerland, where Gabriel undergoes a cure for his lungs (injections of gold).

May, 1931
MB and Gabriel briefly live in Newcastle-on-Tyne.

August, 1931
They move to Chelsea.

January, 1932
They relocate to a cottage, "Tebel Vos," on the cliffs above Sennen Cove, Cornwall.

1932
Publishes *Several Occasions, Death of Felicity Taverner, Traps for Unbelievers* and *Warning to Hikers.*

1933
Publishes *The Macedonian.*

December, 1934
Gabriel Aitken leaves MB permanently, and goes to live with his aunts in Newcastle-on-Tyne.

1935
Publishes *Scenes from the Life of Cleopatra,* and begins work on a novel about Julian the Apostate, of which she drafts fifty-five typed pages.

March 5, 1937
Dies of perforated ulcers in a Penzance hospital.

1937
The Crystal Cabinet: My Childhood at Salterns, edited and shortened by her literary executor Angus Davidson, is published posthumously.

1938
Last Stories is also published posthumously but soon withdrawn due to a threat of a libel suit from Geoffrey Dunlop.

1984–85
Gravestone in Sennen churchyard is restored by Mary Butts's daughter, Camilla, and the words by William Blake added: "I strove to seize the inmost form."

KENNETH IRBY & CHRISTOPHER WAGSTAFF

A Preliminary Checklist of Published Writings by and about Mary Butts

THIS PRELIMINARY CHECKLIST suggests the breadth of the work Mary Butts produced during her brief but very productive writing career. Perhaps of greatest surprise is the large number of diverse and penetrating reviews she contributed to newspapers and magazines during the 1930s. The five sections of this list cover: A) books, pamphlets and translations, B) fiction in periodicals and collections, C) poems and prose poems D) articles, reviews and other miscellaneous prose, and E) selected writings about and relating to Mary Butts. Sections A through D are arranged chronologically, section E alphabetically. We anticipate that other published reviews, essays, and poems will undoubtedly come to light that we have missed or been unable to locate. We are especially grateful to Mary Butts's daughter Camilla Bagg for permitting us to examine and photocopy her mother's two large clippings books which, although incomplete, laid a foundation for the listing of reviews and gave fresh impetus to our search for periodicals. In addition, warm appreciation is due to the research workers in the interlibrary loan services at the University of California, Davis, who assisted us over many months in locating and borrowing various items for our inspection. Lastly, we are happy to report that in 1994 photocopies of nearly all of the articles in part D, as well as most of the reviews of Mary Butts's work which appeared during her lifetime, were placed in a special "Mary Butts Miscellany" collection in the Bancroft Library at the University of California, Berkeley. They are now available to anyone wishing to read them. It is hoped that this collection of research materials will expand and become more complete in the years ahead.

A. BOOKS, PAMPHLETS, AND TRANSLATIONS

A1 *Dieu L'Invisible Roi* by H. G. Wells. "Traduction et préface de M. Butts." Paris: Payot, 1918. 329 p. The preface (pp. ix-ciii) quotes extensively from Wells's *First and Last Things.*

A2 *Speed the Plough and Other Stories.* London: Chapman & Hall, Ltd., 1923. 222 p.

A3 *Ashe of Rings.* Novel. Paris: Contact Editions, Three Mountains Press, 1925. 304 p.

A4 *Ashe of Rings.* New York: Albert & Charles Boni, 1926. 296 p.

A5 *Armed with Madness.* Novel. London: Wishart & Company, 1928. 225 p.

A6 *Armed with Madness.* "With drawings by Jean Cocteau." Larger format on hand-made paper and limited to 100 copies. London: Wishart & Co., 1928. 225 p. Three drawings by Cocteau, including frontispiece.

A7 *Armed with Madness.* New York: Albert & Charles Boni, 1928. 238 p.

A8 *Imaginary Letters.* "With Engravings on Copper from the Original Drawings by Jean Cocteau." First edition of 250 copies, numbered. Paris: Edward W. Titus, 1928. 49 p. Seven drawings by Cocteau, including frontispiece.

A9 *Armed with Madness.* "Cheaper Re-issue." London: Wishart & Co., 1932. 205 p.

A10 *Death of Felicity Taverner.* Novel. London: Wishart & Co., 1932. 268 p.

A11 *Several Occasions.* Stories. London: Wishart & Co., 1932. 231 p.

A12 *Traps for Unbelievers.* Essay. London: Desmond Harmsworth, 1932. 51 p.

A13 *Warning to Hikers.* Essay. The Here and Now Pamphlets, no. 6. London: Wishart & Co., 1932. 36 p.

A14 *Ashe of Rings.* "Afterword by the author. First English Edition (revised)." London: Wishart & Co., 1933. 313 p.

A15 *The Macedonian.* Historical novel. London: William Heinemann Ltd., 1933. 211 p.

A16 *Scenes from the Life of Cleopatra.* Historical novel. London: William Heinemann Ltd., 1935. 286 p.

A17 *The Crystal Cabinet: My Childhood at Salterns.* Autobiography. London: Methuen & Co., Ltd., 1937. 279 p. Frontispiece portrait by Cocteau.

A18 *Last Stories.* London: Brendin Publishing Co., 1938. 265 p.

A19 *Scenes from the Life of Cleopatra.* Photo-offset reprint of 1935 ed. New York: The Ecco Press, 1974. 286 p.

A20 *Imaginary Letters.* "With reproduction of the original line drawings by Jean Cocteau." Afterword by Robin Blaser, including the poem, "Corfe," by Butts. Vancouver: Talonbooks, 1979. 80 p.

A21 *The Crystal Cabinet: My Childhood at Salterns.* Expanded ed. Forward by Camilla Bagg. Afterword by Barbara O'Brien Wagstaff. London: Carcanet, 1988. 296 p. Simultaneously published by Beacon Press, Boston.

A22 *With and Without Buttons and Other Stories.* Selected with an afterword by Nathalie Blondel. Manchester: Carcanet Press Limited, 1991. 216 p. Includes fourteen stories.

A23 *From Altar to Chimney-piece. Selected Stories.* Preface by John Ashbery. Kingston: McPherson & Co., 1992. 293 p. Includes sixteen stories.

A24 *The Taverner Novels.* An omnibus edition of *Armed with Madness* and *Death of Felicity Taverner.* Preface by Paul West. Afterword by Barbara O'Brien Wagstaff. Kingston: McPherson & Co., 1992. 384 p.

A25 *The Classical Novels.* An omnibus edition of *The Macedonian* and *Scenes from the Life of Cleopatra,* including three short stories. Foreword by Thomas McEvilley. Kingston: McPherson & Co., 1994. 360 p.

B. FICTION IN PERIODICALS AND COLLECTIONS

B1 "Lettres Imaginaires." *The Little Review* 6. 6 (Oct. 1919): 8–12; 6. 7 (Nov. 1919): 27–32.

B2 "Magic." *The Little Review* 7. 2 (July-Aug. 1920): 3–6.

B3 "Ashe of Rings." [Chapters 1–5 of the novel.] *The Little Review* 7. 4 (Jan.-Mar. 1921): 3–14; 8. 1 (Autumn 1921): 97–106.

B4 "Speed the Plough." *The Dial* 71 (Oct. 1921): 399–406.

B5 "Change." *The Dial* 72 (May 1922): 465–70.

B6 "Speed the Plough." *Georgian Stories 1922.* London: Chapman & Hall, Ltd., 1922. 46–54.

B7 "Speed the Plough." *Georgian Stories 1922.* New York: G. P. Putnam's Sons, 1923. 44–54.

B8 "Deosil." *The Transatlantic Review* 1. 4 (Mar. 1924): 40–50.

B9 "Deosil." *The Best British Short Stories of 1924.* Ed. Edward J. O'Brien and John Cournos. Boston: Small, Maynard & Co., 1924. 27–37.

B10 "Speed the Plough." *Stories from the Dial.* New York: Lincoln MacVeagh, The Dial Press, 1924. 152–66.

B11 "Speed the Plough." *Stories from the Dial.* London: Jonathan Cape, 1924. 152–66.

B12 "Friendship's Garland." *Contact Collection of Contemporary Writers.* Paris: Contact Editions, Three Mountains Press, 1925. 30–40.

B13 "The Later Life of Theseus, King of Athens." *The Calendar of Modern Letters* 1. 4 (June 1925): 257–65.

B14 "The Later Life of Theseus, King of Athens." *Georgian Stories 1927.* Ed. Arthur Waugh. London: Chapman & Hall, Ltd., 1927. 66–75.

B15 "The Later Life of Theseus, King of Athens." *Georgian Stories 1927.* Ed. Arthur Waugh. New York: G. P. Putnam's Sons, 1928. 80–90.

B16 "The House Party." *Pagany* 1. 1 (Jan.-Mar. 1930): 7–24.

B17 "Scylla and Charybdis." *Pagany* 1. 4 (Oct.-Dec. 1930): 6–17.

B18 "Green." *Pagany* 2. 4 (Oct.-Dec. 1931): 1–13.

B19 "After the Funeral." *The London Mercury* 27. 158 (Dec. 1932): 111–15.

B20 "A Lover." *Life and Letters* 11. 58 (Oct. 1934): 26–37.

B21 "The Warning." *Life and Letters* 11. 61 (Jan. 1935): 396–404.

B22 "The Guest." *Life and Letters To-day* 13. 1 (Sept. 1935): 101–15.

B23 "One Roman Speaks." *The Cornhill Magazine* 152 [n.s. 59]. 910 (Oct. 1935): 448–65.

B24 "In the House." *Life and Letters To-day* 18. 11 (Spring 1938): 83–85.

B25 "Mappa Mundi." *Life and Letters To-day* 18. 11 (Spring 1938): 86–96.

B26 "Honey, Get Your Gun." *Life and Letters To-day* 18. 12 (Summer 1938): 74–80.

B27 "The House." *Life and Letters To-day* 18. 12 (Summer 1938): 61–73.

B28 "Look Homeward, Angel." *Life and Letters To-day* 18. 12 (Summer 1938): 56–60.

B29 "Green." *A Return to Pagany*. Ed. Stephen Halpert and Richard Johns. Boston: Beacon Press, 1969. 344–56.

B30 "Look Homeward, Angel." *The Cornish Review* 16 (Winter 1970): 9–14.

B31 "The Golden Bough." *Antaeus* 13–14 (Spring-Summer 1974): 88–97.

B32 "Bellerophon to Anteia," "The Later Life of Theseus, King of Athens," and "A Roman Speaks." Appendix: Three Stories. *The Classical Novels.* An omnibus edition of *The Macedonian* and *Scenes from the Life of Cleopatra.* Foreword by Thomas McEvilley. Kingston: McPherson & Co., 1994.

C. POEMS AND PROSE POEMS

C1 "The Heavenward Side." *The Outlook* 83 (30 June 1906): 504.

C2 "Vision." *The Egoist* 5. 8 (Sept. 1918): 111.

C3 "Pythian Ode." *The Transatlantic Review* 2. 3 (1924): 235–39.

C4 "Two Poems." ["Give bread give drink"; "On Vexui" (*sic*)]. *Larus* 1. 3 (May 1927): 10–13.

C5 "Picus Martius." *The Hound & Horn* 3. 2 (Jan.-May. 1930): 230–33.

C6 "Heartbreak House." *Pagany* 1. 3 (July-Sept. 1930): 1–4.

C7 "Thinking of Saints and Petronius Arbiter." *Pagany* 2. 1 (Jan.-Mar. 1931): 95–97.

C8 "Rites of Passage." *Pagany* 2. 3 (July-Sept. 1931): 62–63.

C9 "Douarnenez." *Soma* 3 (1932): 45–46.

C10 "Heartbreak House." *Soma* 3 (1932): 46–48.

C11 "Picus Martius." *Soma* 3 (1932): 41–43.

C12 "Thinking of Saints and of Petronius Arbiter." *Soma* 3 (1932): 43–45.

C13 "Corfe." *An "Objectivists" Anthology*. Ed. Louis Zukofsky. Le Beausset, Var, France: To Publishers, 1932. 36–39.

C14 "On An American Wonder-Child Who Translated Homer at Eight Years Old." *Seed* 1 (Jan. 1933): 9–10.

C15 "Corfe." [Final portion, from "Until they came to the world's end," with a note by John Wieners.] *The Floating Bear* 26 (Oct. 1963): 3. Rpt. ed. La Jolla: Laurence McGilvery, 1973. 287.

C16 [With Cecil Maitland.] "House Rhymes by Cecil and Mary." ["The Douglas Credit System"; "Hutson's Meals"; "Love"; "The Bath."] In "Selections from the Journal." Ed. Robert H. Byington and Glen E. Morgan. *Art & Literature* 7 (Winter 1965): 167–69.

C17 "Avenue Montaigne." *Antaeus* 12 (Winter 1973): 151–52.

C18 "Corfe." *Antaeus* 12 (Winter 1973): 144–46.

C19 "Heartbreak House." *Antaeus* 12 (Winter 1973): 147–50.

C20 "Parenthesis." *Antaeus* 12 (Winter 1973): 143.

C21 "Thinking of Saints and of Petronius Arbithe" [sic]. *Antaeus* 12 (Winter 1973): 141–42.

C22 "Two Ways of Not Seeing the World." *Antaeus* 12 (Winter 1973): 140.

C23 "Corfe." Butts, *Imaginary Letters.* In Afterword by Robin Blaser. Vancouver: Talonbooks, 1979. 77–80.

C24 "The Peace of God." *The Writings and the World of Mary Butts.* Conference brochure. University of California, Davis, 1984. n. pag.

D. ARTICLES, REVIEWS, AND OTHER MISCELLANEOUS PROSE

1919

D1 "Aldington's Images of Desire." *The Little Review* 6. 4 (Aug. 1919): 35–36.

1920

D2 Rev. of *The Works of Thomas Vaughan,* ed. A. E. Waite. *The Little Review* 6. 10 (Mar. 1920): 47–48.

D3 "Thomas Vaughan." Reply to S. Foster Damon. *The Little Review* 7. 3 (Sept.-Dec. 1920): 58.

1921

D4 Rev. of *The Wild-flowers of Asklepiades, and Poems of Poseidippos* and *The Poems of Meleager of Gadara. The Little Review* 7. 4 (Jan.-Mar. 1921): 45–47.

1922

D5 "Unpleasant Court Cases, Facts of Life, Plea for Rank and Adequate Knowledge." Interview. *Pall Mall* (20 Dec. 1922): n. pag.

1924

D6 "A Correction." Letter. *The Transatlantic Review* 2. 1 (1924): 98.

1929

D7 "Mr Wescott's Third Book." Rev. of *Good-bye Wisconsin,* by Glenway Wescott. *The Dial* 82 (May 1929): 424–27.

D8 Reply to questionnaire. *The Little Review* 7. 2 (May 1929): 21–22.

1931

D9 "Aldous Huxley." *Scrutinies by Various Writers,* Volume II. Ed. Edgell Rickword. London: Wishart & Co., 1931. 74–98.

D10 "France and Classicism." Rev. of *Introduction to French Classicism,* by H. Caudwell. *The Bookman* 80 (July 1931): 211.

D11 "A Story of Ancient Magic." Rev. of *The Corn King and the Spring Queen,* by Naomi Mitchison. *The Bookman* 80 (July 1931): 210.

D12 "Antiquity?" Rev. of *The Greek Slave,* by Douglas Sladen. *The Bookman* 81 (Nov. 1931): 137.

D13 "Rousseau." Rev. of *Jean-Jacques Rousseau,* by John Charpentier. *The Bookman* 81 (Dec. 1931), Xmas suppl.: 51–52.

1932

D14 "On Gardens." Rev. of *Gardens and Gardening: Studio Gardening Annual (1932). The Bookman* 82 (Apr. 1932): 40.

D15 "A Glimpse of the Victorian Scene." Rev. of *Victorian Days and Ways,* by Mark Perugini. *The Bookman* 82 (May 1932): 119.

D16 "The Past in the Present." Rev. of *Greek By-ways,* by T. R. Glover. *The Bookman* 82 (July 1932): 206.

D17 "The Real East End." Rev. of *The Real East End,* by Thomas Burke. *The Bookman* 83 (Oct. 1932): 24.

D18 "Hesiod, an Hellenic Prophet." Rev. of *Hesiod: Works and Days,* ed. T. A. Sinclair. *The Bookman* 83 (Nov. 1932): 113–14.

D19 Rev. of *Rome: Of the Renaissance and To-day,* by Sir Rennell Rodd. *The Bookman* 83 (Dec. 1932): 254.

D20 "This England." Rev. of *This Unknown Island,* by S. P. B. Mais, and six other books. *The Bookman* 83 (Dec. 1932): 274–80.

D21 "Vision of Asia." Rev. of *The Vision of Asia: An Interpretation of Chinese Art and Culture,* by L. Cranmer-Byng. *The Bookman* 83 (Dec. 1932): 223–25.

1933

D22 Rev. of *Josephus,* by Lion Feuchtwanger. *The Bookman* 83 (Jan. 1933): 405.

D23 "Ghosties and Ghoulies: Uses of the Supernatural in English Fiction." *The Bookman* 83 (Jan. 1933): 386–89; (Feb. 1933): 433–35; (Mar. 1933): 493–94; vol. 84 (Apr. 1933): 12–14.

D24 "The Girl Through the Ages." Rev. of *The Girl Through the Ages,* by Dorothy Margaret Stuart. *The Bookman* 84 (May 1933): 110.

D25 "Aristophanes, the Laughing Philosopher." Rev. of *Aristophanes,* by Gilbert Murray. *The Bookman* 84 (June 1933): 152.

D26 "Taking Thought." Rev. of *Thinking and Doing,* by Harry Roberts. *Time and Tide* 14. 24 (17 June 1933): 738, 740.

D27 Rev. of *A History of Delos,* by W. A. Laidlaw. *The Bookman* 84 (July 1933): 212.

D28 "Our Native Land." Rev. of *This Was England,* by Horace Annesley Vachell, and two other books. *The Bookman* 84 (Aug. 1933): 252.

D29 "Alexander the Great, the Claim to Divinity." Rev. of *Alexander the Great,* by Arthur Weigall. *Sunday Times* (24 Sept. 1933): 10.

D30 "The Dark Tower." Rev. of *A Modern Prelude,* by Hugh I'Anson Fausset. *Time and Tide* 14. 39 (30 Sept. 1933): 1153–54.

D31 Rev. of *Alexander the Great,* by Arthur Weigall. *The Bookman* 85 (Oct. 1933): 78–79.

D32 Rev. of *Ancient Greek Literature,* by C. M. Bowra. *The Bookman* 85 (Oct. 1933): 84.

D33 "It Was Like That." Rev. of *The Testament of Youth,* by Vera Brittain, and *Up the Attic Stairs,* by Violet M. Macdonald. *The Bookman* 85 (Oct. 1933): 44.

D34 "For Special People." Rev. of *Twice Shy,* by D. M. Low, and two other books. *John O'London's Weekly* 30. 756 (7 Oct. 1933): 22.

D35 "King Richard III Defended." Rev. of *King Richard III: A Chronicle,* by Philip Lindsay. *Sunday Times* (8 Oct. 1933): 8.

D36 "A Russian Prophet." Rev. of *Jesus the Unknown* and *The Secret of the West,* by Dmitri Merezhkovsky. *Time and Tide* 14. 41 (14 Oct. 1933): 1228, 1230.

D37 "Gods and Men." Rev. of *Alexander the Great,* by Arthur Weigall. *Week-End Review* 8. 190a (21 Oct. 1933): 411–12.

D38 "Homage to Bertrand du Guesclin." Rev. of *Black Mastiff,* by M. Coryn. *Sunday Times* (5 Nov. 1933): 8.

D39 "'Back to the Land,' A Plea to the Town Dweller." Rev. of *Country Days,* by A. G. Street. *Daily Telegraph* (21 Nov. 1933): 15.

D40 Rev. of *A Bunch of Blue Ribbons,* no author given, and *The Drama of the Weather,* by Sir Napier Shaw. *The Bookman* 85 (Dec. 1933), Xmas no.: 309–10.

D41 "England." Rev. of *Week-Ends in England,* by S. P. B. Mais, and two other books. *The Bookman* 85 (Dec. 1933): 256, 258.

D42 Rev. of *The Herschel Chronicle: The Life Story of William Herschel and His Sister Caroline,* ed. Constance A. Lubbock. *The Bookman* 85 (Dec. 1933): 252–53.

D43 "Magic of Person and Place." Rev. of *The Strange Death of President Harding,* by Gaston B. Means, and eight other books. *The Bookman* 85 (Dec. 1933): 141–43.

D44 Rev. of *Poet and Artist in Greece,* by E. A. Gardner. *The Bookman* 85 (Dec. 1933): 218.

D45 "'This England.'" Letter. *The Bookman* 85 (Dec. 1933): 202.

D46 "The Real Wordsworth." Rev. of *The Later Wordsworth,* by Edith C. Batho. *Time and Tide* 14. 48 (2 Dec. 1933): 1446, 1448.

D47 "The Pleasures of Gardening." Rev. of *A Short History of Gardens,* by H. N. Wethered. *Sunday Times* (3 Dec. 1933): 15.

D48 "On Gardens, Holding the Right Emotion." Rev. of *I Know a Garden,* by Marian Cran. *Sunday Times* (10 Dec. 1933), Xmas book suppl.: 3.

D49 "A Biographical Problem, Katherine Mansfield's Early Life." Rev. of *The Life of Katherine Mansfield,* by R. E. Mantz and J. Middleton Murray. *Sunday Times* (31 Dec. 1933): 6.

1934

D50 "Unparalleled Swift." Rev. of *Swift or The Egoist,* by Mario M. Rossi and J. M. Hone, and *Jonathan Swift,* by W. D. Taylor. *Time and Tide* 15. 2 (13 Jan. 1934): 44–45.

D51 "Values." Rev. of *Whistler's Corner,* by Nora Stevenson, and two other books. *John O'London's Weekly* 30. 772 (27 Jan. 1934): 656.

D52 "The Art of Montagu [sic] James." *The London Mercury* 29 (Feb. 1934): 306–17.

D53 "Where Are We Going?" Rev. of *Camilla,* by Anne Stretton, and two other books. *John O'London's Weekly* 30. 773 (3 Feb. 1934): 690.

D54 "A Man Possessed." Rev. of *The Quest for Corvo,* by A. J. A. Symons. *Time and Tide* 15. 7 (17 Feb. 1934): 212, 214.

D55 "The New Gods." Rev. of *Fire Brigade,* by Raymond Otis, and two other books. *John O'London's Weekly* 30. 775 (17 Feb. 1934): 766.

D56 "Mr. Powys's Dorset." Rev. of *Earth Memories,* by Llewelyn Powys. *Sunday Times* (18 Feb. 1934): 11.

D57 "Alexander the Great, The Real Dilemma." Rev. of *Alexander the Great,* by F. A. Wright. *Sunday Times* (25 Feb. 1934): 11.

D58 "The Isles of Greece." Rev. of *From Olympus to the Styx,* by F. L. Lucas and Prudence Lucas. *The Bookman* 85 (Mar. 1934): 505.

D59 "King Harry." Rev. of *Henry VIII,* by Helen Simpson. *Time and Tide* 15. 13 (31 Mar. 1934): 412–13.

D60 Rev. of *Cornish Homes and Customs,* by A. K. Hamilton Jenkins. *The Bookman* 86 (Apr. 1934): 72.

D61 "The Past Lives Again." Rev. of *Rome for Sale,* by Jack Lindsay, and two other books. *The Bookman* 86 (Apr. 1934): 44–45.

D62 "Roads Through the Centuries, Track to By-Pass." Rev. of *From Track to By-Pass,* by T. W. Wilkinson. *Sunday Times* (22 Apr. 1934): 12.

D63 "Baron Corvo." *The London Mercury* 29 (May 1934): 619–24.

D64 "The Grandeur of Rome." Rev. of *Twelve Centuries of Rome,* by G. P. Baker. *The Bookman* 86 (May 1934): 119.

D65 "Scandal or History." Rev. of *I, Claudius,* by Robert Graves. *Time and Tide* 15. 18 (5 May 1934): 584–86.

D66 "A New Vision." Rev. of *Orthodoxy Sees It Through,* ed. by Sidney Dark. *Time and Tide* 15. 21 (26 May 1934): 675–77.

D67 "Gardens and Gardening." Rev. of *Gardens and Gardening: The Studio Gardening Annual (1934),* ed. F. A. Mercer. *The Bookman* 86 (June 1934): 161.

D68 "The Great Dumas." Rev. of *Dumas, Père,* by G. R. Pearce. *Time and Tide* 15. 23 (9 June 1934): 732–34.

D69 "'A Waste of Shame.'" Rev. of *The Fool of Love, A Life of William Hazlitt,* by Hesketh Pearson. *Time and Tide* 15. 25 (23 June 1934): 802–03.

D70 "An Artist in a New World." Rev. of *The Ordeal of Mark Twain,* by Van Wyck Brooks. *Sunday Times* (22 July 1934): 12.

D71 Rev. of *Country,* by H.J. Massingham. *The Bookman* 86 (July 1934): 189.

D72 "Two Blind Mice." Rev. of *Mr. Finchley Discovers His England,* by Victor Canning. *The Bookman* 86 (Aug. 1934): 255.

D73 "Mr. S. P. B. Mais in America." Rev. of *A Modern Columbus,* by S. P. B. Mais. *Sunday Times* (9 Sept. 1934): 9. [Signed M. B.]

D74 "Mr. Mencken Again, A Question of Ethics." Rev. of *Treatise on Right and Wrong,* by H. L. Mencken. *Sunday Times* (30 Sept. 1934): 12.

D75 "Jig-saw History." Rev. of *Marathon and Salamis,* by Compton Mackenzie. *The Bookman* 87 (Oct. 1934): 62.

D76 Rev. of *Negro,* ed. Nancy Cunard. *The Adelphi* 3rd ser. 9. 1 (Oct. 1934): 185–87.

D77 "'Mr. Ezra Pound Is the Goods.'" Rev. of *Make It New,* by Ezra Pound. *Sunday Times* (28 Oct. 1934): 12.

D78 "Five Also Ran." Rev. of *The Foolscap Rose,* by Joseph Hergesheimer, and five other books. *The Bookman* 87 (Nov. 1934): 129–30.

D79 "Two Artists." Rev. of *Gerald, A Portrait,* by Daphne du Maurier, and *Peter Warlock: A Memoir of Philip Heseltine,* by Cecil Gray. *Time and Tide* 15. 45 (10 Nov. 1934): 1430.

D80 "Mr. Graves's Rome." Rev. of *Claudius the God,* by Robert Graves. *The Bookman* 87 (Dec. 1934), Xmas suppl.: 36.

1935

D81 "King Henry the Fifth, Behind the Curtain of History." Rev. of *King Henry V,* by Philip Lindsay, and *Henry V,* by J. D. Griffith Davies. *Sunday Times* (6 Jan. 1935): 8.

D82 "A Swedish Childhood." Rev. of *Memories of My Childhood,* by Selma Lagerlöf. *Time and Tide* 16. 2 (12 Jan. 1935): 55.

D83 "Spring Storm." *Manchester Guardian* (11 June 1935): 16.

D84 "Seven Detective Stories, New Poirot Novel." Rev. of *Death in the Clouds,* by Agatha Christie, and six other novels. *Sunday Times* (14 July 1935): 8. [Signed M. B.]

D85 "Four Detective Novels." Rev. of *The Man Who Was Too Clever,* by Anthony Gilbert, and three other novels. *Sunday Times* (21 July 1935): 8. [Signed M. B.]

D86 "Modern World and Religion." Rev. of *Religion and the Modern State,* by Christopher Dawson, and two other books. *Sunday Times* (18 Aug. 1935): 9.

D87 "Adventure and Detection, Stories by Beginners." Rev. of *Better than Warfare,* by Louis Christie, and two other novels. *Sunday Times* (1 Sept. 1935): 7. [Signed M. B.]

D88 "Conspiracies and Crime." Rev. of *Murder in Fancy Dress,* by Inez Haynes, and five other novels. *Sunday Times* (8 Sept. 1935): 7. [Signed M. B.]

D89 "The Eighteenth Century." Rev. of *Oliver Goldsmith,* by Stephen Gwynn, and *William Cowper,* by Gilbert Thomas. *Time and Tide* 16.38 (21 Sept. 1935): 1339–40.

D90 "Imperial Rome." Rev. of *Augustus. A Novel,* by Gunther Birkenfeld, and *Magnificent Hadrian,* by Sulamith Ish-Kishor. *Time and Tide* 16. 40 (5 Oct. 1935): 1403–04.

D91 "The Funeral March of a Marionette." Rev. of *The Funeral March of a Marionette,* by Susan Buchan. *Time and Tide* 16. 41 (12 Oct. 1935): 1450.

D92 "America in the 'Gilded Age.'" Rev. of *"King Lehr" and the Gilded Age,* by Elizabeth Drexel Lehr. *Sunday Times* (20 Oct. 1935): 16.

D93 "Dorset Essays, Scenes and Memories." Rev. of *Dorset Essays,* by Llewelyn Powys. *Sunday Times* (24 Nov. 1935): 16.

D94 "The Finer Corvo." Rev. of *Hubert's Arthur,* by Rolfe, Baron Corvo. *Time and Tide* 16. 49 (7 Dec. 1935): 1800, 1802.

D95 "Green Fingers." Rev. of *The Living Garden,* by E. J. Salisbury. *Sunday Times* (8 Dec. 1935): 12.

1936

D96 "Parzival." Rev. of *The Story of Parzival and the Grail,* Wolfram von Eschenbach, by Margaret Fitzgerald Richey. *Time and Tide* 17. 2 (11 Jan. 1936): 57–58.

D97 "Americans on England, Pilgrims of the Past." Rev. of *Americans on England,* by Professor R. B. Mowat. *Sunday Times* (2 Feb. 1936): 13.

D98 "Queen Victoria's 'Wicked Uncle.'" Rev. of *Ernest Augustus, Duke of Cumberland and King of Hanover,* by Herbert Van Thal. *Sunday Times* (9 Feb. 1936): 11.

D99 "Mount Athos." Rev. of *The Monks of Athos,* by R. M. Dawkins. *Time and Tide* 17. 11 (14 Mar. 1936): 385–86.

D100 "The Lady on the Black Horse." Rev. of *Miracles and Adventures,* by M. A. Sinclair Stobart. *Time and Tide* 17. 12 (21 Mar. 1936): 417–18.

D101 "The Fortunes of a Family." Rev. of *The Five Sons of "Bare Betty,"* by Col. the Hon. Arthur C. Murray. *Sunday Times* (29 Mar., 1936): 11.

D102 "Cleopatra's Daughter." Rev. of *Cleopatra's Daughter,* by Beatrice Chanler. *Time and Tide* 17. 14 (4 Apr. 1936): 488–89.

D103 "Flickering Genius." Rev. of *A Flame in Sunlight, Thomas de Quincey,* by Edward Sackville-West. *Time and Tide* 17. 19 (9 May 1936): 680–81.

D104 "Caesar and His Times." Rev. of *Caesar's Mantle,* by Ferdinand Mainzer, trans. by Eden Paul and Cedar Paul. *Sunday Times* (24 May 1936): 10.

D105 "Chartres—The Symbol." Rev. of *Mont-Saint-Michel and Chartres,* by Henry Adams. *Time and Tide* 17. 24 (13 June 1936): 856.

D106 "Great Drama and Small." Rev. of *Thomas Cranmer,* by Charles Williams, and *Garibaldi,* by John Drinkwater. *Time and Tide* 17. 31 (1 Aug. 1936): 1103.

D107 "The Eighteenth Century." Rev. of *Oliver Goldsmith,* by Stephen Gwynn, and *William Cowper,* by Gilbert Thomas. *Time and Tide* 17. 38 (21 Sept. 1936): 1339–40.

D108 "The Real Voltaire." Rev. of *Voltaire,* by Alfred Noyes. *Time and Tide* 17. 46 (14 Nov. 1936): 1596.

1937

D109 "The Heresy Game." *The Spectator* 158 (12 Mar. 1937): 466–67.

D110 "Eminent Romans." Rev. of *Marcus Agrippa,* by F. A. Wright, and *Augustus Caesar,* by Bernard M. Allen. *Time and Tide* 18. 15 (10 Apr. 1937): 470, 472.

1965

D111 "Selections from the Journal." Ed., with intro., Robert H. Byington and Glen E. Morgan. *Art and Literature* 7 (Winter 1965): 166–79.

1969

D112 Letter. *A Return to Pagany.* Ed. Stephen Halpert and Richard Johns. Boston: Beacon Press, 1969. 339.

1985

D113 Three letters. Ed. Barbara O'Brien Wagstaff. *Northern Lights* 2 (1985–86): 23–27.

E. SELECTED WRITINGS ABOUT AND RELATING TO MARY BUTTS

E1 Acton, Harold. *Memoirs of an Aesthete.* London: Methuen & Co., Ltd., 1948.

E2 Adeane, Louis. "Mary Butts." *World Review* (Nov. 1951): 23–27.

E3 Agate, James. "Cleopatra as a Schoolmistress." *Daily Express* (6 June 1935). Rev. of *Scenes from the Life of Cleopatra.*

E4 Arnold, Lilian. "Russian and English." *John O'London's Weekly* (10 Dec. 1932): 438. Rev. of *Death of Felicity Taverner.*

E5 Bagg, Camilla. Foreward. *The Crystal Cabinet: My Childhood at Salterns.* Boston: Beacon Press, 1988. iii-viii. Also in Carcanet ed.

E6 Baker, Frank. "A Note on Mary Butts." *The Cornish Review* 16 (Winter 1970): 4–8.

E7 ———. "Mary Butts." *I Follow But Myself.* London: Peter Davies, 1968.

E8 Beach, Sylvia. *Shakespeare and Company.* New York: Harcourt, Brace & Co., 1956.

E9 Beer, Patricia. "Very Like Poole Harbour." *London Review of Books* (5 Dec. 1991): 16. Rev. of *With and Without Buttons.*

E10 Blakeston, Oswell. "Plutarch's Siren." *Books and Bookmen* 16. 6 (Mar. 1971): 29.

E11 ———. "The Lady Who Enchanted Cocteau." *Little Caesar* 12 (1982): 19–22.

E12 Blaser, Robin. Afterword. *Imaginary Letters.* Vancouver: Talonbooks, 1979. 61–76.

E13 ———. Pῖκοσ ὁ καὶ Ζεύσ. *The Writings and the World of Mary Butts.* Conference brochure. University of California, Davis, 1984. n. pag.

E14 Blondel, Nathalie. Rev. of *The Crystal Cabinet. Poetry Nation Review* 15. 3 (1988): 53–55.

E15 Blunden, Edmund. "Alexander." *Time and Tide* (29 Apr. 1933): 501–02. Rev. of *The Macedonian.*

E16 Boulton, Cecil. "Mary Butts' Bright Novel, *Ashe of Rings,* 'Dostoevski Served With a Little Milk.'" *New York Evening Post* (5 June 1926): 5. Rev. of *Ashe of Rings.*

E17 Bowen, Stella. *Drawn from Life.* New ed. with intro. by Julia Loewe. London: Virago, 1984.

E18 Browne, Wynyard. "A Great Novel." *The Bookman* (Dec. 1932): 306. Rev. of *Death of Felicity Taverner.*

E19 ———. "Greek and Barbarian." *The Bookman* (Apr. 1933): 44–45. Rev. of *The Macedonian.*

E20 Bryher. "Recognition Not Farewell." *Life and Letters To-day* 17. 9 (Autumn 1937): 159–64.

E21 Bunting, Basil. "Uno dei mali dell' Inghilterra." *Il Mare,* 1933. Rev. of *Death of Felicity Taverner.*

E22 Byington, Robert H. and Morgan, Glen E. "Mary Butts." *Art and Literature* 7 (Winter 1965): 163–65.

E23 Cage, John and Hoover, Kathleen. *Virgil Thomson: His Life and Music.* New York: Thomas Yoseloff, 1959.

E24 Charters, James. *This Must Be the Place: Memoirs of Montparnasse.* Ed. Morrill Cody. London: Herbert Joseph Ltd., 1934.

E25 Conant, Oliver. "Countryside Modern." *New York Times Book Review* (26 July 1992). Rev. of *With and Without Buttons* and *From Altar to Chimney-piece.*

E26 Crowley, Aleister. *The Confessions of Aleister Crowley: An Autobiography.* Ed. John Symonds and Kenneth Grant. London: Routledge & Kegan Paul, 1979.

E27 Dolin, Anton. *Autobiography.* London: Oldbourne, 1960.

E28 "A Dorset Childhood." *Times Literary Supplement* (29 May 1937): 404. Rev. of *The Crystal Cabinet: My Childhood at Salterns.*

E29 Duchêne, Anne. "Landowners and Lasses." *The Times Literary Supplement* (18 Oct. 1991): 1. Rev. of *With and Without Buttons.*

E30 Duncan, Robert. "Re Mary Butts." *The Writings and the World of Mary Butts.* Conference brochure. University of California, Davis, 1984. n. pag.

E31 Fausset, Hugh I'A. "A 'War-Fairy-Tale.'" *The Manchester Guardian* (22 Sept. 1933): 5. Rev. of *Ashe of Rings.*

E32 Ford, Hugh. *Published in Paris: American and British Writers, Printers, and Publishers in Paris, 1920–1939.* New York: Macmillan Publishing Co., 1975.

E33 Goldring, Douglas. "Literary Expatriates." *The Nineteen Twenties.* London: Nicholson & Watson, 1945.

E34 ———. "Mary and Cecil." *South Lodge.* London: Constable & Co. Ltd., 1943.

E35 ———. *Odd Man Out: The Autobiography of a "Propaganda Novelist."* London: Chapman & Hall, 1935.

E36 Grant, Joy. "Glimpses and Grievances." *The Times Literary Supplement* (23 Dec. 1988). Rev. of *The Crystal Cabinet: My Childhood at Salterns.*

E37 Guggenheim, Peggy. *Out of This Century.* New York: Universe Books, 1979.

E38 Hainley, Bruce. "Quite Contrary: Mary Butts' Wild Queendom." *Voice Literary Supplement* (May 1994): 21–23.

E39 Hall, Edward Fitch. "Modern Witchcraft." *New York Herald Tribune* (8 Aug. 1926): 8. Rev. of *Ashe of Rings.*

E40 Hamnet, Nina. *Laughing Torso.* New York: Ray Long & Richard R. Smith, Inc., 1932.

E41 Hartley, L. P. "The Literary Lounger." *The Sketch* (3 July 1935). Rev. of *Scenes from the Life of Cleopatra.*

E42 Hope, David. *Mary Butts, Fire-Bearer.* Sennen, Cornwall: Sennen Pamphlet Series, no. 1, 1937, 5 pgs.

E43 Ingram, H. F. "Poole's Forgotten Genius: The Story of Mary Butts." *Poole and Dorset Herald* (23 Feb. 1966): 2.

E44 ———. "Poole's Forgotten Genius: The Story of Mary Butts, Part II." *Poole and Dorset Herald* (2 Mar. 1966): 2.

E45 Kessler, Jascha. "Beauty and the Beast: Rediscovering Mary Butts." *The Bookpress* 3.7 (Oct. 1993): 1, 12–14.

E46 L., D. "In a Napkin." *The Review of Reviews* (June 1923). Rev. of *Speed the Plough and Other Stories.*

E47 Lanchester, Elsa. *Elsa Lanchester, Herself.* New York: St. Martin's Press, 1983.

E49 Lindberg-Seyersted, Brita, ed. *Pound/Ford: The Story of a Literary Friendship.* New York: New Directions, 1982.

E50 Lindsay, Jack. *Fanfrolico and After.* London: The Bodley Head, 1962.

E51 Lohrke, Eugene. "Cups and Spears." *New York Herald Tribune* (10 June 1928): 16. Rev. of *Armed with Madness.*

E52 "London After the War." *New York Times Book Review* (9 Aug. 1925): 7. Rev. of *Ashe of Rings.*

E53 M., A. N. "Change for Change's Sake." *The Manchester Guardian Weekly* (16 Mar. 1923): 212. Rev. of *Speed the Plough and Other Stories.*

E54 M., T. "A Memorable Novel." *The Manchester Guardian* (9 Dec. 1932): 7. Rev. of *Death of Felicity Taverner.*

E55 McAlmon, Robert. *Being Geniuses Together. An Autobiography.* London: Secker & Warburg, 1938. Rev. ed. with supplementary chapters by Kay Boyle. New York: Doubleday, 1968.

E56 Macaulay, Rose. "Stories Old and New." *The Daily News* (12 Apr. 1923): 7. Rev. of *Speed the Plough and Other Stories.*

E57 McKinley, Mary Ann. "Rediscovering an English Femme Maudit." *New Letters Book Reviewer* (Fall 1993): 4, 14. Rev. of *From Altar to Chimney-piece.*

E58 Medley, Robert. "Paris 1926." *Drawn from the Life: A Memoir.* London, Boston: Faber & Faber, 1983.

E59 "Miss Mary Butts: Imaginative Gifts." *The Times,* London (13 Mar. 1937): 14b. Obituary.

E60 Moore, Marianne. "A House-Party." *The Dial* 85 (Sept. 1928): 258–60. Rev. of *Armed with Madness.*

E61 ———. "A Study of Greatness." *The Manchester Guardian* (16 Mar. 1933): 5. Rev. of *The Macedonian.*

E62 "New Novels. *Death of Felicity Taverner.*" *Times Literary Supplement* (29 Dec. 1932): 988.

E63 "New Novels. *The Macedonian.*" *Times Literary Supplement* (20 July 1933): 494.

E64 "New Novels. *Scenes from the Life of Cleopatra.*" *Times Literary Supplement* (27 June 1935): 414.

E65 O'Brien, Kate. Rev. of *Death of Felicity Taverner. The Sunday Referee* (Dec. 1933).

E66 O'Riordan, Conal. "So Far as I Can See: Ideas in the Light of Experience I.—Of a New Author." *The New Writers* (16 Mar. 1923). Rev. of *Speed the Plough and Other Stories.*

E67 Pekar, Harvey. Rev. of *The Taverner Novels* and *From Altar to Chimney-piece. Review of Contemporary Fiction* (Fall, 1992): 181–82.

E68 Plomer, William. *At Home.* London: Jonathan Cape, 1958.

E69 ———. *In a Bombed House: 1941. An Elegy in Memory of Anthony Butts.* Printed for private circulation, 1942. Poems.

E70 ———. *Museum Pieces.* New York: The Noonday Press, 1954. Fiction.

E71 Poli, Bernard. *Ford Madox Ford and the "Transatlantic Review."* New York: Syracuse University Press, 1967.

E72 Raynor, John. "In Memoriam: Mary Butts." *The Cornish Review* 16 (Winter 1970): 8.

E73 Roberts, R. Ellis. "The Real Cleopatra." *News Chronicle* (19 June 1935). Rev. of *Scenes from the Life of Cleopatra.*

E74 ———. Rev. of *Several Occasions. The New Statesman and Nation* (12 Mar. 1932): 338, 340.

E75 ———. "Reviews and Impressions of Alexander." *The Guardian* (28 Apr. 1933). Rev. of *The Macedonian.*

E76 Rodker, John. *Memoirs of Other Fronts.* London: Putnam, 1932. Fiction.

E77 Rose, Francis. "Villefranche—Cocteau and Bérard." *Saying Life.* London: Cassell, 1961.

E78 Ross Williamson, Hugh. "Mary Butts." *The Bookman* (Dec. 1931): 188–89.

E79 ———. "Religion and Science." *The Bookman* (Apr. 1932): 5–6. Rev. of *Traps for Unbelievers.*

E80 ———. "A Writer's Childhood. The Testament of Mary Butts." *John O'London's Weekly* (11 June 1937): 388. Rev. of *The Crystal Cabinet.*

E81 Royde-Smith, Naomi. "Mary Butts." *Time and Tide* 18. 12 (20 Mar. 1937): 378.

E82 S., de A. Rev. of *Armed with Madness. The Manchester Guardian* (15 June 1928): 7.

E83 Sackville-West, Edward. "A Poetical Autobiography." *The New Statesman and Nation* (12 June 1937): 974. Rev. of *The Crystal Cabinet: My Childhood at Salterns.*

E84 Sell, Joseph. Rev. of *Scenes from the Life of Cleopatra. Bystander* (12 June 1935).

E85 "Short Stories. *Last Stories.*" *Times Literary Supplement* (8 Oct. 1938): 649.

E86 "Sophisticated Fantasy." *New York Times Book Review* (13 May 1928): 9, 17. Rev. of *Armed with Madness.*

E87 "The Soul in Fiction." *The Observer* (12 Feb. 1933): 8. Rev. of *Death of Felicity Taverner.*

E88 Spilleth, Meg. "The Effects of Childhood." *The Minnesota Daily* (28 Sept. 1988). Rev. of *The Crystal Cabinet: My Childhood at Salterns.*

E89 Squire, J. C. "The Modern Revival of the Short Story: Miss Mary Butts' Success." *The Daily Telegraph* (8 Mar. 1932). Rev. of *Several Occasions.*

E90 ———. "A Subtle Pen." *The Sunday Times* (27 Nov. 1932). Rev. of *Death of Felicity Taverner.*

E91 Steen, Marguerite. "The Glory that was Greece." *Everyman* (Mar. 1933). Rev. of *The Macedonian.*

E92 Symonds, John. "Cakes of Light for Mary Butts." *The Great Beast: The Life and Magick of Aleister Crowley.* London: Macdonald, 1971.

E93 "Tale of Two Worlds." *The New Statesman and Nation* (24 Dec. 1932): 837. Rev. of *Death of Felicity Taverner.*

E94 Thomson, Virgil. "Langlois, Butts, and Stein." *Virgil Thomson.* New York: Alfred A. Knopf, 1966.

E95 Upchurch, Michael. "Rediscovering Mary Butts." *Washington Post Book World* (20 Sept, 1992): 11. Rev. of *The Taverner Novels* and *From Altar to Chimney-piece.*

E96 Vernon, Frank. "Books We'd Like to Burn: Writers' Contorted View of Morality." *John Bull* (28 Apr. 1923). Rev. of *Speed the Plough and Other Stories.*

E97 Wagstaff, Barbara O'Brien. Afterword. *The Crystal Cabinet: My Childhood at Salterns.* Boston: Beacon Press, 1988. 275–82. Also in Carcanet ed.

E98 ———. "Brightness Falls from the Air." Afterword. *The Taverner Novels.* An omnibus edition of *Armed with Madness* and *Death of Felicity Taverner.* Kingston: McPherson & Co., 1992. 367–73.

E99 ———. "Alchemist of Reality: Recovering Mary Butts." *Poetry Flash* (Apr. 1984): 4, 9.

E100 ———. Untitled statement. *The Writings and the World of Mary Butts.* Conference brochure. University of California, Davis, 1984. n. pag.

E101 Warren, C. Henry. "Love of Nature?" *The Bookman* (May 1932): 116–17. Rev. of *Warning to Hikers.*

E102 Waugh, Evelyn. *The Diaries of Evelyn Waugh.* Ed. Michael Davie. London: Weidenfeld & Nicholson, 1976.

E103 Wescott, Glenway. "The First Book of Mary Butts." *The Dial* 75 (Sept. 1923): 282–84. Rev. of *Speed the Plough and Other Stories.*

E104 Wieners, John. "Mary Butts, Inhabit her Ashe Family of Rings." *Floating Bear* 26 (Oct. 1963): 3.

E105 Wineapple, Brenda. "Shadow of the Left Bank." *Belles Lettres* (Summer 1992): 32, 34. Rev. of *The Taverner Novels.*

E106 Wolfe, Humbert. "'Her Infinite Variety.'" *The Observer* (2 May 1935). Rev. of *Scenes from the Life of Cleopatra.*

E107 ———. "King of the World." *The Observer* (12 Mar. 1933): 5. Rev. of *The Macedonian.*

E108 Woolf, Virginia. *The Diary of Virginia Woolf.* Ed. Anne Olivier Bell and intro. Quentin Bell. New York and London: Harcourt Brace Jovanovich, vol. 2, 1978; vol. 3, 1980; vol. 4, 1982.

E109 ———. *The Letters of Virginia Woolf.* Ed. Nigel Nicolson and Joanne Trautmann. New York and London: Harcourt Brace Jovanovich, vol. 2, 1976; vol. 4, 1978; vol. 5, 1979; vol. 6, 1980.

E110 Wright, Patrick. *On Living in an Old Country: The National Past in Contemporary Britain.* London: Verso, 1985.

Contributors

Louis Adeane's principal poetical work is *The Night Loves Us: Thirty-Two Poems* (Delphic Press, 1946). Other poems can be found in *I Burn for England: An Anthology of the Poetry of World War Two* (Frewin, 1966) and *For Those Who Are Alive: An Anthology of New Verse* (Fortune Press, 1946).

Camilla Bagg, Mary Butts's daughter by her first husband, John Rodker, lives in Reading, England, and has spent many years in local government as a councillor in rural affairs. She edited and wrote the foreword to the reissue of Mary Butts's *The Crystal Cabinet* (1988).

Robin Blaser lives in Vancouver, British Columbia. With Robert Duncan and Jack Spicer, he initiated a far-reaching poetry renaissance in Berkeley, California, in the late 1940s. Until his retirement in 1986, he was on the faculty of Simon Fraser University. *The Holy Forest,* his collected poems, was published by Coach House Press in 1993. He edited *The Collected Books of Jack Spicer* (Black Sparrow, 1975) and wrote an afterword to an edition of Butts's *Imaginary Letters* (Talonbooks, 1979).

Bryher (1894–1983), born Annie Winnifred Ellerman, daughter of the English shipping magnate, Sir John Ellerman, authored both fiction and nonfiction. Her early novel, *Two Selves,* was printed by Robert McAlmon's Contact Press in 1923. From 1935 to 1950 she published the literary review *Life and Letters To-Day.* She encouraged and gave financial support to many writers, including Dorothy Richardson and H.D. In addition to selecting the material for Mary Butts's posthumous *Last Stories* (1938), Bryher had planned to issue a Butts festschrift.

Harcourt Wesson Bull discovered Butts's *Ashe of Rings* as a college student and spent time with her in southern France in the spring of 1928. He lived in Sennen, Cornwall, for about six months during 1935. After he returned to his native New England, he and Mary Butts corresponded until her death. His memoir in this volume would appear to be his only published writing.

Robert H. Byington is professor of literature at the University of North Carolina at Wilmington, where he served as chairperson of the English Department until 1989. For a number of years he has been working in the field of folklore.

Robert Duncan (1919–1988) continued the great modern tradition begun by Ezra Pound, H.D., and William Carlos Williams, his major collections of poetry being *Derivations, The Opening of the Field, Roots and Branches, Bending the Bow,* and *Ground Work,* the last four published by New Directions. The University of California Press is preparing his collected works, to be published in seven volumes.

David Hope resided for a time in Sennen, Cornwall, where he knew Mary Butts. Other biographical information is unavailable. Apparently, the Sennen Pamphlet Series had only one issue, devoted to Hope's appreciation of Butts.

Kenneth Irby lives in Lawrence, Kansas, where he teaches in the English Department at the University of Kansas. His many books of poetry include *Relation* (Black Sparrow, 1970), *Catalpa* (Tansy, 1977), and *Call Steps* (Station Hill/Tansy, 1992). He co-edited Carl Ortwin Sauer's *Seventeenth Century North America* and has prepared an edition of Mary Butts's collected poetry.

Gerrit Lansing lives in Gloucester, Massachusetts, where he published the magazine *Set* from 1961 to 1963. His poems and reviews have appeared recently in *Sulfur, Notus,* and *Conjunctions.* His works of poetry include *The Heavenly Tree Grows Downward* (Station Hill, 1977) and *'Analytic Psychology' or The Soluble Forest is Swimming Across* (Institute of Further Studies, 1983).

Hugh Ross Williamson (1901–1978) was a minister, theologian and an authority on the first half of the seventeenth century. From 1930 to 1934 he was editor of *The Bookman,* and, for a year, acting editor of *Strand* magazine. Following service as an Anglican priest from 1943 to 1955, he united with the Catholic Church in 1955. His non-fiction works include *The Poetry of T. S. Eliot* (1932), *John Hampden* (1933), *King James I* (1936) and *George Villiers, Duke of Buckingham* (1940). Among his many novels are *The Silver Bowl* and *James, By the Grace of God.*

BARBARA O'BRIEN WAGSTAFF lives in Berkeley, California, where she teaches in the Freshman Program at the University of California and works as a free-lance editor. She has written afterwords to the Beacon Press edition of *The Crystal Cabinet* (1988) and *The Taverner Novels* (McPherson, 1992).

CHRISTOPHER WAGSTAFF teaches in the Freshman Program at the University of California at Berkeley. He edited *Robert Duncan: Drawings and Decorated Books* (1992) and has curated exhibitions of the work of Jess, Harry Jacobus, and other painters. He scripted and co-directed the documentary film "Mary Baker Eddy: A Heart in Protest" (1988), with Julie Harris and Robert Duvall. He is now working in the field of religious studies.

GLENWAY WESCOTT (1901–1987) was born in Wisconsin. Following the publication of his first two novels, *The Apple of the Eye* (1924) and *The Grandmothers* (1927), he went to England to meet Ford Madox Ford. For many years he lived in Germany and France, and is especially well remembered for the novella *The Pilgrim Hawk* and the collection of stories *Good-bye Wisconsin.*